ECONOMICS OF HEALTH CARE
FINANCING: THE VISIBLE HAND

B

132

ECONOMIC ISSUES IN HEALTH CARE

General editors

Professor Gavin Mooney
Health Economics Research Unit
University of Aberdeen
Foresterhill
Aberdeen AB9 2ZD

Dr Alistair McGuire
Centre for Socio-Legal Studies
and Pembroke College
University of Oxford
Oxford OX2 6UD

ECONOMICS OF HEALTH CARE FINANCING: THE VISIBLE HAND

Cam Donaldson

Health Economics Research Unit
Department of Public Health
University of Aberdeen

and

Karen Gerard

Division of Epidemiology and Public Health
University of Newcastle-upon-Tyne
and formerly Health Economics Research Unit
University of Aberdeen

MACMILLAN

First published 1993 by
THE MACMILLAN PRESS LTD
Houndmills, Basingstoke, Hampshire RG21 2XS
and London
Companies and representatives
throughout the world

ISBN 0–333–53869–2 hardcover
ISBN 0–333–53870–6 paperback

A catalogue record for this book is available
from the British Library.

Reprinted 1994

Printed in Hong Kong

Contents

Acknowledgements

There are many people to thank for their help in producing this book.

First, we would like to thank the series editors, Gavin Mooney and Ali McGuire, for helping us through the final stages of the production process.

We would also like to thank our colleagues in various institutions; many of our ideas were formed and much writing was done while at these places. Therefore, we are grateful to our colleagues at the Department of Public Health at the University of Sydney, at the Centre for Health Economics Research and Evaluation at Westmead Hospital in Sydney, and at the Centre for Health Economics at the University of York. Special help at each of these sites was provided by Monika Bhatia, Jackie Dettman, Julie Glanville, Alan Maynard and Owen O'Donnell.

The following people provided us with valuable information on particular countries: Tamas Angelus (Hungary), Toni Ashton (New Zealand), Joan Artells (Spain), Ivar Sønbo Kristiansen (Norway), Ken Lee (USSR), Marian Matulewicz (Poland) and Frans Rutten (The Netherlands).

Thanks are also due to our colleagues in the Health Economics Research Unit: in particular Doreen Adams, Anne Bews and Shelley Farrar.

Finally, this book could not have been written without the support and inspiration provided by Tony Culyer of the University of York, and by Gavin Mooney. Much of the work presented here originated from a project on health care financing, carried out with the Institute for Health Services Management under Tony's supervision. All that Gavin did was to make us believe we could write a book in the first place!

PART 1

Markets and Market Failure in Health Care

CHAPTER 1

Health Care Financing Reforms: Moving into the 1990s

INTRODUCTION

Many governments are changing their methods of financing health services (or are at least talking about it). These changes are often in part based on political ideology but are also, it is claimed, the results of economic or financial pressures. Implicit in many of the changes is a genuine desire to do better with the health care resources at the disposal of nations. But do they actually work out like this?

Despite the involvement of large amounts of public and private money and resources, and besides the potential effect on the welfare of large numbers of the population, scant regard is paid to the economic principles and economic evidence on the costs and effects of such change. There is a wide body of literature on the economics of health care financing, which is rather inaccessible and difficult for any interested person to draw together. The main aim of this book is to allow such individuals to gain easier access to the economic literature and principles of health care financing. In this there are four strands. First, we set out the economic principles of markets and market failure which underpin different methods of financing health care. Second, we outline different methods of funding health care. In the third part of the book we assess the evidence from economic studies of the different methods. Finally, we examine some future challenges for research and policy making regarding health care financing.

To introduce the rest of the book, we focus in this chapter on two issues. First, changes in financing arrangements which are taking place in different regions of the world are highlighted. The reader should note that it is not the intent here to review the arrangements per se but rather to focus on change. The nature of such change sets an agenda for the remainder of the book. Thereafter, we indicate how each chapter contributes to the overall assessment of the changes that are going on.

3

THE CHANGING WORLD OF HEALTH CARE FINANCING

Western Europe

In Western European health care systems, the basic funding arrangements
are of two main sorts: directly from tax revenues (such as in Denmark,
Norway, Sweden and the UK) and funding from social insurance contributions (such as in France and Germany) (Jönsson, 1989) (Note 1). Some
systems, like those in Italy and Spain, use a mixture of the two, although the
trend in recent years has been towards the former. The Dutch system is
slightly different again, relying not only on social insurance but also on a
large degree of private insurance for routine care for those over a certain
level of income.

So, even within a small geographical area of the world, basic funding
arrangements differ. In Western Europe these reflect not only economic
considerations but also cultural differences and the history of health care
financing in the countries involved. More important than this, however, are
the changes in financing arrangements which these countries are considering
and whether these will make things better or worse for the populations
involved.

Some of these changes are at a system level (i.e. involve changing the
whole of the basic funding arrangements) and can be evaluated with varying
degrees of difficulty. Others are at much more of a micro-level (i.e. they
mean considering different ways of raising funds or altering arrangements,
but still remaining within the basic system of fund raising). For many
micro-level changes, such as patient charges, a great deal of information
exists which can help in determining whether or not such changes are for
the better.

Regarding basic-system changes, the governments of both Italy and Spain
have made commitments to move towards systems funded mainly from
taxation (Italian Ministry of Justice, 1978; Ministerio de Sanidad y Consumo, 1989). Progress towards this is being made in both countries. About 50
per cent of funding in Italy is still dependent on social insurance, with about
10 per cent of funding from private insurance and patient charges. In Spain,
about 20 per cent of funding is still accounted for by social insurance and a
further 21 per cent by private insurance and charges, although the exact
contribution of private insurance and charges is unknown.

Other major reforms, but not involving the basic systems of raising
finances, include attempts to inject more competitive elements into health
care financing, such as in the Netherlands and the UK (van de Ven, 1989;
Secretaries of State, 1989a and b). In these countries, competition will be in
health care provision rather than in financing. In the UK district health
authorities (DHAs) will perform the task of purchasing care on behalf of
the communities they serve. DHAs will be permitted to purchase care from

NHS hospitals, independent NHS hospital trusts opting out of DHA control and/or the private sector. Thus, providers will compete for funds from DHAs on the basis of cost and quality. In the Dutch system, providers will receive funding from health care insurers.

Also, in these two systems, reforms based on the US health maintenance organisation (HMO) model have been introduced. For instance, in the UK, some general practitioners have been allocated budgets with which to purchase certain types of hospital care on behalf of those on their lists (Secretaries of State, 1989a and b).

There are many more micro-level changes going on in Western European countries. Patient charges for health care exist in Italy and in Spain, to a greater degree in the latter. In Norway, such charges are levied for visits to general practitioners (GPs); patients pay about 35 per cent of the fee (Kristiansen, 1990). Charges for visits to GPs are also being considered in Denmark. Most countries operate systems of charging (at least in part) patients for GP drug prescriptions, and the amounts involved have increased recently in France and the UK. In Germany, there is a small daily charge for the first 14 days in hospital and for inpatient rehabilitation, and these too are expected to increase as a result of the 1989 health law reform (Henke, 1989). A hospital day charge has been recently introduced in France.

Specifically regarding the payment of doctors, there are various arrangements across Western Europe. In most cases, hospital doctors are salaried, although in France (private hospitals), and in Belgium and Luxemburg, the system is fee-for-service (FFS) based (Directorate General for Research, 1988). GPs are reimbursed in a mixture of ways; totally FFS in Germany (Kirkmann-Liff, 1990), some salaried and some FFS in Norway (Kristiansen, 1990); capitation combined with FFS and/or allowances (e.g. for group practice) in Italy and the UK (Directorate General for Research, 1988; Donaldson and Gerard, 1989a), and HMO-style arrangements in the UK (for some practices) and the Netherlands as mentioned above.

Hospital funding also varies and some recent changes have been observed. In Denmark, Italy, Norway, Sweden and Spain, hospitals can receive most of their revenues through a block grant from the central pool of funding, be it taxation or social insurance (Jonsson, 1989). Recent innovations, however, have included more competition between providers to attract funds (as in the Netherlands and the UK), experiments with clinical budgeting (also in the Netherlands and the UK) and the introduction of patient-based reimbursement (as in Germany) (Henke, 1989).

Eastern Europe

Before 1989, the health care systems of Eastern Europe were based on the principle of 'free' access, financed by monies from general revenues of governments. These general revenues were devolved to more local levels, as is still the case. In Hungary, local taxation has recently been introduced to supplement funds from general revenues (Angelus, 1990). Through restructuring and openness it has become clear that Eastern European health care faces many problems: perverse incentives (such as hospital funding being based on bed days and, in primary care clinics, on attendances), shortages of supplies and equipment, and duplication of services between primary care clinics and hospital. In some cases, like that of the former USSR, the intention is to increase funding, but along with reforms aimed at increasing the 'flexibility' of the system. It is likely that the private sector in financing and provision will increase in size.

In Poland, reforms recently discussed have included provision of a limited health package by the state plus a system of voluntary health insurance for services beyond the basic package. It is unclear whether or not 'top-up' insurance will be related to people's health states (i.e. experience-rated). An alternative proposal has been to have not a basic package, but a system funded totally from insurance contributions from employers. How disadvantaged groups would be covered by this system is not clear (Indulski *et al.*, 1989).

In the former USSR, the greatest innovation is the experiment in primary-care clinics (or polyclinics) and hospital funding taking place in Leningrad, Kushiben (Volga) and Kemerono (Siberia) (Hakansson *et al.*, 1988). Hitherto, hospital budgets went from the Ministry of Health to the hospitals and polyclinics separately. In the experiment, however, polyclinics hold the budget, the hospital being paid by the polyclinic for services carried out on the polyclinic's patients. The polyclinics will receive a fee for each patient registered, and so will have an incentive to attract patients. Polyclinics and hospitals will retain surpluses. The aim is to achieve greater efficiency in health care, in particular to reduce length of stay, which has been rising.

In Hungary, reforms have been largely structural (e.g. a new Ministry of Social Affairs and Health in 1986), but financial aspects include a social insurance system made up largely of employers' contributions (although it is not clear if this supplements or replaces income tax), experiments with diagnosis-related groups (DRGs) in the hospital sector, more emphasis on patient charges (particularly for drugs), and people being allowed to insure privately on top of state contributions (Angelus, 1990).

North America

The Canadian health care system is based on public insurance and has been relatively stable over the last 20 years, since the introduction of public health care insurance. The most frequent debates have been about the introduction or extension of patient charges (Barer *et al.*, 1979). The switch in Canada, from a US type of system to public insurance, provides some useful comparisons at the global level, with extremely large sample sizes (22 million people in the Canadian group and about 250 million in the US).

The USA and Turkey are the only countries in the OECD which do not have universal coverage of their populations, whether through tax-funded schemes or through private health care insurance. In the USA the public health care system is in two main parts (although this varies slightly from state to state): Medicaid for low-income persons and financed from federal and state general taxation revenue; and Medicare for those aged over 65 years, those on renal dialysis and those who are permanently disabled (financed by a combination of payroll taxes on earnings up to a ceiling, premiums paid by elderly people and general revenues) (Ginsburg, 1988). Medicare also requires direct charges from patients for doctors' bills (a \$75 annual deductible and a 20 per cent user charge thereafter), and hospitalisation (a deductible of \$400 in 1985 and a daily user charge for the sixty first through to the ninetieth day). Within the US Medicare system a prospective pricing system for hospital episodes was introduced in 1983. Diagnosis-related groups (DRGs) have been used to fix prices paid by Medicare for hospitalisation, price being determined by the patient's diagnosis.

The US private sector is dominated by private health care insurance, and many policies require substantial out-of-pocket payments from enrolees. Other recent developments include HMOs and preferred provider organisations (PPOs). These affect both hospital financing and doctor reimbursement. Payment of doctors, however, remains dominated by fee for service (FFS).

Despite recent developments, mostly aimed at cost containment, one in six of the US population remains uninsured or underinsured (publicly or privately), which has led to recent calls for a system of universal health care insurance (Enthoven and Kronick, 1989a; Enthoven and Kronick, 1989b; Navarro, 1989).

Latin America

Latin America is dominated by social insurance systems (Akin, 1988). Workers usually pay a fixed percentage of wages to the system and most are self-financing. Sixteen Latin American countries use such systems, with varying degrees of success regarding coverage: as many as 80 per cent of the population are covered in Argentina and as few as 7 per cent in Honduras. The proportion of the population covered is rising in most countries.

Two-tier systems exist in all countries, with more wealthy members of society receiving access to better facilities through private health insurance. Several countries claim to have had problems with 'overconsumption' of services and have, therefore, introduced different methods of financing. Argentina's social insurance funds (private, not-for-profit entities) have varying levels of patient charges attached to them. Brazil has recently introduced a DRG system for funding hospital care. Uruguay has been at the forefront of experimentation with prepaid health care plans, such as HMOs.

Australasia

The stability of the Australian and New Zealand health care systems over the past few decades has contrasted greatly. The New Zealand health care system, the first to establish a National Health Service, has remained very stable until recently. The Australian health care system, on the other hand, is a constant source of political debate and has been subject to many fundamental changes since 1945, not least during the most recent decade.

In 1984, a universal public health insurance system (Medicare) was reintroduced in Australia. A previous version (Medibank) had operated for 12 months in 1975–6, but had been gradually dismantled under Liberal administrations until the return of a Labor government in 1983. In the system prior to Medicare, private insurance was widespread, as was use of patient charges. Elderly people and some poor people were covered by the public sector, but many people remained uninsured (Deeble, 1982; Palmer and Short, 1989). In opposition since 1983, the Liberal Party has advocated a return to the previous system, along with assurances that it will not be more costly and that universal coverage will be maintained. Recent budget proposals include the introduction of charges for general-practitioner consultations and general-practice grants to replace FFS payments.

In New Zealand, a change of government has resulted in two great changes to the health care system. The first is the introduction of provider competition, as in the UK and the Netherlands. Four new regional health authorities (RHA) are to be created. They will purchase care on behalf of their population (about 800 000 people each) from competitors from public, private and voluntary sectors. People can opt out of RHA cover to a private sector plan, taking a weighted cash allocation with them, so there is also some competition in financing. Secondly, patient charges are to be introduced for outpatient visits and inpatient stays; these charges could cost the average family the equivalent of £UK300 per annum (Ashton, 1991; Dearden, 1991).

Less-developed Countries (LDCs)

LDCs find tax raising difficult for two main reasons: the political undesirability of raising taxes from an already poor population, and the difficulty of collecting taxes anyway. (This is a 'catch 22'; if countries do not have a system of collection they will never be able to formalise things, but why have a system if funds collected do not cover the cost of collection?)

Basic sources of finance remain the central revenues of government, insurance schemes which can be organised easily (for example, for large numbers of civil servants), and private finance through user charges and insurance (although the size of this is often not known). In recent years, however, two main sources of enhanced funding have been advocated or implemented — community financing and increased (or at least more formal) use of patient charges (Carrin and Vereecke, 1992).

Community financing is often more organisational than financial; self-help on a mutual basis (Abel-Smith and Dua, 1988; Myers, 1988; Asian Development Bank *et al.*, 1988). People who live together in some form of local community get together to undertake collective action to achieve common goals. Community financing can take several forms. One type is socially organised community insurance schemes, such as the health card scheme in Thailand, in which cards are sold to participants in exchange for 'free' contact with a health worker for a fixed amount of episodes of illness per annum. The health worker decides an appropriate course of action. Money can be used to make loans to cardholders for water supply, sanitation and nutrition projects. Non-use of the card for one year can result in substantial discounts (a 'no claims bonus'?) the following year. Other possibilities are drug banks, in which the community may pay preferential subsidised rates, but organises the bank and has an input to decision making on prices, as in Nepal and Thailand. Also, the giving of gifts in cash or kind can be used in the construction of health facilities, or healthy water supplies, as in Bangladesh.

Patient charges are often politely referred to as 'cost recovery' in LDCs (Griffin, 1988; Asian Development Bank *et al.*, 1988). Thus, there is often emphasis on raising funds as well as on preventing 'overuse'. Their use is increasing, although they still account for less than 10 per cent of recurrent expenditure in LDCs. They are used mainly for small, well-defined items like drugs and outpatient visits. A wide range of countries have them in use or are thinking about them; they include Bangladesh, Burma, China, Malaysia, Sudan and Thailand. In many countries they are income-assessed: for example, India, Indonesia, Pakistan, the Philippines and Zaire (Griffin, 1988).

So it is apparent from this brief introduction that, in various regions of the world, health care financing is changing. Some changes are fundamental, others are at the micro-level. Below we indicate the structure of the book for analysing and assessing the likely impact of these changes.

OUTLINE OF THE BOOK

The first part of the book, Chapters 2 and 3, deals with the economic reasoning behind the health care systems which different countries have. Some commentators have claimed that government intervention in health care financing should be far less than it is today (Logan *et al.*, 1989), with more being left to market forces. Indeed, no matter what system of financing is in operation, market forces will always exist. How they operate will depend on the structure of the basic financing system. Therefore, as market forces can never be ignored in the health care financing debate, in Chapter 2 we deal with the issue of defining 'markets'. Before discussing market failure and building in major modifications, such as government intervention, it is useful to strip markets bare and describe how they would work in ideal conditions.

Towards the end of Chapter 2, and more fully in Chapter 3, the reasons for the failure of markets in health care financing are outlined. It will be seen that government intervention in health care financing is not only inevitable but also to the benefit of the community. The main problems with which financing systems, and therefore governments, have to deal come to light explicitly in this chapter: devising financing mechanisms which avoid 'moral hazard', whereby, as a result of being insured (publicly or privately), the attitudes consumers and providers of health care change so that they have no incentive to moderate 'overuse' of services 'because the insurer will pay'; 'adverse selection' and the problem of ensuring access to care for less-well-off groups in need; determining how much societies care about the access of less-well-off groups; and problems of asymmetry of information, which leads to consumer ignorance of much health care and puts the doctor in a particularly powerful position in the health care market.

Government intervention does not necessarily imply that the form of intervention will be uniform across different countries. The different basic systems of health care financing and their objectives are, therefore, outlined in Part 2, which encompasses Chapters 4 and 5. It will be seen that within the different systems outlined in Chapter 4 there exist many arrangements of micro-level type. These arrangements are not exclusive to one type of system; for instance, patient charges can be tried in public as well as privately-orientated systems. The objectives of health care systems against which changes in financial arrangements should be measured are outlined in Chapter 5. These objectives cover efficiency and equity, and it will be seen that there is a greater consensus over defining the former rather than the latter type of objectives.

The evidence on different arrangements in dealing with the main problems of financing is dealt with in Part 3. As moral hazard is the area of concern here which is most well researched by economists and others, it is dealt with in Chapters 6 to 8. In Chapter 6 different ways of dealing with moral hazard on the part of the consumer are examined. Chapters 7 and 8 concentrate on the supply side of the market, examining mechanisms for countering moral hazard among doctors and in hospitals respectively.

The challenges of adverse selection and achievement of equity are returned to in Chapter 9. Different financing systems obviously have implications for equity as well as efficiency.

Part 4, the final part, looks to the future. In Chapter 10 we ask, 'Given the financing arrangements that exist, how can the techniques of economics be used in the future to improve things?' The chapter is thus about using approaches which take account of costs and benefits in order to set the budget for health care; the approaches are economic evaluation and examining determinants of health (of which more details follow later).

Finally, in Chapter 11, we conclude on the state of current evidence. No hard and fast answers are given. But the following questions will be addressed:

- What should be the nature of the financial intermediary between the consumer and the provider?
- What form should the 'insurance premium' take?
- What is the role of out-of-pocket payments made by the consumer at the point of use?
- What should be the financial arrangements for providers?

In answering these questions, financing arrangements are judged in terms of efficiency and equity. Some arrangements are judged less desirable than others and future areas for health economics research are identified.

CHAPTER 2

Markets and Health Care

INTRODUCTION

Free markets in health care are rare, almost all health care systems in the world operating with some level of government intervention. Yet, market forces were not 'invented'. They are as old as civilisation and will continue to exist for a long time. They can operate either in an unregulated form or in an adjusted form based, in turn, on the regulatory framework which has been imposed upon them. These are significant observations because they mean that current debates and proposed 'solutions' to questions concerning optimal ways of financing and allocating health care must inherently consider the applicability and shortcomings of 'market' forces.

Although free (i.e. unregulated) market solutions are upheld as efficient, the reality is that they do not work as well for some economic goods and services as for others. Notwithstanding this, the market is an important concept and the starting point in economic analysis. It contributes to the understanding of exchange and distribution of resources within any sector of an economy. Thus, it is appropriate to commence this book with due consideration of how well markets work in the case of financing and allocating health care resources. In particular, we begin with an analysis of the 'perfect' market system (also referred to as 'perfect competition') for health care. It is important to give serious consideration to the theory underlying perfect markets for four main reasons:

(1) The perfect market system is one which would unequivocally work best for health care, but only under certain ideal conditions. A perfect market delivers the highly desirable outcome of maximum consumer satisfaction or well-being (also referred to as 'utility') with the resources available to society. How such an outcome arises will be explained below. The usefulness of this perfect-competition model is that, even if it cannot be attained, it serves as a standard against which the success or failure of alternative financing mechanisms, whether market- or publicly orientated, can be measured. The question then becomes one of how close other systems come to achieving this standard.

(2) Some economists are of the view that all health care should be financed through competition, except for public health interventions (e.g. immunisation programmes) and subsidisation for the poor (Green, 1986;

12

Logan *et al.*, 1989) (Note 2). Therefore, it is important to be aware of the economic theory upon which such arguments are based so as to be able to construct arguments either in favour of or against such a mode of financing.

(3) Market theories of demand and supply are fundamental building blocks of modern microeconomics. Even if one doubts the usefulness of market forces in the financing and allocation of health care, it is important to know how a perfect market would work, as economic theories of why some markets (including health care) fail to work stem from that very knowledge.

(4) Some health care systems may rely on a mixed economy, relying on elements of both government intervention and competition. So it is conceivable that market forces can play a part in the allocation of some health care resources, even where government intervention is present.

The aims of this chapter are, first, to explain what a market is and how a perfect market for health care would work under its ideal conditions, and, second, to make clear what these ideal conditions are. This will then lead into the third chapter, which examines the possible consequences of breakdowns in, or failure of, these ideal conditions.

WHAT IS A MARKET AND HOW DOES IT WORK?

We can examine what markets are and how they work using the economic concepts of demand and supply. Markets are made up of a demand side, and a supply side with consumers acting on the side of demand and producers on that of supply. A market is simply an adjustment mechanism for supply and demand which permits the exchange of goods and services between consumers and producers without the need for government intervention. Markets adjust using price signals. At the given market price, producers offer their products for sale and consumers spend their (disposable) income according to their wants and desires. In a perfect market situation this will mean no producers or consumers are left unsatisfied by the resultant exchange and distribution; at the given market price producers are able to sell all that they want (so maximising their profits) and consumers are able to purchase all they wish (so maximising their utility). Economists refer to this outcome as 'a cleared market' or 'market equilibrium'.

Thus, if market forces lead to the achievement of (or close approximation to) a societal objective of utility maximisation, it would be desirable to leave markets unfettered by government intervention. As government intervention in administering the allocation of resources to different groups in society is not costless in itself, it is better that such intervention be avoided, and the resources used in such intervention put to some other desirable use.

Markets avoid the need for resources being taken up in such administration by conveying information from consumers to producers, and from producers to consumers, via 'market signals'. These signals help to ensure that the optimum solution (cleared markets) is found. Market signals are the prices and quantities of goods and services provided in the economy. For example, a consumer may want to purchase a particular type of car, but cannot afford the price, and therefore does not make the purchase. In response to this, the salesperson may reduce the price of the car to a level which the consumer can now afford. The consumer responds by purchasing the car. In this situation, the consumer has responded to two price signals, initially by not buying the car and then by making the purchase. The salesperson has responded to a quantity signal, the sight of an unsold car in the showroom, by throwing out a new price signal to which our consumer and other consumers can respond. In another example, a fish-shop owner may be left with some unsold fish near the end of the working day. In response to this quantity signal, the shop owner could lower the price of fish for the last hour of trading. More fish will then be sold as consumers, responding to the new price signal, buy more fish than they otherwise would have done.

In the above examples, quantity and price signals were transferred from producers to consumers and vice versa via the costless mechanism of the market. This 'invisible hand' theorem was one of the insights of the renowned Eighteenth-century economist, Adam Smith, put forward in his famous book, *The Wealth of Nations* (Smith, 1776). Through the invisible hand, consumers maximise their satisfaction by freely spending their money on goods which, presumably, contribute more to their utility than any others at that point in time. Through the same process, producers sell their products and by doing so maximise their profits.

In perfectly competitive markets, all such transactions are desirable. This is because, in perfect markets, such transactions take place under certain ideal conditions, some of which will now be introduced. In the above examples, producers have to lower prices in order to sell their products. This means that such producers are inadvertently competing with other producers on whose products consumers could have spent their money. In the theory of perfect competition, it is assumed that all producers seek to maximise their profits. Each producer is so small, and one of so many, that, individually, they cannot exercise control over any aspect of the market except for their own costs of production. Without the possibility of collusion with others, producers are forced to compete with each other on the basis of price. Another basic assumption of this 'classical' model of economic behaviour is that consumers are fully informed and knowledgeable and will, therefore, possess the ability to seek out the producer with the lowest prices (Note 3). This situation results in producers having an incentive to operate at minimum cost so as to be able to set prices low enough to attract as many consumers as possible. Producers not operating at least cost will have this reflected in higher prices, to which consumers will respond by switching their demands elsewhere. High-cost producers will go out of business. Those remaining in business will be technically efficient in their production, either by maximising output for a given cost or by minimising costs for a given level of output.

If this model is applied to the health care market it means that, by definition, fully informed and knowledgeable consumers will weigh up the costs and benefits of health care relative to other goods. They will spend that amount of money on health care which maximises their well-being. This will result in the appropriate amount of resources being allocated to health care overall and to different types of health care (i.e. there will be allocative efficiency). At the same time, health care producers, seeking to maximise profits, will produce consumers' most highly valued types of health care at least cost, so behaving in a technically efficient manner. This combination of technical and allocative efficiency ensures that consumers' well-being is maximised at least cost to society.

Thus, self-interest is the basis of the market; consumers seek to maximise utility and producers seek to maximise profit. So, it seems that, under certain conditions, the pursuit of self-interest is not necessarily a bad thing; the market delivers maximum utility from the resources available to society. Many of the assertions of Smith (1776) reflect this. The following are two such assertions which have been quoted by ten Have (1988) and Culyer (1985) respectively to demonstrate the economic view of how markets function:

Assertion 1
'In almost every other race of animals, each individual, when it is grown up to maturity, is entirely independent, and in the natural state has occasion for the assistance of no other living creature. But man has almost constant occasion for the help of his brethren, and it is in vain for him to expect it from their benevolence only. He is more likely to prevail if he can interest their self-love in his favour, and to show them that it is to their own advantage to do for him what he requires of them. . . . It is not from the benevolence of the butcher, the brewer, or the baker that we expect our dinner, but from their regard for their own self-interest. We address ourselves, not to their humanity, but to their self-love, and never talk to them of our own necessities, but of their advantages.'

Assertion 2
'But it is only for the sake of profit that any man employs a capital in the support of industry; and he will always, therefore, endeavour to employ it in the support of that industry of which the produce is likely to be of the greatest value, or to exchange for the greatest quantity either of money or of other goods. . . . As every individual, therefore, endeavours as much as he can . . . so to direct that industry . . . every individual necessarily labours to render the

annual revenue of the Society as great as he can. He generally, indeed, neither intends to promote the public interest, nor knows how much he is promoting it. . . . He is in this, as in many other cases, led by an invisible hand to promote an end which was no part of his intentions. . . . I have never known much good done by those who affected to trade for the public good. It is an affectation, indeed, not very common among merchants, and very few words need to be employed in dissuading them from it.'

Remember that these assertions rest on two value judgements, one of which we have already introduced: that consumers are fully knowledgeable and informed, and therefore are the best judges of their own well-being; and that the prevailing distribution of income is fair, enabling consumers to be appropriately empowered by their prevailing level of disposable income. The latter judgement does emphasise the fact that the distribution of resources in markets is a result not only of consumers' willingness to pay for goods but also of their ability to pay.

Even given these restrictions, Smith's insight is remarkable in that consumers' utility can be maximised without any need to expend some of society's resources on some kind of centralised planning mechanism organised by government. On the issue of the distribution of income, it may be possible to redistribute income and still rely on the invisible hand of the market to allocate resources efficiently (Arrow, 1963).

It is because of assertions like those above that Smith is often seen as the champion of self-interest. After all, the self-interest of suppliers matched by the self-interest of consumers leads to an optimal outcome for society because 'man is led, as if by an invisible hand, to promote ends which were no part of his original intention' (Skinner, 1986, p. 40). However, Smith merely observed self-interest to be characteristic of people rather than a virtue, and, as such, is often misquoted. This paradox of private gain yielding social good can work only under certain ideal conditions, to which we will return later in the chapter. Smith also recognised this limitation, which makes his insights even more remarkable in terms of their relevance to the modern day. Therefore, two more of his observations are discussed, one later in this chapter and the other in Chapter 3.

In the meantime, a more formal analysis of how a perfect market in health care works can be described with reference to Figure 2.1. In this diagram supply and demand are described in terms of their relationship to price and quantity. The price of health care is represented on the vertical axis and the quantity of health care demanded and supplied per unit of time (say, per annum) is represented on the horizontal axis. The demand for health care is expressed as a downward-sloping curve. This reflects the general view that as the price of a good falls, more of that good will be demanded. The underlying assumption is that all other things, such as consumers' tastes, income, and the prices of other goods, remain constant. Each point on the demand curve, therefore, represents how much health

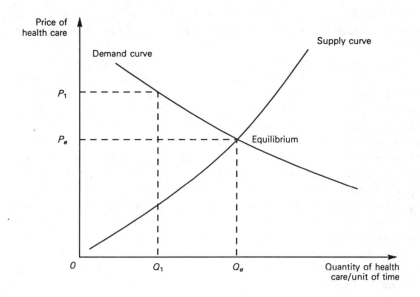

Figure 2.1 Demand for and supply of health care

care consumers want to buy at each price, given their tastes, their incomes
and the prices of other goods. Looked at another way, it represents how
much consumers are willing to pay for different quantities of health care. At
Q_e, consumers are willing to pay only P_e for one more unit of health care,
whereas, at the level of provision of Q_1, consumers would have been willing
to pay a higher price, P_1, for one more unit of health care as a result of it
being more scarce.

It can be argued that health care itself is not a 'good'. Rather, the
demand for health care is derived from a demand for health improvements
or health maintenance. In contributing to a consumer's utility, health
improvements and health maintenance have *value in use*. Health *per se*
cannot be traded, either between individuals or by a single individual over
different points in time. Nevertheless, health contributes to utility. As health
itself cannot be traded (or exchanged) in the market place for other goods,
it has no *value in exchange*. Health care normally has no value in use.
(Unless people like being operated on for reasons other than to lengthen, or
enhance the health-related quality of, their life!) However, it can be traded
and, when leading to health improvement or health maintenance, has value
in exchange.

This is important because, if we are to assume the existence of a fully
informed consumer, then the implication is that the consumer has perfect
knowledge of the relationship between health care and its contribution to

health improvements or the maintenance of health, and therefore has the ability to judge the value in exchange of health care as well as the value in use of health.

The supply curve for health care in Figure 2.1 slopes upwards from left to right. This is because, normally, the amount supplied to any market will respond positively to the price received by producers. The higher the price, the more will be supplied. This is the case because the more a producer expects to receive for their product, the greater is their incentive to produce more, assuming the cost of each extra unit produced increases less than the extra revenue received. In addition, some new producers who could not compete at lower prices (because they could not cover their costs) will now be attracted into the market, further increasing supply at higher prices. Each point on the supply curve therefore represents how much health care producers are willing to sell at each price, given technology, unit production costs and levels of government regulation.

The market 'clears' where demand is equal to supply. This is at the point of equilibrium in Figure 2.1, where price is equal to P_e and quantities demanded and supplied are equal to Q_e. As the quantity of health care supplied to the market by producers is equivalent to the quantity demanded by consumers, there is no waste.

Given all the assumptions built in above, competitive forces will always ensure that equilibrium is reached. To illustrate this, take the situation in Figure 2.2 at price P_1, where supply is greater than demand. Suppliers of health care will notice that this is the case, as they will have produced health care which remains unsold or will have staff and equipment which are idle. In such a situation, suppliers will respond to this quantity signal by lowering prices, thus enticing consumers to increase their demand for the unused health care. In the face of falling prices, consumers will increase their demand for health care. At the same time, some producers will go out of business because they cannot cover their costs at lower prices and others will contract the scale of their production. Demand will continue to increase and supply will contract until the two are equal at the point of equilibrium. This is similar to the example of the fishshop owner above. Excess fish were available towards the end of the day, so price was lowered to ensure that more fish were sold.

At P_2 in Figure 2.2, a situation of excess demand prevails. In this situation, consumers respond by bidding up prices. This results in an increase in the supply of health care, and a decrease in demand as some consumers are bid out of the market. A good example of this is in housing markets in a boom period. Houses tend to be in short supply, and consumers respond by bidding up prices. This forces some consumers out of the market and at the same time encourages more people to offer their houses for sale, so increasing supply. Again this process continues until demand is equal to supply. The housing market is an interesting case in which the invisible

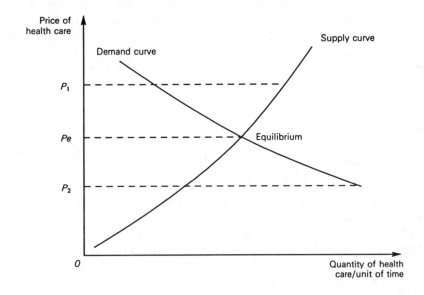

Figure 2.2 Market equilibrium

hand is rendered visible. This is done by the transfer of price and quantity information via estate agents and newspaper columns. These modes of transferring information develop because the cost to individual consumers of collating data on the availability and prices of housing would otherwise be too great. Thus, where the market fails in transferring signals from sellers to buyers, another market develops to fulfil that function.

Until the growth of private health insurance in developed countries during the 1930s and 1940s, much health care was provided in the fashion of markets described above. Arms-length transactions took place between doctors and patients and those who could pay the market price got care while those who could not did not receive care. Of course some less well-off people (usually working-class males) were covered by government insurance schemes, and others gained access to care through charitable organisations (Gray, 1991). However, even today many people (often the better-off in societies) pay for health care via market transactions.

MARKETS: THE PANACEA FOR HEALTH CARE ILLS?

Should health care be organised in this way? If markets worked perfectly, in the way described above, the answer to this question would be an unqualified 'yes', provided that any problems of equity in the distribution of income could be overcome (e.g. progressive taxation, through which taxation takes an increasing proportion of income as income rises, to redistribute income to the poor). No alternative system would achieve the same level of utility from health care, or, if it did, it could only be done at greater cost. For this reason the perfect market is regarded as the 'gold standard' of transaction mechanisms.

The problem is that, when examining the realities of markets, the answer to the question 'Should health care be organised using the market mechanism?' is not so clear cut. This is because perfectly functioning markets require a number of crucial assumptions to hold true, the reality being that there is no market in which all of the assumptions do hold true. The relevant questions then become:

(1) How many of these assumptions break down in health care relative to other goods?

(2) To what extent do the assumptions break down?

(3) Once one or more of the assumptions break down, should the market remain unregulated, or is there a way of 'helping' markets to work?

(4) Is there an alternative way of financing and organising health care which is more likely to meet social objectives than an unregulated market, whatever these objectives may be?

The first two of these questions are dealt with in the following chapter, in which the issue of market failure is discussed. The third is dealt with throughout the remainder of the book: by considering how complete market failure in health care might be; in Part Two, by describing alternative methods of financing health care and considering some possible objectives for health care; and then, in Part Three, by comparing how different health care financing mechanisms perform in the pursuit of these objectives. The implication of the third question is that, although there is no commodity which meets all of the assumptions required of a perfect market, an unregulated or regulated market may still be the preferred mode of exchange because it approximates the objectives of utility maximisation at least cost better than does any alternative mode.

Before addressing the extent to which the assumptions of perfect markets break down, we need to know exactly what the crucial assumptions of the perfect market are. Some have already been introduced in the previous section, but an explicit listing would be more helpful in structuring the arguments to follow in the next chapter. It is to this which we now turn.

THE CRUCIAL ASSUMPTIONS

In order to achieve the optimal outcomes of utility maximisation at least cost, perfect markets require five main conditions to hold true: certainty; no externalities; perfect knowledge on the part of the consumer; consumers to act free of self-interested advice from suppliers; and several small suppliers to promote genuine competition, and therefore prevent collusion on the part of suppliers. Each of these assumptions is discussed in more detail below. In order to set up the arguments to be presented in detail in the following chapter, a brief counter-argument to each assumption is presented here.

Certainty

The assumption of certainty is that consumers know exactly what they want, when they want it and where they can get it. This means health care consumption can be planned in the same way as one's weekly consumption of foodstuffs. Clearly the consumption of some items of health care can be planned in this way. Once someone becomes aware of being shortsighted, they can plan how often to have an eye test and when to purchase the next set of spectacles or contact lenses. However, it is also clearly the case that many items of health care consumption cannot be planned in this way. This is because deteriorations in health are often sudden and/or unexpected. In addition, the health care required to offset such health problems may be expensive and unaffordable, either in a one-off payment, or, if the condition persists, over a period of time. In such situations, health insurance markets are likely to develop to counter the financial burdens of the uncertain effects of ill-health. Such markets experience some problems similar to those encountered with publicly financed health services, as well as others which give rise to the need for some government regulation. Such problems are discussed in the next chapter.

No Externalities

Externalities are spillovers from other people's production or consumption of commodities which affect an individual in either a negative or a positive way, but which are out of the individual's locus of control. The costs and benefits of such spillovers cannot be accounted for in market transactions, because when such transactions take place consumers and suppliers consider only costs and benefits to themselves. A commonly used example of an externality is a neighbour's beautiful garden from which one reaps benefits without having to contribute directly to the costs of producing such benefits. If the supplier of a positive externality does not reap the full rewards from production of their commodity, then that commodity will tend to be underproduced. The gardener in question would have produced an even more beautiful garden or helped others in enhancing their gardens if payment could have been received for doing so. The most obvious example of a negative externality which exists in modern economies is that of ozone depletion. If producers of commodities leading to negative externalities do not have to bear the costs of such externalities, too much of these commodities will be produced. Without producers and consumers bearing the cost of the reversal or prevention of ozone depletion, too many ozone-depleting commodities will be produced and consumed.

In health care, there may be various forms of positive externalities. For example, some people may benefit from other people's consumption of needed health care. An obvious example here is vaccination, which has direct effects on risks to one's own health. Benefit may also arise from knowing that someone else is receiving needed health care even if this does not impact on one's own health status. As unregulated markets do not account for externalities, such markets may lead to underproduction of health care. On the other hand, negative externalities in health care include iatrogenic illness. In this case market transactions could lead to over-production of health care.

Perfect Knowledge

The assumption of perfect knowledge on the part of the consumer infers that the consumer of health care is aware of her or his health status and that all the options available to contribute to an improvement in health. Equally important is the assumption that the consumer knows how each of these options will contribute to better health and is able to judge the relative quality of each (i.e. the consumer has knowledge of the technological relationship between health care and health improvements or health maintenance).

Again, it may well be the case for many minor common ailments, and also some chronic conditions, that consumers are aware not only of their health status but also of the treatment options available. However, this is unlikely to be the case for more acute conditions, such as breast cancer or appendicitis. Even in the case of minor and chronic ailments, information on new developments in treatment may get through to health care providers long before it reaches consumers.

The accumulation of knowledge is also determined by the regularity with which one uses the market. Again, consumers of health care are less likely to make regular use of the market than consumers of foodstuffs. Further-more, some element of knowledge accumulation is determined by 'learning from mistakes'. Given the technological relationship between health care and health, and without chances to make regular use of the health care market or to learn from mistakes, consumers may often be in a position from which they cannot judge what life would be like either in the absence of health care or if health care was consumed (Weisbrod, 1978). When the consumer is in the position of considering whether or not to purchase health care, it is the difference between these two states of the world which is of importance to them. In such situations, the advice of a more qualified and knowledgeable 'expert' who is familiar with the market, in this case a doctor, is required. The need for an expert is further enhanced by the nature of the decision faced by the consumer: with many commodities, making the wrong decision does not have drastic consequences and the choice can often be repeated and rectified at very little cost, whereas, with health care, errors in decision making may have serious consequences and the choice may not be repeatable!

Consumers Act Free of Self-interested 'Advice' from Doctors

Following on from the assumption of perfect knowledge, consumers can act freely in their own interest when making decisions about what and what not to consume. Suppliers, acting in their own interest, provide commodities most highly valued by consumers relative to their prices. But, given a lack of perfect knowledge on the part of consumers of health care, doctors are often placed in the position of providing expert advice to consumers about care to be provided by themselves or their colleagues. Thus, the supplier of care is able to influence substantially demand for that care. It is asking a lot of doctors placed in such a situation if they are required to act simultaneously on behalf of their own and their patients' interests. For instance, there may be situations in which doctors actually have an incentive, financial or otherwise, to provide care of no value or of little value relative to its cost.

Numerous, Small Producers with No Market Power

In perfect markets it is assumed that producers are small and numerous, and therefore do not have any market power. They compete with each other only on the basis of price. In order to attract consumers, producers have to keep prices as low as possible. Thus, the costs of commodities, including health care, are minimised. This process breaks down in health care because the need for experts to advise patients results in the requirement for licences (medical and other health-related qualifications) to permit doctors and other health care professionals to practise. In a position of being able to grant licensure to prospective colleagues, doctors are empowered with a degree of market control which permits them to restrict entry to their profession, and therefore to restrict the competitive forces which act to minimise health care costs. If entry to the profession is limited then the amount of health care provided will be less than would otherwise have been the case because there are fewer doctors. With supply limited, the price of health care will be higher than it would otherwise have been (Note 4). Despite this, it is argued that licensure is required in order to maintain standards. Possible ways out of this seeming dilemma may be to remunerate doctors in a way that encourages provision of good-quality care at low cost and to involve governments (as representatives of consumers) in negotiating with doctors on the numbers of qualified staff required.

CONSUMER IS SOVEREIGN?

If all of the above assumptions held true, there would be very little acrimony over the issues of how much societies should spend on health care overall or about levels of spending on different types of health care. This is because, as pointed out by McGuire *et al.* (1988), consumers of health care will:

(1) have to judge the cost of health care;
(2) bear the cost of health care;
(3) have to judge the benefits of health care;
(4) receive the benefits of any health care consumed;
(5) make decisions, because a rational and knowledgeable consumer will purchase only health care whose benefits are greater than its costs.

Armed with knowledge and the ability to switch demands from one small provider to another, consumers determine the appropriate level of price at which supply will equal demand. At that level of supply and demand the size of the health care sector is determined. With rationing by price, there will be no queues for care. There can be no (justified) complaints when the level of spending on health care and its quality are dictated by the preferences of fully knowledgeable consumers. If some people are denied access to care, and this is thought to be unjust, the solution is to redistribute income and to let the market do the rest, once again relying on fully knowledgeable consumers.

This dominance of consumers' preferences is known as consumer sovereignty. Whether consumer sovereignty is widespread is open to debate. It is not known whether consumers actively or passively accept many of the products which are available in the market place. Perhaps consumer sovereignty enters the decision-making process at an early stage when marketing experts are assessing the potential of a product. Often-quoted examples of the power of consumers to dictate to producers are the failures of the Ford Edsel motor car in the 1950s and of New Coke in the 1980s, both in the USA. Consumers did not take to these products and they were subsequently, and quickly, withdrawn from the market. In the latter case, the original Coke (or what became known as Classic Coke) was reintroduced, as it was supposedly of greater utility to consumers. Despite such famous occurrences, it should be noted that examples of such consumer power are few and far between. They demonstrate that consumers can be powerful but not that consumer sovereignty is widespread.

CONCLUSIONS

We have attempted to demonstrate in this chapter how markets for health care would work under idealised conditions. The reality, of course, is that no market possesses such idealised conditions. The nearest to an ideal market is probably the stock market, in which both sellers and buyers are armed with good knowledge of the world market in shares, which is kept up to date by computer technology. In such markets, consumers can be relied upon to judge cost and quality and producers to minimise costs.

As we have already hinted, such idealised conditions seldom, if ever, exist in health care. This does not, of itself, necessitate government intervention in the health care market. Many commodities are traded in markets which are not perfect but remain free of government 'interference'. The question, then, is the degree of imperfection. The following chapter explores in more detail the failure of the crucial assumptions of perfect markets and introduces possible policy responses to such failures. If such imperfections are accepted, extensive government intervention in health care is difficult to avoid, if maximisation of the community's welfare is the objective of such care.

CHAPTER 3

Market Failure in Health Care

INTRODUCTION

It takes but a moment's thought to realise that not many markets possess all of the ideal characteristics outlined in the previous chapter. Thus, many commodities are not traded in perfect markets. Even in the most market-orientated economies a common, everyday commodity like food is subjected to some level of government intervention in its financing, and sometimes in its provision. On the demand side of the market, income subsidies are provided to certain groups of people to give them the ability to purchase the basic necessities of life, including food. On the supply side, many countries have farming subsidies and employ a food inspectorate to monitor the standards of food and its packaging, and to impose restrictions on certain food imports while promoting their own exports.

For the most part, government intervention in markets does not go beyond these levels. In the case of foodstuffs, once consumers have been subsidised and producers inspected, they are free to make transactions between one another in a largely unregulated environment. It is assumed that consumers are the best judges of their own welfare. However, in health care, government intervention is much more extensive than this. Intervention in the health care market often involves governments in purchasing care on behalf of consumers and even in providing such care.

The aim of this chapter is to introduce the economic arguments used to justify such extensive government intervention in health care. This involves examining why the market in health care fails. Although no markets work perfectly (according to the ideal assumptions outlined in the previous chapter), it may still be that leaving the resource allocation process to be determined by market forces remains the best way of getting as close as possible to the ideal outcomes of the perfect market. Many imperfect markets remain fiercely competitive, which may be of benefit to consumers. The basic reasoning underlying *extensive* government intervention in health care, however, is that none of the ideal assumptions of perfect markets works in the case of health care. Thus, market failure in the allocation of health care is so complete that extensive government intervention is more likely to result in the achievement of societal objectives than are market forces supplemented by minimal government intervention.

The implication of this is that there are important, and sometimes distinctive, characteristics of the commodity health care which render it more susceptible than other commodities to government intervention. These characteristics, and their consequences, are outlined in the following three sections of this chapter. They are as follows:

- Risk and uncertainty associated with contracting illness, which, in an unregulated market, will lead to the development of insurance markets and the consequent problems of diseconomies of small scale, moral hazard and adverse selection.
- Externalities.
- Asymmetrical distribution of information about health care between providers and consumers, combined with problems of professional licensure.

This taxonomy of the characteristics of health care which lead to market failure in its financing and (sometimes) provision follows that of Evans (1984) and McGuire *et al.* (1988), to whom the reader is referred for a more comprehensive and technical discussion. Although one may recognise each of the above characteristics in other commodities, it is our contention that health care is unique in that it possesses *all* of these characteristics. One (or even two) of these characteristics existing in a commodity may not justify extensive government intervention. However, it is argued in this chapter that all of these characteristics occurring in one commodity would render market failure so complete as to result in government intervention being the optimal solution for its financing, though not necessarily its provision.

Throughout the chapter, possible policy responses to market failure will be introduced and some discussion of their relative merits may take place. However, for the most part, these responses are discussed in detail in forthcoming chapters. After discussing the various aspects of market failure in health care, data on the extent of government involvement in the financing of health care will be presented. It will be seen that, even in market-orientated economies, a substantial proportion of health care is publicly financed. However, government financing of health care can take many different forms, and, depending on the amount of government intervention, markets in health insurance may also develop. The different kinds of health care systems which may develop as a result of government intervention are described in the next chapter.

RISK, UNCERTAINTY AND THE FAILURE OF PRIVATE HEALTH CARE INSURANCE

Uncertainty and the Demand for Insurance

For the individual, illness is unpredictable. In general terms, it may be possible to predict the prognoses associated with various chronic conditions and to predict in probabilistic terms how people of varying ages, circumstances, and pre-existing conditions will fare in terms of their future health status. But, at the level of the individual, future health status is likely to be uncertain.

It follows from this that one cannot plan one's future consumption of health care in the way that one could do so for commodities like food. As a result of this inability to plan when a future event will occur, an unregulated market would respond by developing insurance mechanisms, whereby an individual, or family, could make payments to some risk-pooling agency (usually an insurance company) for guarantees for some form of financial reimbursement in the event of illness leading to the insured person incurring health care expenses. Some insurance against loss of income may be taken out by the insured person, but, despite the desirability of doing so, it is difficult to insure against anxiety, pain and suffering resulting directly from illness. This is because of difficulties in valuing anxiety, pain and suffering in monetary terms, and because insurance companies could never obtain reliable and objective estimates of how much anxiety, pain and suffering an illness leads to (Note 5). On the other hand, health care expenditures incurred are a fairly reliable signal that an illness has occurred, and they are more readily quantifiable. Therefore, it is *health care* insurance which is mostly taken out by insured people, although it is commonly referred to as *health* insurance (Evans, 1984). People cannot insure against ill-health itself but rather the financial costs of ill-health. Thus, health care insurance embodies the wider concept of income maintenance.

If insurance policies are actuarially fair, premiums paid will equal health care expenditure incurred. However, this assumes that insurance companies make no profit and incur no administration costs. These assumptions do not hold, but people still take out (actuarially unfair) insurance, paying premiums which are 'loaded' so as to cover administration and profit. The reason for this is that, in general, people are risk-averse; they do not like risk and gain utility from covering the uncertainty of large financial losses. This is a utility gain for which they are willing to pay.

For example, in a community of ten people it might be known that each person has a one-in-ten chance of incurring health care expenditures of £1000 per annum. If all are risk averse, each would take out an insurance policy, paying £100 per annum each if it were actuarially fair. However, if administrative costs were £10 per annum, would each person be willing to pay the actuarially unfair premium of £101 each? The answer is probably 'yes'.

People are also more likely to insure against larger losses which are unpredictable than against smaller losses which occur more regularly and therefore more predictably. For instance, of those people who visit a dentist every six months for a check-up, some may not find it worth their while insuring against the predictable and inexpensive check-up itself, but would rather insure against the unpredictable and more expensive consequence of requiring treatment subsequent to the check-up. This does not mean, of course, that no one will insure against relatively small potential losses; many people do insure against such losses. The reason for this may be related not only to uncertainty itself, but also to the anxiety associated with incurring financial costs. However, as one would expect, the value of insurance is in providing cover against the uncertainty of financial losses – especially large ones.

From the foregoing, it is apparent that insurance is a sensible institutional response to the problem of uncertainty in the incidence of large health care expenses. How, then, do health care insurance markets fail, and why should the public sector intervene in such markets? Such market failure arises from three sources: diseconomies of small scale, moral hazard, and adverse selection.

Diseconomies of Small Scale

Before explaining this term 'diseconomies of small scale', it is best to explain the term 'economies of scale'. The bigger an organisation, the easier it becomes, normally, for that organisation to distribute a fixed cost across its products, so reducing the cost per unit produced. This is an example of an economy of scale. In health care insurance, an example of an economy of scale is marketing costs, which may amount to the same total figure no matter how many people are insured with a particular company. Thus, the more people covered the smaller will be the marketing costs per person, an economy which may then be fed back to consumers in reduced premiums. The same may be true for administrative tasks such as the processing of bills and the collection of premiums.

Diseconomies of small scale arise in markets with several competing insurance companies, each with its own administrative and marketing costs. In a large company, such administrative costs would be reduced because they would be spread over more customers. However, a large monopoly insurer may be exploitative. An alternative policy response would then be to have a public monopoly so that low costs are maintained without the risk of exploitation. Some costs, such as those of marketing, of checking for eligibility of rebates and of premium collection, may be drastically reduced or cut out altogether if premium collection is 'piggy-backed' on to the taxation collection system.

Diseconomies of small scale result in market failure because it is conceivable that a person would not be willing to pay for insurance which is inflated by the cost of small-scale competition or by an exploitative monopolist, but would be willing to vote for a system involving the collection of premiums through some public mechanism, such as taxation. One of the reasons why market mechanisms are often thought to be better than some form of government intervention is that neoclassical theory assumes that such costs are zero, or at least very small. The cost of producing the information to make the market work is ignored.

Evans (1984) has demonstrated that expenditure on administration as a percentage of total health care expenditure in the US is 5.2 per cent compared with 1.5 per cent in Canada. Thus, the more privately orientated health care system appears to be administratively more costly. If we exclude the public sector from the USA calculations, private sector administrative costs are 13.4 per cent of private sector reimbursement (Richardson, 1987). A 1983 estimate of administrative costs in the USA was 22 per cent of total health care expenditure, a figure replicated later in an update of this work (Himmelstein and Woolhandler, 1986; Woolhandler and Himmelstein, 1991). The recent process of introducing more competition into the USA health care system itself is thought to have resulted in increased administrative costs as a result of greater spending on advertising and on hospital utilisation review (Evans, 1987; Quam, 1989). Evans (1990) has described the effect of such activities as follows:

'A large and growing share of the American total is spent, not on doctors and nurses, but on accountants, management consultants, and public relations specialists. Their contribution to the health of the American public is difficult to discern (unless one is trained in neoclassical economics and is able to see with the eye of faith).'

Richardson (1987), referring to data for Australia, claims that, in 1982–3 (the year before the introduction of universal health care insurance) management expenses of private funds amounted to 14.8 per cent of benefits paid to claimants, while in its first full year of operation, the corresponding figure for Medicare (Australia's second universal public health insurance scheme) was 4.7 per cent. Thus, the evidence suggests that diseconomies are likely to exist when care is financed through small-scale competition in the private insurance sector.

Moral Hazard

In insurance-based health care systems the problem of potential 'excess' demand exists because of what has become known as 'moral hazard'. Excess demand results in the benefits from resources used in health care provision being exceeded by the benefits forgone (or opportunity cost) from the use of these resources in an alternative which is not currently funded (Note 6). The levels of demand, and therefore provision, are greater than would be the case in a perfect market with fully-informed consumers. Moral hazard is basically a change in the attitudes of consumers and providers of health care which results from becoming insured against the full costs of such care.

Moral hazard can be divided into 'consumer moral hazard' and 'provider moral hazard'. Each has two aspects. Consumer moral hazard arises on the one hand because the very fact of being insured reduces the (financial) costs of treatment at the point of consumption and hence makes being ill a less undesired state, a state less energetically to be avoided. Consequently, the incentive to adopt healthier lifestyles is diminished and the probability of requiring care rises. This is likely to be more significant in certain other spheres (for example, automobile insurance), but it also applies to health. The other aspect of consumer moral hazard is the effect being insured has when sickness occurs and services are demanded: a zero or reduced price at the point of use encourages a higher rate of use than would otherwise be considered efficient; there is a wedge driven between paying for the cost of what is provided and the value of, or willingness to pay for, what is provided. Thus, the market fails to transmit efficient price signals to consumers.

Consumer moral hazard is the form in which moral hazard is most often characterised (Pauly 1968; 1983). The phenomenon can also be explained diagrammatically. According to Figure 3.1, and from our previous discussion of demand theory in Chapter 2, it can be seen that a zero price of health care at the point of delivery would result in the overconsumption of health care relative to what would occur under normal market mechanisms. At a prevailing market price of P_e, the amount of overconsumption is represented by the amount $OQ_1 - OQ_e$. This overconsumption results in a welfare loss to society represented by the area ABQ_1 as a result of the benefits, to patients, of health care consumed being less than the cost of such care. For instance, the benefit of care consumed at Q_2 is represented by the distance between Q_2 and point C, while the cost of such care is P. More benefit (or welfare) to society could be obtained by shifting the resources used up by these excess demands out of the activities covered by health insurance and into some other health-inducing activity or even out of health care altogether.

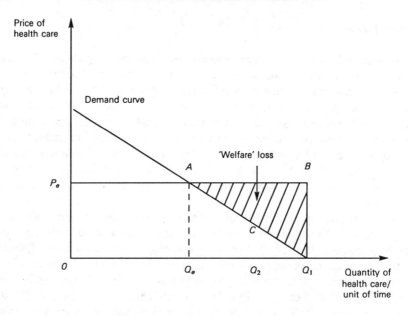

Figure 3.1 Effect of insurance on demand for health care

It should be noted here that the characterisation of moral hazard as described is very neoclassical. In particular, the implication is that the demand curve in Figure 3.1 is that of a fully informed and rational consumer. However, we have already questioned this assumption and do so again in the section below on licensure and asymmetry of information. It will be argued in that section that the doctor (or supplier of care) can have considerable influence over demand for care. Thus, the traditional neoclassical view of the independence of supply and demand is broken. As it is not known where the demand curve of a fully informed consumer would lie, it is difficult to see how the welfare loss associated with excess demand can be measured. The relevance of the demand curve of a less than fully informed consumer influenced by advice from suppliers is difficult to judge.

Provider moral hazard can result from a simple lack of awareness of costs or from the use of fee-for-service (FFS) remuneration methods for doctors in which fees depart from 'market prices'. In systems that use FFS methods of remuneration, doctors are paid a fee for items of service provided to patients. For example, a surgeon may receive a fee for a particular operation carried out, a radiologist for reading a mammogram, and a general practitioner for a consultation or for providing a more specific item of service like a vaccination.

The conventional wisdom is that, in such systems, doctors have a financial incentive to provide care in excess of that which would be arrived at by trading with fully informed consumers. This phenomenon is also known in the literature as 'supplier-induced demand' (Evans, 1974; Rice, 1983; Cromwell and Mitchell, 1986) and will be more fully explored in the section below on asymmetry and licensure, and also particularly in Chapter 7. However, the important point is that in FFS systems problems of how much care is provided arise only when fees depart from the 'true competitive prices' which the doctor would have received. Thus, in accordance with the conventional wisdom, if the fee is greater than the true competitive price there will be an incentive to overprovide. But, contrary to conventional wisdom, if the fee is below the true competitive price, then there will be an incentive to underprovide care.

These phenomena cannot be tempered by consumers because, firstly, they often do not have the knowledge to be able to judge what is appropriate and what is not, and, secondly, it can be seen from the discussion above that consumers also have no financial incentive to moderate such behaviour anyway because a third party, the insurance company, will be paying for the costs of care. It is commonly found in the USA that a further 'wedge' is driven between the cost of providing care and the value derived by consumers, because it is often the employer who negotiates and pays insurance premiums. Thus, there are two 'third parties' to whom health care costs can be passed by both consumers and providers: insurance companies and employers. The effect that moral hazard (of all kinds) has on rising premiums which are ultimately borne by the consumer is thus accentuated by being partially disguised to the consumers themselves.

Similarly, in publicly-orientated systems, such as the UK and Scandinavia, health care providers do not incur the full opportunity cost of provision of many aspects of care (for example, diagnostic tests), thus rendering them prone to provider moral hazard arising from a lack of awareness of costs but not from payment by FFS. In many cases doctors are either not interested in or are not given information on the costs of items of resource use consequent upon their actions. In this case it is the health authority, and ultimately the taxpayer, who pays for care. Once again, therefore, the effects of moral hazard on health care costs in a centrally funded system are partially disguised to consumers. The market fails both to transmit information on costs to, and to impose responsibility for costs on, the supplier of health care.

It is worth noting that the danger of 'overutilisation' due to moral hazard can be exaggerated. There are powerful grounds for supposing that the rate of utilisation chosen at prices reflecting the full cost of care would be too low anyway (see Culyer and Simpson, 1980, for a review). This arises because of the external benefits of health care in the form of the reduction in the probability of infection from communicable diseases for the rest of the community. Presumably, too, many people care sufficiently about others for them to experience a vicarious benefit from the knowledge that their health needs are better cared for than would otherwise be the case (Culyer, 1986). This issue is covered in detail below in the section on externalities.

Moral hazard is the aspect of insurance markets which has received most attention from economists. This is reflected in the fact that Chapters 6 to 8 of this book are devoted to an examination of the evidence on different policy responses to this phenomenon. Policy responses to moral hazard do not have to be financial. Traditional organisational responses to preventing overuse of expensive hospital services in many developed countries have involved the use of primary-care doctors as the 'gateway' to such services. Likewise, in less-developed countries a similar policy is to use 'barefoot doctors', as in Papua New Guinea and, of course, China. Such organisational considerations are, unfortunately, beyond the scope of this book.

Financially, consumer moral hazard has typically been countered in the following ways: use of copayments (or user charges), whereby the insured person pays some fraction or absolute amount of the supplier's charge; fixed periodic per capita prepayment by consumers directly to the provider of comprehensive health care, such as a health maintenance organisation (HMO); provision of incentives for consumers to demand care from selected providers, offering low-cost packages of care, as in the case of preferred provider organisations (PPOs); placing financial limits on indemnity; non-price rationing by doctors according to judgements of need, usually resulting in consumers incurring waiting 'costs' for elective treatment.

The first four of these have been implemented mainly in private insurance-based systems, such as the USA, with the fifth being characteristic of publicly provided and financed health care, such as in the UK National Health Service. The principles underlying HMOs and PPOs are outlined in more detail in the next chapter. Given our comments above on the relevance of the neoclassical approach to moral hazard, some of these 'solutions' can be questioned in principle—particularly user charges. So-called 'solutions' may simply bring along another set of problems. This also highlights the importance of evidence on the effects of all of the above on costs and health outcomes. This evidence is presented in Chapter 6.

Provider moral hazard has been typically countered by four main methods: firstly, non-pecuniary incentives resulting mainly from the pressure of peer review, which can also be bolstered by financial reward for 'good practice'; secondly, use of a salaried service in order to cap payments to providers of care; thirdly, financial limitations imposed at a 'global' level by clinical or institutional budgets, at a case-by-case level by prospective reimbursement for patients within diagnosis-related groups (DRGs), or by fixed periodic prepayments to HMOs' primary-care doctors for provision of their own care or even for the purchase of hospital care on behalf of their patients; fourthly, direct government regulation as a means of controlling providers, such as the limited list for pharmaceutical prescribing by general practitioners in Norway, with financial penalties imposed on those who unjustifiably prescribe outside the list.

Each of these methods of controlling provider moral hazard is reviewed in Chapters 7 and 8. In Chapter 7, evidence is presented on how different methods of payment affect doctor behaviour, while in Chapter 8 the effect of different reimbursement mechanisms on hospital behaviour is reviewed.

Adverse Selection

Adverse selection results from asymmetry of information in the insurance market: that is, buyers of insurance tend to have more of an idea of their risk status than sellers of health care insurance. Initially, in a competitive market, if the insurance companies have no idea of individual risk status, a premium could be set reflecting the general health risks of the insured population. Thus, the premium paid by everyone who takes out insurance would be the same, reflecting the 'average' risk level of the insured population. This is what is called 'community rating'.

For some members of the insured population who perceive their own risk level to be lower than average, this community rating premium will be too high. They will then elect not to take out health care insurance and will not be covered in the event that the unexpected happens. The effect of this decision, however, means that the average risk level of those remaining insured will rise, because it is people of lower-than-average risk who have dropped out of insurance. Thus, to cover the projected health care costs of this population, premiums must rise. Once again, the result of this is that those perceiving their risk status to be lower than the average of those remaining insured will drop out of insurance, and the process will carry on. This process, whereby the best risks are selected out of the insured group, is called 'adverse selection'.

In a competitive system other phenomena would be expected to follow from adverse selection. The presence of a low-risk, uninsured group of people presents the potential for insurance companies to tailor premiums to levels of individual, rather than population, risk. This is 'experience rating'. If fine distinctions can be made, a premium will reflect assumed future risk level based perhaps on some idea of past history of personal and family health as a predictor for the future. As a result of this process, higher-risk groups (typically the lower-paid, elderly people and the chronically sick) will be required to pay higher experience-rated premiums to maintain coverage, premiums which they may not now be able to afford. The process by which low-risk individuals are drawn into low-premium plans is often referred to as 'skimming' or 'creaming off'.

How, then, does adverse selection constitute market failure? Two groups of people may be left uninsured as a result of adverse selection: those of low risk who start off the vicious circle by pulling out of insurance at community rates; and those in high-risk groups who cannot afford experience-rated premiums. Adverse selection constitutes market failure for the former group but (perhaps, surprisingly) not, on its own, for the latter. For the former group, the market fails because both insurer and customer would be willing to enter into a contract, but the necessary information required for such a transaction to be entered into is not transmitted from one party to the other via the market. The transaction is prevented by asymmetry of information about risk status. Low-premium insurance policies could be offered, but, because of asymmetry, insurance companies would have no a priori information on potential customers which would not allow them to prevent some high-risk people taking up such policies. Therefore, such policies will not be offered. Despite this failure of the market, society may not wish to respond anyway, because the failure mainly affects a small and privileged group.

For the high-risk group, the market does not fail. Quite simply, their financial resources cannot cover the cost of insurance. As Evans (1984) points out, these people 'cannot afford Mercedes Benz's either, but that is no failure of automobile markets'. Despite this, it is this aspect of adverse selection which presents the more serious social problem.

By far the majority of uninsured or underinsured people will come from this group. In the USA it has been estimated that, in 1977, 50 million people were inadequately covered against the event of catastrophic illness (Farley, 1985) and, more recently, that 37 million people (17 per cent of the population) have no cover whatsoever (Wilensky, 1988). Those families with experiences leading to catastrophic health expenditures (over 5 per cent of family income) are more likely to be inadequately covered than average families, largely because of the interaction of low income, poor insurance and poor health (Wyszewianski, 1986; Quam, 1989). Hayward et al. (1988) found that, among those with medical problems, those without insurance are 1.9 times as likely to have needed supportive medical care, drugs or other supplies, but not to have obtained them, and were 2.3 times more likely than insured people to have their illness result in a major financial problem. Newacheck (1988) has found that uninsured children receive 50 per cent less ambulatory doctor visits and that less than half of USA citizens with incomes below the official poverty line meet Medicaid eligibility criteria, although the aim of Medicaid is to provide public coverage for 'poor' members of US society. Concern for the plight of the uninsured and underinsured in US society was highlighted by the recent series of articles on this subject in the *Journal of the American Medical Association* (Moore, 1991; Friedman, 1991).

In Australia, it was estimated that about 15 per cent of the population had no private or public insurance cover prior to the introduction of the first compulsory public insurance scheme there in the early 1970s (Deeble,

1982). This was despite the fact that one vulnerable group, elderly people, received automatic cover as a designated priority group. The uninsured group was made up largely of Southern European migrants and those in low-income groups. The same was also true before the introduction of the second Australian public insurance scheme in 1984 (Palmer and Short, 1989) (Note 7).

Thus, the USA and Australian experiences indicate that, even in health care systems based on private health insurance but in which some attempt is made to provide coverage for those in special groups (such as elderly people in Australia and low-income people in the USA Medicaid schemes), a substantial degree of adverse selection still exists. As we have said above, however, this does not, on its own, represent market failure for this group. The market has not failed in its transmission of information between suppliers and demanders of health care insurance. Whether this social problem is defined as market failure depends on externalities: that is, how much members of society care about the exclusion of others from access to needed health care. To continue Evans's analogy, members of society are less likely to care about the access of less-well-off people to Mercedes Benz cars than about access for these people to needed health care! Thus it is adverse selection and externalities acting in conjunction which determine society's response to this problem (Note 8). Therefore, it is the issue of externalities to which we now turn in order to identify whether anything should be done about the effects of adverse selection on high-risk groups and, if so, what the possible policy responses might be.

EXTERNALITIES

As described in the previous chapter, externalities are spillovers from other people's production or consumption of commodities which affect an individual in either a negative or a positive way, but which are out of the individual's locus of control. The costs and benefits of such spillovers cannot be accounted for in market transactions because, when such transactions take place, consumers and suppliers consider only costs and benefits to themselves. If producers of commodities leading to negative externalities do not have to bear the costs of such externalities, too much of these commodities will be produced. If the cost of a negative externality is added to the other costs of producing a commodity, the price is likely to rise. It then follows that less of that commodity will be demanded. Depending on the size of the negative externality, it can be seen that unregulated market forces may lead society away from its optimal provision of various goods and services.

In health care, there may be certain positive externalities whereby people benefit from other people's consumption of the commodity. Benefit may arise from knowing that others can consume a public health intervention, such as vaccination, which has direct effects on risks to one's own health (a 'selfish' externality) (Note 9). Benefit may also arise from knowing that someone is receiving needed health care which does not necessarily impact on one's own health status (a 'caring' externality). This caring externality is often characterised by the concern some benevolent, rich and healthy members of society may have for those who are poor and/or unhealthy, although clearly the poor can be similarly concerned. Our final statement from Smith (1759; Note 10)), as quoted by Skinner (1986), demonstrates that even he recognised the existence of externalities, though (as may be expected, given the historical context) not explicitly for health care:

> 'How selfishly soever man may be supposed, there are evidently some
> principles in his nature which interest him in the fortune of others, and render
> their happiness necessary to him, though he derives nothing from it except for
> the pleasure of seeing it.'

From this concern, Smith was of the view that governments should protect individuals by involvement in road building, public education, help for the destitute, provision of a system of justice and provision of 'cultural' activities for workers to offset the effects of economic advance. The economic theory underlying caring externalities in health care was developed largely by Culyer (1971).

As unregulated markets do not account for individuals' willingness to pay for external benefits, such markets will lead to underproduction of health care. Once this willingness to pay, or demand, is added to that generated by private individuals accounting for only their own costs and benefits, it follows that more health care would be demanded. More formally, assuming a two-person society, then, in Figure 3.2, if MV^B represents a poor individual's demand curve for health care (that is, the value placed on additional amounts of care as represented by individual A's willingness to pay for them), at price P_e for health care, the amount of health care allocated to A would be Q_e. However, assuming that individual B (a rich person) also gets some value from A's receipt of health care, then presumably B would be willing to pay for this (as represented by the demand curve $MV_A{}^B$, the marginal value to B of A's consumption of health care). Adding these two marginal value curves together results in the curve representing the total marginal value of A's consumption of health care (MSV^A, the marginal social value of A's consumption). It can be seen that at price P_e provision of care to A after accounting for externalities would be Q_1. It follows that the market was previously underallocating resources to health care, in this case by an amount $OQ_1 - OQ_e$ per annum.

It should be noted at this point that, as characterised, our externality model relies on the benevolence of the rich. It may be that democratic

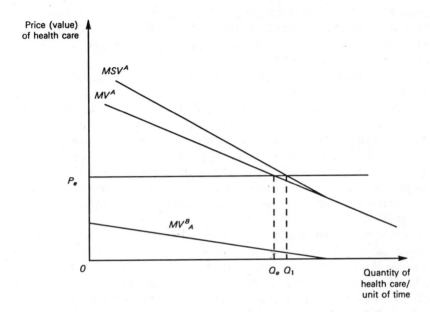

Figure 3.2 Modelling the effect of externalities

systems lead to the election of governments mandated to take money from the rich, whether the rich like it or not. Of course, this is much more difficult to depict in the form of simple neoclassical diagrams like Figure 3.2, and depends on society's broader equity objectives. What these objectives might be in relation to health care is discussed in Chapter 5.

Returning to our simpler model, relying on benevolence, the question then is how to affect the transfer from individual B to individual A, to allow A to purchase his or her required health care. The problem of leaving this to the market is that the amount of the transfer will be less than if contributing individuals made the transfer through some other means. For instance, relying on the goodwill of people to seek out those who are sick so as to contribute to the cost of their health care is impractical and too costly, in terms of time and effort, for those who would like to contribute. Likewise, charities suffer from a similar experience because people often do not 'get round to' making a contribution.

Yet, if the exercise is rendered costless apart from the actual contribution made, more individuals would be prepared to make that contribution. The most efficient way of achieving this is through some mechanism of public health insurance or taxation. In such cases, governments bear the administrative costs of the transfer and more people will be willing to make the transfer. A progressive taxation system of premium collection has the added advantage of transferring not only wealth from those who are healthy to those who are not, but also from those who are rich (and frequently have better health) to those who are poor (and have poorer health). Thus, a progressive taxation system may be a very efficient way of transferring monies to achieve health improvements from the consumption of health care and other commodities. One problem with universal public health care insurance and taxation is that it is compulsory to participate in the system of transferring monies. However, given that neither a free market nor a public system of financing care will satisfy everyone, it is a choice between two evils. It would seem from survey results that even in the privately orientated USA, the majority of the USA population would prefer to have a health care system which provides cover for all, which in turn implies some kind of compulsory participation by consumers, employers or both (Navarro, 1989).

It could be argued that, rather than responding to externalities through publicly financed health care systems, a possible policy response is simply to subsidise those deemed to be 'in need' and to 'leave the rest to the market' as in the case of foodstuffs outlined at the very beginning of this chapter. A cash subsidy for health care, however, has several problems associated with it. First, there is the problem of defining who is in need (and what that concept means) and estimating their treatment expenses in advance. Secondly, there is the 'bleeding cheat' problem, as a result of which recipients of the subsidy may not spend it on what was intended (Archibald and Donaldson, 1976). In this case, the need for health care is so unpredictable that people may spend the money on something they perceive to be more urgent than health care insurance. Culyer (1991) has argued that a general subsidy is more likely to be appropriate for goods and services that are highly income-elastic (i.e. highly responsive to changes in income) at low levels of household income. Such goods (e.g. food) are the most basic of necessities for which people will spend the subsidy in the intended way. This is unlikely to be the case with health care. Vouchers could be used to tie consumption to health care, but such a system can be administratively cumbersome (see Chapter 4).

Secondly, subsidising consumers of health care on the demand side ignores the influence of doctors on the supply side. A lack of perfect knowledge on the part of consumers results in asymmetry of information between the consumer and the provider of health care. Consequently, the former often seeks advice from the latter. This puts providers in a situation where they are not only suppliers but also demanders of care. Continually to subsidise consumers' costs of health care in such a situation, and particularly when providers are rewarded on an FFS basis, could result in a continual cycle of rising fees and further subsidies which would simply, and possibly substantially, increase the costs of health care to the community with little or no additional benefits to patients.

In addition, to maintain standards, licensure exists, whereby the only doctors who can practise are those appropriately qualified. This results in a situation of monopoly in which doctors (many would say rightly) are not subjected to competition from non-qualified practitioners (or 'quacks'). Combining this with the problem of asymmetry of information between doctors and patients could result in doctors manipulating the health care market to their own ends and to the detriment of patients and the community, as in the case of escalating health care costs at little or no benefit to patients described in the previous paragraph. If this problem did not exist then the problems of uncertainty and externalities alone would not justify the level of government intervention which exists in many countries. It is this problem of licensure and asymmetry of information to which we now turn in more detail.

LICENSURE AND ASYMMETRY OF INFORMATION

The Need for a Profession

There has never been, at least in modern times, a free market for doctors' services. Such a market could exist but it would involve no regulation on the supply side. Thus, unqualified practitioners (or 'quacks') would be free to practise and consumers would make choices between all practitioners on the basis of their own assessments of quality and price. In health care, such a market would be problematical in that consumers have little knowledge of how health care will affect their health. Leaving consumers free to make choices in an unregulated market could result in mistakes being made (many of these being very serious). Such mistakes can be made by consumers in other markets, but mistakes in other markets are often less serious and amenable to remedy at small cost. This may not be the case with health care, where mistakes can be serious and unredeemable (even fatal). Hence, societies tend to care more about such mistakes than those made when consuming other products (that is, the externality effect is greater). Also, in many other markets, consumers use the market so much that they obtain the opportunity and thereby the ability to learn from mistakes, and, again, this is not possible in many areas of health care. Therefore, the need for standards and control over conduct in the health care market is universally accepted because consumers are unlikely to be informed enough to protect their own interests. This results in licensure whereby those permitted to practise must hold some minimum qualification. Inadvertently, however, this gives some degree of market power to those holding licenses to practise, in this case doctors. This degree of power may be enhanced when it is the profession itself which decides on numbers of entrants.

Thus, as Evans (1984) has pointed out, any debate about free markets in health care is really based on rhetoric rather than the actual nature of things. The actual nature of things is such that the true question is one of who should have direct control over health care financing and provision, doctors or governments. Given patients' lack of knowledge and the nature of the doctor's role in advising patients, providing care and receiving recompense for that care, it is our contention that this role should be played by governments as representatives of the community and purchasers of much care on its behalf. Given their special position, doctors may have an incentive to overprovide care, the cost of which is not justified in terms of benefits to patients. Indeed, some of this care may be of no benefit whatsoever. It is the nature of the problem of asymmetry and the consequent 'special' position of doctors in the health care market which is discussed in more detail in the following subsection.

The Problem of Asymmetry

In health care, ignorance on the consumer's part is not matched by ignorance on the part of the provider. Therefore, an asymmetry exists. In other production processes, like food production, some regulatory processes may be applied, such as in monitoring standards of products. But, in such cases, the consumer is still judged to be the best judge of their own welfare. This is not necessarily so in health care, because of the technical relationship between health care and improvements in health. Basically, consumers desire improvements in or maintenance of health status. However, improvements in health status cannot be purchased in the market. The consumer is forced to purchase health care in order to achieve an improvement in health. Health care itself is normally of no value, but is linked to health improvements via a 'technological' relationship about which doctors know more than consumers.

So, the market fails in its ability to inform the consumer of the contribution of health care to health status. In the words of Weisbrod (1978):

> 'What a buyer wants to know is the difference between his state of well-being with and without the commodity being considered. For ordinary goods, the buyer has little difficulty in evaluating the counter-factual – that is what the situation will be if the good is not obtained. Not so for the bulk of health care. . . . The noteworthy point is not simply that it is difficult for the consumer to judge quality before the purchase . . . but that it is difficult even after. . . .'

The debate about the need for government intervention, beyond subsidies, in the health care market follows from this aspect of market failure, in combination with externalities and problems of private health care insurance. This debate focuses on two issues: first, the need for licensure, which has been discussed above; and, secondly, whether doctors act as perfect agents, so eliminating the need for government intervention beyond subsidies and legislation permitting the introduction of licensure.

Are Doctors Perfect Agents?

Given the lack of ability of consumers to judge what types, amounts and qualities of health care to consume, or even to judge when care is needed, the doctor is placed in a position of advising the patient on their consumption. That is, the doctor acts as an 'agent' on the patient's behalf. This places the doctor in a unique position of influence in which they can act as both demander and supplier of health care. There are many other areas of the economy in which suppliers of care provide 'advice' to consumers, but they differ from health care in certain respects:

– advice from an expert third party may be bought in to protect the consumer from the supplier (e.g. when purchasing a car);
– one is often more sure of what the outcome should be after the purchase is made (e.g. the engine should start after the car has been fixed);
– the consequences of mistakes are less stark;
– other people tend to care less about mistakes made in other markets than about those made in health care (so, once again, the externality effects are different).

The question then is one of whether the doctor acts as a 'perfect agent' on the patient's behalf. As Williams (1988) eloquently points out, if the doctor is a perfect agent:

'The DOCTOR is there to give the PATIENT all the information the PATIENT needs in order that the PATIENT can make a decision, and the DOCTOR should then implement that decision once the PATIENT has made it.'

The idea is that doctors objectively supply information to the patient, who can then make a decision which maximises utility. Thus, as Evans (1984) says:

'The perfect agent cannot at the same time be an economic principal – unless she is also a perfect schizophrenic. The provider has interests of her own – income, leisure, professional satisfaction, which are partially congruent and partly in conflict with those of the patient. The 'perfect agent' would need a split brain, one half advising the patient solely in the patient's interest, the other half reacting to the patient's resulting consumption choices in a self-interested, own-welfare maximising way. Economic analyses which assume self-interested, profit or income maximising providers must either implicitly assume such schizophrenia as well, or else assume away the asymmetry of information problem and the agency relationship entirely (thus removing any justification for regulation). Not surprisingly, such analyses rarely spell out their assumptions in detail.'

Clearly the role of perfect agent places a great burden on doctors, so much so that Williams (1988) claims that the more recognisable form of his characterisation of the agency relationship is one of imperfect agent in which the words 'DOCTOR' and 'PATIENT' are reversed, and

'The PATIENT is there to give the DOCTOR all the information the DOCTOR needs in order that the DOCTOR can make a decision, and the PATIENT should then implement that decision once the DOCTOR has made it.'

It seems then that doctors are not perfect agents. Indeed there is evidence that doctors do in fact possess the power to induce demand for their own services. The evidence is from systems based on FFS remuneration. Thus, the implication is that patients are encouraged to consume services of little or no benefit, on the recommendation of doctors, for which doctors then receive a fee. If this care is in fact of little or no value to patients in terms of health gains (or some more general measure of well-being), then such demand inducement constitutes an inefficient use of health care resources. Such resources could be used to greater benefit elsewhere in the health care sector or outwith health care altogether.

It is difficult to interpret much of the evidence on supplier-induced demand because it is not clear whether induced demand is for services whose benefits are greater than their costs. This is because of the great problem of measuring benefits in health care. Variations in treatment for the same condition within the same types of health care system are great. It is still not known what is the best level of provision and it is, therefore, difficult to determine what is excessive (Loft and Mooney, 1989; Andersen and Mooney, 1990).

The evidence on supplier-induced demand has been reviewed in more detail by Donaldson and Gerard (1989a) and Rice and Labelle (1989) and is based on international comparisons, population studies and quasi-experiments. Internationally, countries whose payment systems for doctors are based on FFS tend to experience higher rates of utilisation of services, even after controlling for differences in age, sex and population (Vayda, 1973; McPherson *et al.*, 1981; Vayda *et al.*, 1982; McPherson *et al.*, 1982; Vayda *et al.*, 1984). Population studies have noted the correlation between increased doctor-to-population ratios in specified geographical areas and increases in service use, and even in fees (Cromwell and Mitchell, 1986). Quasi-experimental work has demonstrated similar results regarding changes in utilisation in response to changes in fees (Rice, 1983). This evidence is reviewed in more detail in Chapter 7, along with other means of remunerating doctors which may be of use in controlling such provider 'moral hazard'.

RELEVANCE OF ECONOMICS TO GOVERNMENT INTERVENTION

Collectively, the above arguments present a compelling case for government intervention in health care beyond provision of subsidies. Returns to the community will be greater than could be achieved by an unregulated market. However, what is less clear is the extent to which such arguments have formed the basis of policy making regarding the introduction of publicly orientated health care systems around the world. Many systems were already in place by the time such arguments were well formulated, mainly by Culyer (1971) and Evans (1984), although much health and social policy has been formulated using less well-defined arguments which were, nevertheless, along the same lines; for example, the establishment of the UK NHS (Foot, 1965).

Also, ideological considerations have not been discussed, the debate in this chapter focussing more on purely economic justifications of government intervention. It has been argued, for instance, that, in most Western countries, two major factors which have led to the introduction of publicly financed health care systems providing universal coverage are the coexistence of a strong labour movement and a socialist (or labour or social-democrat) government (Navarro, 1989). Indeed ideological considerations could be incorporated into the economic calculus, in that people place various degrees of value on the pursuit of justice and equality. Such considerations, however, would take us further into the field of political economy than we have space for here (Note 11). Also, such considerations are much less the preserve of economics than the arguments presented above. What can be said, though, is that basic values and the way policy is formulated differ from country to country, and therefore a health care system which suits Canadians may not suit Americans (Note 12) and a system which suits the British may not suit Australians. What people want from their doctors and from their health services will also vary from country to country. Such ideological and cultural factors should obviously have weight alongside economic considerations in deciding on the optimal health care system for any country.

Despite this, it does seem evident that the above arguments on market failure have been taken into account in previous policy formation, although not explicitly in the form expressed in this chapter. The introduction of the UK National Health Service (NHS) was based on the principle that

'. . . everybody in the country . . . should have an equal opportunity to benefit from . . . medical and allied services' (*A National Health Service*, 1944).

This was later revised to the desire to have

'. . . equal opportunity of access to health care for people at equal risk' (Department of Health and Social Security, 1976).

The occurrence of adverse selection and caring externalities could easily underlie such principles (Note 13). This has certainly been the case in Australia, where 16 per cent of the population were not covered by public or private insurers prior to the introduction of the second Australian universal public insurance system, Medicare (Palmer and Short, 1989):

'The introduction of Medicare in February 1984 was designed to ensure that all Australians have access to medical and hospital services on the basis of need' (Blewett, 1988).

The same is true in Canada, where the reaction to the inability of private insurers to cover the high risk and/or poor, where the health needs were greatest, was

'. . . to set up universal public systems in each province which would, through cross-subsidisation, be able to include these groups'. (Evans, 1987)

Likewise, the importance of government involvement in regulating fee structures has also been recognised in Australia and in Canada (Deeble, 1982; Evans, 1984). For private or public insurers to guarantee payment of medical fees which are set by the medical profession itself would simply result in a climate of continual fee increases being met by private and public payers. This could increase health care costs, perhaps substantially, at little or no benefit to patients.

The response of these countries to this phenomenon has been slightly different. In Australia, the government sets its own fee schedule and reimburses only a fixed percentage of the fee (85 per cent for general practitioner care and 75 per cent for hospital care, while for the latter the 'gap' between 75 and 100 per cent can be privately insured against). In general practice, doctors can accept the 85 per cent government coverage as full payment, thus waiving the patient's obligation to make up the other 15 per cent of the fee. Doctors are also free to charge above the government fee level, but this extra amount cannot be privately insured against. Consequently, fees tend to be driven down to the levels funded by the government, thus giving the government effective control over their level. In Canada the approach is more direct. Each province produces a schedule of fees to which doctors must adhere. Both systems lead to much conflict between the medical profession and the government. Another problem is that although such regulation gives each government control over fee levels, it does not have direct control over the volume of services provided. Presumably, institutional constraints, such as hospital capacity and the number of hours in a day, help to check the volume of services provided, particularly if governments have a large element of control over investment in such institutions (as is the case in Australia and Canada). However, continual negotiation between the medical profession (as suppliers of care) and governmental bodies (as negotiators of price on patients' behalf) seems to be successful in preventing cost escalation.

CONCLUSIONS

We hope that in this chapter we have demonstrated that as well as strong social and ideological arguments in favour of extensive government intervention in health care, there are powerful economic grounds for such intervention.

Health policy makers in governments have to consider many questions when deciding whether to intervene in this market and on the form of the intervention. However, paramount among the questions to be asked are:

(1) Can the nation afford to spend a large proportion of its resources on the diseconomies and potential excesses of a private health care (insurance) system?

(2) Is it acceptable that, while such excesses exist, large groups in society have no cover and, in many cases, no access to care?

(3) Who should protect such groups?

Governments in most, if not all, developed nations have responded positively to such questions, necessarily going beyond simplistic, subsidy-based 'solutions'. The extent to which government intervention in health care has taken place in OECD countries is demonstrated by the data presented in Table 3.1. Even in what Evans (1990) has called 'the rhetorically "free-enterprise" USA' it can be seen that, in 1984, 41 per cent of health care was publicly funded, the equivalent percentage figure being much higher in almost all other OECD countries.

What the above example of the development of different FFS arrangements in Australia and Canada highlights, however, is that such intervention can take many different forms, reinforcing our comments on the importance of ideological and cultural factors. We have already implied that not every country would want an NHS. In addition, some forms of financing, like charging patients for care, exist in all systems, although to differing degrees. The next question, then, is what kind of basic systems exist and what mechanisms exist within these systems to meet the basic challenges presented by moral hazard (on the part of consumers and providers) and adverse selection. This is the subject matter of Chapter 4.

Table 3.1 Percentage of total health expenditures which are government funded

Country	1970	1980	1984
Australia	55.8	62.5	84.5
Austria	59.1	62.3	60.9
Belgium	87.0	87.4	91.6
Canada	70.2	74.4	74.4
Denmark	86.3	85.2	83.4
Finland	72.1	78.2	78.8
France	71.7	72.0	71.2
Germany	74.2	79.3	78.2
Greece	53.9	83.9	79.3
Iceland	47.4	82.6	82.7
Ireland	77.8	93.5	86.9
Italy	86.4	87.8	84.1
Japan	69.8	70.8	72.1
Netherlands	84.3	78.6	78.3
New Zealand	–	83.5	78.4
Norway	91.6	98.4	88.8
Portugal	–	68.9	71.1
Spain	54.7	73.5	72.3
Sweden	86.0	92.0	91.4
Switzerland	–	65.4	–
UK	87.0	90.4	88.9
USA	37.0	42.5	41.4

Source: OECD (1987).

Part 2

Health Care Systems and Their Objectives

CHAPTER 4

Alternatives for Funding Health Care

INTRODUCTION

Having established, we believe, that some level of government intervention is inevitable and unavoidable in health care, it then becomes important to consider the extent and form of that intervention. In this chapter, alternative methods of funding health care are outlined along with possible advantages and problems associated with each. Although the objectives of such systems are implicit in the descriptions, possible objectives of health care systems are considered explicitly in the next chapter.

Most Western countries operate a system of government approval for grants for proposed capital investments. For the most part, hospitals (or local health authorities) pay no charges once the grant is allocated. In countries such as the UK this process is highly centralised, operating through the NHS. In others (Finland, France and Germany) the process involves regional and national governments. In Canada (at provincial level) and Sweden (at local government level) the process is more explicitly localised. In the USA, many capital costs are incorporated in payment rates (including DRGs), although government does provide subsidies through tax exemptions (OECD, 1987). Relatively little has been written on the subject of optimal methods of capital funding in the health care sector. Consequently, we deal with this issue no further than beyond this point.

It should also be noted that two alternatives have already been discussed: perfect markets and unregulated private health insurance. The former will not be described in this chapter. However, it is possible to modify private health insurance systems in attempting to control for moral hazard and adverse selection without necessarily involving governments. Therefore, possible modifications to private health care insurance will be outlined.

In the absence of adequate empirical evidence, no financing system is necessarily the correct one. Once the inevitability of government intervention is accepted, this can take many forms. In Canada and Australia, for instance, it was natural to move from the well-established systems of private insurance to systems based on public insurance; or at least to give the image of being based on public insurance (Note 14). In Australia, a private health

51

care insurance system still exists to provide top-up cover over and above the universal public insurance scheme. In many Northern and Eastern European countries, on the other hand, systems funded largely from direct taxation have developed, as well-established private insurance markets did not exist when initial steps towards extensive government intervention were taken. These are further reasons why a system which has been developed, and is working well, in one country may not be acceptable to the population of another country.

Describing each alternative financing system is made easier by outlining two key issues in advance; these are common to all systems. First, we examine the complicated nature of the public–private mix in finance and provision which may arise in different systems, and, secondly, different methods of paying providers (doctors and hospitals) are briefly reviewed. The systems which are then outlined are private health care insurance (including modifications, such as preferred provider organisations), direct taxation, public health care insurance, and health maintenance organisations (HMOs). Some other possible, but largely untried, methods of financing are then outlined. Each method is described in terms of three characteristics: principal sources of finance; methods of paying doctors; and methods of paying other providers, mainly hospitals. We conclude this chapter with a summary of how each method counters the problems of moral hazard and adverse reaction.

PUBLIC–PRIVATE MIX IN FINANCE AND PROVISION

The organisation of financial intermediaries may be on a monopolistic, oligopolistic or competitive basis. In a monopolistic system, the financial intermediary is usually a public agency such as a government, a quango or a health corporation. In an oligopolistic system (i.e. one in which there are a small number of large intermediaries) finance can be controlled by public agencies or private agencies, such as insurance companies, or a combination of these. In a competitive system, a large number of small private intermediaries would exist. The closest practical example of this latter system is one based on the vertically-integrated HMO (see the section explaining HMOs later in this chapter), which provides a package of primary and tertiary care in return for a prepaid premium.

The provision of services, however, does not necessarily have to match the financial organisation. For instance, hospital care in many European countries represents a large, vertically integrated health system, in which finance and provision are combined within one organisation. Thus, both finance and provision are public as in the case of quadrant (1) in Figure 4.1. In many countries, general practice would fall into quadrant (2), such care

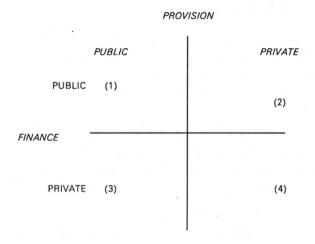

(1) Public finance and public provision   (3) Private finance and public provision
(2) Public finance and private provision   (4) Private finance and private provision

Figure 4.1   Public/private mix in health care financing and provision

being provided by self-employed doctors who, nevertheless, happen to receive almost all of their income from the public purse. A system based on HMOs, on the other hand, represents a similarly integrated (but privately funded) system which could fit into quadrants (3) and (4), buying in care from private or public providers. Also, it is important to recognise that systems do not have to be vertically integrated in these ways: a third-party private payer, such as an insurance company, could also fit into segments (3) and (4). The basic point is that public finance does not have to match public provision, nor private finance private provision. Public provision could be financed by private arrangements (private insurance, direct charges, etc.) and private provision by public finance (e.g. prospective payments made by government agencies directly to private hospitals).

The arguments presented in the previous chapter provide a stronger case for government intervention in *financing* rather than in *providing* health care. Control of financial arrangements permits governmental bodies more direction of the health care system in the pursuit of societal objectives: as the collective purchaser of care on the community's behalf, a public body can dictate terms of provision with equal power to both public and private providers (Evans, 1987). Simply providing public services does not guarantee use by those groups for whom they are intended, because less ill, rich or privately insured patients may be more 'attractive customers' for such hospitals than those more in need of care.

REWARDING THE PROVIDERS

The incentives that affect doctors are not, of course, only financial. Personal pride in a professional job well done and the pressure of peer review (and the information on good practice that it can provide) are among the other features of the professional environment that can reward or penalise professional behaviour in non-pecuniary ways.

Of the financial incentives, fee-for-service (FFS) rewards according to the volume of service provided. FFS remuneration *can* lead to 'induced' and unnecessary demand by patients (for fee-yielding services) on the recommendation of their doctors, and also to cost inflation. Whether or not it does depends on whether fees are set above or below what they would have been in a truly competitive environment.

Capitation (usually found in the context of general practice) pays according to the to the number of patients registered with an individual doctor. This can provide a financial incentive to increase list sizes which could lead to utilisation or consultation levels with which the doctor cannot cope efficiently. Doctors may also have an incentive to refer patients on to hospitals or specialists for which they do not have to pay from the capitation fee. On the other hand, it provides no financial distortion of the purely professional role, given the list size and the available facilities: the doctor simply exercises professional judgements as best they can about patients needs and how best these are to be met. Salaried systems are similar in effect, save that they afford no incentive to increase list size. They also, however, carry the association of 'employee', which in many countries has usually been an anathema to doctors, particularly to general practitioners, though not to hospital doctors. Salaried systems, depending on their structure, may also lead to discontinuity of care as doctors move around in order to gain promotion. These alternatives do not, of course, have to be seen as mutually incompatible. It is possible to combine salary, capitation and FFS in a single remuneration system.

Reimbursement of institutions like hospitals can be done in a variety of ways under either public or private insurance. Retrospective reimbursement involves the insuring agency in paying the provider for all 'reasonable' expenditures incurred on behalf of an insured person or group over the previous period. It notoriously encourages cost inflation and, possibly, unnecessary provision, particularly if coupled with FFS. This is because a hospital will have little incentive to curb expenditure if it is known that all such expenditure will be met by the funding body.

Prospective reimbursement is in principle better able to contain costs, and lends itself much better to forward financial planning by both the institutions to be reimbursed and the financing agencies. Prospective reimbursement can be based on population formulae, as in the UK, or according to planned workload with appropriate cost schedules for a variety of case types. In systems, such as the UK one, in which the overall budget is global, there will be no incentives to allocate resources to those areas which are most productive.

The prospective payment system, which is becoming widely used in the USA public sector, is based on costings of diagnosis-related groups (DRGs). Funding is not global, but is based on individual cases. The cost units require careful estimation and continual updating. If used only partially, or if inaccurately done, they can lead to 'patient shifting', whereby cases which are costlier than the estimate, or costlier than the average embodied in the estimate, are shifted into a less controlled part of the system (e.g. from inpatient to outpatient) or simply not treated at all. Likewise, 'cost shifting' can take place whereby costs of care are shifted on to patients (e.g. private patients) not covered by the DRG reimbursement system.

The remainder of this chapter looks in greater detail at five or more ways of financing health care: private health care insurance; direct taxation; public health care insurance; health maintenance organisations; and other sources of finance. Within each of these, different ways of providing care and of paying providers might be employed. But their descriptions are made easier by having covered each of these issues separately, and briefly, in advance.

PRIVATE HEALTH CARE INSURANCE

The uncertainty surrounding the incidence of ill-health and the efficiency of treatment mean that health care is an appropriate case for insurance. Insurance can help individuals and groups (consumers and professionals alike) to adjust in preferred ways to these uncertainties. As has been seen, this may be achieved by government intervention providing comprehensive public insurance, by a combination of government and private finance or by a comprehensive range of private finance. For a given premium a set of health care risks may be insured against. In the case of pure private insurance, the insurance company covers specified risks of ill-health to the consumer and incurs the consequential expense of (one hopes effective) health care. Private insurance companies usually operate in a market with a small number of large companies (an oligopolistic structure). Although such a structure may achieve economies of scale, there is an incentive for companies to act together to strengthen their power in the market and in doing so keep premiums high and in line with each other.

In a situation of pure insurance (i.e. insurance without extra charges) the consumer pays a premium which might cover the use of all approved health care should the consumer fall ill. This premium is paid either in full by the consumer or shared by their employer (or perhaps by social security funds in the case of unemployed people). Premiums may also be tax-deductible.

Having taken out insurance, the price facing the consumer at the point of using health care will often be zero.

As was explained in Chapter 3, community rating is likely to yield, under private insurance, to experience rating (unless prohibited), because other agencies will offer cover at lower premiums to the uninsured good risks. The poor, the medically indigent and the chronic sick will in any case not usually be covered by such agencies and will, in an entirely private system, be dependent on charity care. Governmental response for some at-risk groups (poor people, elderly people) then becomes almost inevitable (e.g. Medicare and Medicaid in the USA).

Moral hazard also exists in private insurance-based health care systems. With a third party (i.e. the insurance company) paying health care bills on a full reimbursement basis and employers contributing heavily to premiums, neither the consumer nor the provider has an incentive to be cost-conscious (see Chapter 3 for definitions of consumer and provider moral hazard). The consumer faced with free or low cost health care at the point of consumption has little or no financial incentive to restrain demands on the service. Likewise, doctors have no financial incentive to moderate such demands. Indeed if reward is on an FFS basis, as is often the case, they may have an incentive to generate demand for their services (the phenomenon of supplier-induced demand). Even today, in parts of the hospital sector in the USA, moral hazard is further exacerbated by the existence of retro-spective cost reimbursement of hospitals by insurance companies. Such a method gives no incentive to be cost-conscious.

To combat the problem of moral hazard, cost-sharing or co-payment schemes have been introduced by insurance companies. Essentially, the aim of these schemes is to place some financial burden on the consumer to eliminate or at least reduce 'unnecessary' use of health care. Individual schemes differ according to the nature of the financial arrangement but take four main forms: a flat rate charge for each unit of service; co-insurance (the insured individual has to pay a certain proportion of each unit of health care consumed); a deductible akin to the 'excess' in some motor vehicle insurance policies (the individual pays 100 per cent of all bills in a given period up to some maximum amount beyond which insurance benefits are paid in full); or a combination of the last two.

Depending on the level of charges for health care, people in low-income groups or high-utilisation groups may be excluded from consumption as a result of lack of ability to pay. Thus, further government intervention may be required. There is also likely to be some anxiety about the effect on individuals' health if they are deterred from 'non-trivial' utilisation.

Cost sharing need not, however, reduce the overall impact of supplier-induced demand. Doctors may, for example, switch their demand-inducing abilities from lower-income groups to those more able to pay. With the presence of supplier-induced demand, cost containment does not seem so obviously achievable through cost sharing. Even worse, serious health problems may be left untreated as more minor (but able-to-pay) cases replace more serious (not-able-to-pay) cases. The end result could be that the same amount is spent on health care but to less effect in terms of improvement or maintenance of the community's health.

Of course, some advocates of charges claim that doctors could discriminate between groups on the basis of ability to pay, so that everyone would be able to afford the charge. However, this argument does not make sense. If everyone can afford the charge, there will still be much strain on the health care system. Again, the incentive for doctors, in such a situation, would be to concentrate on those more able to pay. Service use would remain the same, but more would be spent on health care because charges would be higher, and care would be going to those less in need.

In addition, and like the diseconomies of scale described in Chapter 3, the billing of patients and the collection of payments under cost-sharing schemes, checking against fraud and so on, are likely to be administratively expensive.

To combat moral hazard in the hospital sector, DRGs are now used (or are being considered for use) in many countries as a means of controlling costs. For instance, since October 1984, US federal government payments for hospitalised patients over the age of sixty-five in the Medicare programme have been changed to fixed amounts of money by type of case which are set prospectively, rather than all 'reasonable' expenses being reimbursed retrospectively. This has changed the incentives for non-government hospitals, to which they have responded. Hospitals are experiencing some decline in utilisation. However, patients may have increased their use of other services not covered by the DRG system, e.g. ambulatory visits to doctors' surgeries (see Chapter 8). Governmentally financed programmes in a primarily private market can also realise some of the gains from 'countervailing power' obtainable in more thoroughly collectivist systems, particularly by 'squeezing' doctors and hospitals in the way the USA DRG system has done.

Consumers in a private insurance system are given a central role in choosing the nature and extent of their own health care coverage. They are able to purchase additional health care insurance according to their own preferences and, of course, ability to pay. The provision of high-quality 'hotel' and other peripheral services is typically greater than in governmental systems.

Preferred Provider Organisations (PPOs)

One recent major reform in private health care insurance markets in the USA has led to the growth of PPOs. PPOs have arisen in the USA as a result of attempts by insurance companies to enter into competition with HMOs (see page 63 for an explanation of HMOs). Premiums either are paid by employers or are shared between employer and employee. Price at the point of use of services is zero. Insurers contract selectively with providers (e.g. primary care doctors and hospitals who provide care below a certain cost per case). The contract is on the basis of both a negotiated fee schedule, which the preferred providers accept as payment in full and acceptance of utilisation review. User charges and deductibles tend to be lower in PPOs than under previous private insurance arrangements (Zwanziger and Auerbach, 1991).

Once more, adverse selection and experience rating will almost inevitably develop within a care system based on PPOs, leaving the more costly groups without cover for health care unless they are subsidised. There is also no financial risk to primary care providers with respect to the volume of services provided. With FFS as the basis for payment the doctor can, to some extent, still manipulate utilisation. However, this has a limit, because if cost per case rises above a certain limit, then the doctor may not be selected as the preferred provider at the next review. The incentive for hospitals to keep costs down arises because a set of prices has been agreed in advance.

Patients can choose between a limited set of providers or choose another provider on less favourable terms, so incentives also exist on the demand side. One specific advantage of PPOs is that they have enabled employers in the USA to move quickly to control health care costs for employees who are already under FFS schemes. Companies either organise schemes themselves or persuade insurance companies to do it. Insurance companies co-operate because this provides a means of competing with HMOs.

DIRECT TAX SYSTEM

Health care finance may be provided by a public monopoly, as in the UK National Health Service. Under such a system, finance is raised by taxation, either in the form of general taxation, hypothecated taxation (i.e. ear-marked taxes specifically for health services) or a general public insurance system (i.e. covering more benefits than only health care and with contributions that are not experience-rated). The Australian health care system provides a good example of an income-related hypothecated tax in the form of the Medicare levy. However, it has never been the intention that this levy should cover all of the public sector's health care costs, the majority being met from direct taxation.

The consumer's contribution to the financial intermediary (i.e. their 'premium') under the direct taxation system is, therefore, part of their total tax payment. But there may also be out-of-pocket contributions depending on the service in question and the individual's circumstances. The NHS principle seems to be that the tax payment covers all basic health care finance, so that the consumer is able to use the health service at zero price. Where charges are levied the usual view seems to have been that they are nominal (that is, small enough not to impose financial hardship and also such as to have no significant effect on a person's health by deterring the consumption of effective health care). In the NHS, waiting lists, waiting times and general practitioner consultations act as important rationing devices for controlling the moral hazard that is inherent in any system having zero (or near-zero) prices at the point of use. In publicly financed systems in less-developed countries (LDCs) charges are also nominal, but have an important revenue-raising role because the lack of infrastructure in such countries renders tax collection difficult.

A system of direct taxation removes the problem of adverse selection because of the absence of competition between financial intermediaries. By detaching premiums from expected risk levels and making them compulsory, a tax system redistributes wealth from those with low *ex ante* expectations of illness to those at high risk. Individuals are effectively charged one form of community rate; one which is dependent on ability to pay but not on previous experience of ill-health. A tax-financed system redistributes according to two indicators of individual well-being, health status and income. It *can* thus be more efficient than any form of redistribution based on income alone. That it *can* be does not of course guarantee that it *will*. It also provides the means of effectively capping total expenditure, provided that there is the political will to contain expenditure. It is also virtually free from 'loading' problems, representing probably the most efficient way of collecting monies to finance the health care system (often referred to as 'piggy-backing' onto the existing system of tax collection).

The use of nominal charges may be seen to provide an incentive to the consumer to restrain some demand, particularly so-called 'unnecessary' ('frivolous' or 'trivial') demand. If that is all that is deterred then nominal charges can be seen as a mechanism which does not deter seeking care for genuine need and therefore does not adversely affect a person's health. Such charges do however raise a number of specific issues: how nominal is 'nominal'? What is frivolous and who defines it? How costly is it to operate a system of 'nominal' charges? What effect on the character of the patient–professional relationship do charges have? How best can one protect the poor, for whom even 'nominal' charges may deter utilisation, without also introducing a cumbersome, stigmatic and expensive bureaucracy?

Collective financing of health care may or may not be linked to public ownership of health services. In the UK NHS, almost all hospitals are publicly owned and hospital doctors are contracted by regional health authorities (RHAs) on a salaried basis. Primary care services on the other hand are less formally organised and general practitioners are private providers remunerated with a combination of FFS and capitation. Access to pharmaceuticals is not cash-limited.

Within the public sector, however, there is no systematic financial signalling system of the sort a well-ordered market would provide. This would inform participants about intersectoral costs, such as GP versus hospital outpatient care, and internal costs which could form the basis of clinical budgets or prepayments per case. Thus, in NHS-type systems, decisions about the optimal balance of services have more usually to be taken either in the face of considerable ignorance about likely cost and likely benefit or only after study in depth. The *system* does not generate a pricing mechanism for routine 'managerial' choices. Nor does it provide a continuing environment of penalties or rewards for inefficient or efficient behaviour. Those who commit resources (the doctors) usually do so in ignorance both of the financial cost of each clinical decision and of the true opportunity cost in terms of the health services that have *not* been provided to others. The budgeting systems that constrain doctors are also typically constructed in extreme ignorance about both costs and benefits. This ignorance can simultaneously lead to claims by some that the total health service financial cake is not effectively used and by others that the service is underfunded. Moreover, it is impossible decisively to refute or support either of these claims – at least, not with current levels of knowledge about costs and benefits.

Experience of markets in health care elsewhere, on the other hand, does not encourage one to be confident that they handle things significantly better. One can, however, have a market in health care finance without a market in health care provision, and a market in provision without one in finance. To suppose that one must necessarily accompany the other is just inaccurate, and the effects of each may be quite different, as pointed out above.

In Chapter 3, it was argued that a market in finance could not work according to societal objectives. However, recent proposals in the UK are resulting in an attempt to implement a market in health care provision in that country, particularly in hospital care (Secretaries of State, 1989a and b). In the UK, district health authorities, armed with revenue from central taxation, will play the role of financing, or purchasing, care on behalf of their local community. They will be permitted to purchase such care from NHS hospitals, from independent hospital trusts or from the private sector, either within or outside the district (Note 15). The aim is for these different types of hospital to compete for funds from district health authorities on the basis of cost and quality. As a monopsony buyer of services, a district health authority should, in theory, have a considerable amount of influence over setting standards of care required (Note 16). Such a system, in which provider markets operate within a single but largely universal system of finance, is known as an internal market.

Some general practices have also been given budgets for the purchase of certain forms of hospital outpatient care and elective surgery on behalf of their patients. The aim is to prevent inappropriate referrals, with general practitioners making judgements based on the cost and quality of hospital care. The 'Dekker' reforms of the Dutch health care system also include proposals for an internal market whereby insurers will purchase services from suppliers of health and social care on the basis of cost and quality (van de Ven, 1989). As yet, internal markets remain unevaluated. They are examined in more detail in Chapter 8.

Additional features can be added into NHS-type systems, such as the strengthening of community representation on decision making and 'watchdog' bodies, and perhaps the use of charges for 'hotel' services. Whether these are 'enough' is a moot point, as is whether it is possible to introduce more market-orientated policies without losing the main advantages of public finance and without introducing stigma, dual standards of medical care, and other features that – in many European countries – seem to be disturbing to the bulk of the population.

PUBLIC HEALTH CARE INSURANCE

A public insurance system can be administered by a monopolistic agent such as a quango, a regional government, or a national government. One of the best-known systems of public health insurance is that existing in Canada. Others exist in Australia, France and Germany. In Canada, consumers pay a uniform premium for hospital and medical care and part of their pharmaceutical and dental costs. Some elements of cost, such as capital expenditure, are financed from tax revenues. Children, elderly people and poor people receive different levels of subsidy for pharmaceuticals and dental care in different provinces. Except in the cases of exempt groups, wealth is transferred only from low to high risks and not (directly – although risk and income tend to be negatively correlated) from persons with high incomes to those with low ones. Premiums can be related to income in the form of a payroll tax; usually, everyone above a certain level of income pays a fixed percentage of their income to the insurance fund. This kind of system is often known as social insurance. It exists in Germany and is common in Latin America. In some countries (e.g. Italy) substantial proportions of health care funding come from both social insurance (about 45 per cent in Italy) and from the central taxation fund (also about 45 per cent in Italy).

In Canada, because private insurance is, for the most part, not permitted, hospitals and doctors have to contract with a public monopsony buyer of care, thus giving provincial governments considerable power over rates of payment. In other countries, such as Australia, private insurance is permitted as a top-up to the basic system, so expanding choice over date and location of treatment for a limited group in society.

For purposes of equity, premiums can either be indexed to income or, as is possible with private insurance, be made tax-deductible. Premiums can be deducted directly, paid by employers; or, for the unemployed, paid through social security. Payroll taxes, unless related proportionately to pay, can have the effect of raising the cost to employers of low-paid (typically less skilled) workers relative to higher-paid workers. The resulting fall in demand for the less skilled leads to still lower wages for the already low-paid and/or more unemployment. Moreover, arrangements would have to be made to ensure cover for the unemployed (voluntary or involuntary), the retired, and those not in the labour force, including dependents of those who are.

One difficulty with payroll taxes, as with national insurance, relates to the incidence of the part paid by employers: is it a cost to employers (as superficially seems the case), or, if it is shifted, does it fall mainly on consumers via higher prices (forward shifting) or on workers in the form of lower wages (backward shifting)? The general belief among economists who have examined this question is that a generally imposed payroll tax falls on labour, regardless of who pays it (employee or employer). Ultimately, of course, both lower wages and higher prices imply that the burden falls on the general public, but it would impinge differently according to consumption patterns and employment status. It is also worth pointing out that a lump sum payroll tax whose final incidence is on employers is effectively a further tax on capital and corporate income and would tend to be progressive; if it were to fall on either employees or consumers it would tend to be regressive (taking a higher proportion of income as income falls).

Care would normally be provided free at the point of use of services under public-health care insurance, although it would be possible to introduce co-payments and charges for 'hotel' services. General practitioners could be paid on the basis of salary, capitation or fee for service (or some combination). There is the possibility of tight government control over fee schedules. Hospitals could be reimbursed in a variety of ways: retrospectively, prospectively, by size of the population served, item by item, globally, with or without peer review and with or without monitoring of outcome and the quality of care. Some hospital income may also come from FFS, nominal charges to patients, and for charges for 'hotel' and other on-site and peripheral services.

Competition *can* take place in a public-health insurance system, for it is possible to envisage the presence of public and private service providers but with the private sector being subject to the same system of payment as the public sector (e.g. internal markets). The crucial aspect of a public health insurance system is monopoly of finance. The lack of competition between financial intermediaries prevents adverse selection and experience rating.

There may also be economies of scale and the avoidance of the recording, billing, collection and enforcement costs (e.g. checking for fraud) of private insurance systems. Once again, advantages may be gained from competition among providers of care because the public insurance agency (as in Canada, a provincial government) acts as the collective purchaser of services on the community's behalf (Evans, 1987). This is similar to the internal market system in the UK NHS.

HEALTH MAINTENANCE ORGANISATIONS (HMOs)

Health maintenance organisations (HMOs) are a product of private insurance systems. However, their prominence in recent years does warrant a separate section of this chapter. HMOs provide (or arrange and pay for) comprehensive health care for a fixed, periodic per-capita payment (or 'premium') which is paid by the consumer (usually with a subsidy from employers or social security). Consumers do not usually pay charges at the point of use. The premium is set in advance and is independent of the volume of services provided to the individual during the period. Providers can be salaried or paid by FFS.

Adverse selection and experience rating will inevitably arise if, as is likely, competition develops. Doctor demand inducement is not likely to be very prevalent, because not only do doctors compete for custom, usually on an annual basis, but also the annual HMO budget is fixed in advance. Doctors, therefore, will be cost-conscious, with the residual between the budget and expenditure accruing to the HMO, and thereby to the doctors. High-spending doctors will then be financially penalised.

Organisationally, HMOs can be of one of four types; a staff model, in which all doctors are employed and/or contracted directly by the HMO; a group model, in which the HMO contracts with an independent group practice to provide services: a network model, in which more than one independent group is contracted to provide services; and an independent practice association (IPA) in which the HMO contracts several doctors in independent practice (Hillman *et al.*, 1989). Thus, there are many financial and organisational variations on the basic HMO model.

Consumers select the health care plan of their choice on an annual basis. Therefore more choice is thought to exist. Because consumers usually receive only a fixed subsidy towards payment (or a fixed percentage of the premium), they too have an incentive to be cost-conscious. Additionally, some HMOs do have user charges, particularly for drugs (Harris *et al.*, 1990).

In the Leningrad experiment in Russia, hospital budgets for thirty-seven specialties have been transferred to polyclinics on the basis of average cost per case. Polyclinics are the main providers of primary care and are also

involved in some specialised outpatient investigation, treatment and rehabilitation. Their staff are salaried. Previously, with hospitals run on a
separate budget, there was an incentive for polyclinics to refer patients on
to hospital. This HMO-style experiment is aimed at improving the appropriateness of such referrals (Hakansson *et al.*, 1988).

This vertical integration of financing for primary and tertiary care is also
the aim of the UK and Dutch internal market reforms outlined above. The
Russian and UK reforms are more supply-side orientated, however, as
consumers cannot choose their DHA or polyclinic; they are covered as a
result of being resident in a particular catchment area.

OTHER FINANCING MECHANISMS

Vouchers for health care are often voiced as an alternative method of
financing although very little is documented about them. Vouchers are a
system of tied subsidy, entitling the holder to trade the voucher in return for
a service. They may be graduated according to the means of the holder, they
may be able to be supplemented out of the holder's own pocket, and they
may vary according to the services (and the period of time to which they
relate) to which they entitle the holder.

The principal advantages of a voucher system in theory are that it serves
consumer choice (the voucher holder may shop around for the insurance
agency of choice, including financially integrated service organisations like
HMOs, of choice) and controls adverse selection (by supplementing ability
to pay).

In practice, given any likely public requirement about the comprehensiveness of the benefits of insurance cover, the 'standard' voucher is likely to
be set at the equivalent of a community-rated premium with out-of-pocket
'topping up' restricted to the 'hotel' type facilities, which may be insurable
but are unlikely candidates for public subsidy. In the absence of private
insurance, such a scheme seems to require a universal system of HMOs as
the counterpart on the provider side.

It is possible to conceive of a voucher for family practitioner services only
(general medical practitioners in particular), in which case it is directly
equivalent to the capitation system (with similar differentiation possible
according to, say, age of the consumer). But the general practitioner's
income would be channelled indirectly via the consumers rather than paid
via a public agency. Consumers could remain as free (or as restricted) as
they currently are to select the practitioner of their choice — and the
general practitioners as free to accept patients. Practitioners could receive
the voucher either when the patient presented or when the patient 'registers'
with the practitioner of choice. The patient would necessarily, however, be
tied to the doctor of choice for the period of validity of the voucher.

If vouchers covered pharmaceuticals, diagnostic tests not performed in the general practice and other such condition-specific services, the risks of moral hazard and adverse selection could become important and general practitioners would have an incentive not to accept patients whose costliness was expected to exceed the value of the voucher—unless topping up or extra billing were permitted (which would in practice discriminate against the poorer risks, who tend typically also to be the worst off in terms of income).

Since the advantages of vouchers can be achieved in other ways, it seems that they are not an attractive alternative to other methods of channelling resources to medical care, which may also be administratively less cumbersome. Setting and updating the value of vouchers is an enormous task. There is, however, no practical experience of vouchers for health care insurance on which to draw, so this conclusion is necessarily conjectural.

The various other means proposed for finance (lotteries, on-site services, charitable donations) can be seen only as supplementary. They are inappropriate both in scale and predictability to the major funding problem, and may be administratively costlier than the alternatives discussed above. None has received the systematic analysis, either theoretical or practical, of the insurance methods. Each may have a useful minor role, especially when harnessing local goodwill and voluntary effort. They can also, however, distort health care planning: for example there may be sponsorship of capital projects that have been neither incorporated into the integrated planning of services nor fully taken into account as regards their longer-term revenue consequences (i.e. once a machine has been bought from charitable donations, the money has to be found to staff and operate it). Such methods need to be employed selectively and can hardly be seen as more than marginal for either the public or the private provision of health care.

Other methods, such as the issue of debt, and equity finance, are already available in the private sector and could become significant if there was a major shift from public towards private provision—especially for-profit provision.

CONCLUSIONS

This short review of the main ways of paying for health care has focused on many issues of recent concern in many countries. The main questions addressed were:

– What financial intermediary stands between the consumer and the service provider?

- What form does the 'insurance premium' take and according to what principles is it set?
- What payments out of pocket are made by the consumer at the point of use?
- How are professional providers to be paid?
- How are institutions to be reimbursed?

Several plausible answers can be given to each of these questions and the chapter has identified the principal pros and cons associated with each. A final selection cannot (or should not) be made solely by weighing up these purely qualitative issues. There is empirical evidence with a bearing on a number of them, and this is the subject of more detailed review in Chapters 6 to 10.

Table 4.1 characterises the main options for raising finance and, within each, some principal variants regarding the control of moral hazard by consumers, doctors and institutions and for dealing with adverse selection. Although HMOs have been described in a separate section of this chapter, they are really a product of private insurance systems and are aimed at controlling both consumer and provider moral hazard. Other methods, such as charges, can be used in all types of system. The options under public insurance and direct taxation systems are identical, except that public insurance systems can include compulsory community-rated premiums plus an experience-rated subsidy.

As the most researched area in the field of health care financing, the issue of different methods of controlling moral hazard on the part of consumers and providers is covered in Chapters 6 to 8. Thus, the evidence on different methods of paying providers (specifically doctors and hospitals) and that on roles for pricing mechanisms are reviewed in those chapters. Modifications to voluntary insurance, free care at the point of delivery and HMOs are also compared throughout these chapters. How different systems cope with the problem of adverse selection and equity in health and health care is the subject matter for Chapter 9. In Chapter 10, the issue of how much should be spent on health care is addressed.

Before all of this, however, if governments are to intervene in health care funding, it is wise to consider what the objectives of such intervention might be. The act of government intervention in itself cannot solve the problems of markets raised in Chapter 3. Government intervention can take many forms, as we have seen in this chapter. To determine the success of different schemes, it is necessary to know what it is they are trying to achieve. This is the subject matter of the next chapter.

Table 4.1 Options arising from funding arrangements for health services: controlling moral hazard and adverse selection

	Basic system for raising finance		
	Private insurance	*Public insurance*	*Direct taxation*
Controlling consumer moral hazard	Charges HMOs PPOs Fixed indemnity (i.e. cover for approved packages only)	Charges Non-price rationing	Charges Non-price rationing
Controlling provider moral hazard	Doctors: Fee for service Capitation Salary Competition (through HMOs etc.)	Doctors: Fee for service Capitation Salary Payments for good practice Budgets	Doctors: Fee for service Capitation Salary Payments for good practice Budgets
	Hospitals: Retrospective budgets Prospective budgets Payment by case (DRG) Payment by day Competition (through HMOs etc.)	Hospitals: Retrospective budgets Prospective budgets Payment by day Internal markets	Hospitals: Retrospective budgets Prospective budgets Payment by day Internal markets
Controlling adverse selection	Compulsory community-rated insurance plus experience-rated subsidy Vouchers Charges plus catastrophic insurance Special schemes for poor, elderly and disabled people	Integral part of the system (100% coverage of population) Can involve compulsory community-rated insurance plus an experience-rated subsidy	Integral part of system (100% coverage of population)

CHAPTER 5

Economic Objectives of Health Care

INTRODUCTION

In this chapter the economic objectives of health care systems are explored in some detail. The point of doing this is to come up with some operational definitions that can be systematically used to judge performance. The key economic objectives relate to efficiency and equity. Defining the term efficiency is somewhat more straightforward than defining the term equity, so this chapter is deliberately devoted more to the equity debate than to the efficiency one. This imbalance is further justified by the fact that, up to now, we have given more space (in Chapters 2 and 3) to the notions of efficiency than to notions of equity.

Once we are equipped with some reasonable definitions, it is possible to conduct an empirical review of the performance of some health care systems. Subsequent review chapters therefore concentrate on efficient consumer behaviour (Chapter 6), efficient provider behaviour (Chapter 7 on doctors, Chapter 8 on hospitals) and equity (Chapter 9).

This chapter is divided into three parts. The first part is a brief introduction to efficiency criteria. The remainder provides a more extensive discussion about equity. After defining efficiency objectives, the confusion surrounding equity is addressed. Evidence on the existence of this confusion is demonstrated by highlighting equity criteria that emerge from policy statements. Economic and philosophical definitions of equity are briefly reviewed before we finally settle on some objectives. In the penultimate part of the chapter we consider the extent of interaction between efficiency and equity objectives. In concluding, we list the efficiency and equity objectives to be used in reviewing empirical evidence on methods of health care financing.

EFFICIENCY

In Chapter 2 it was demonstrated that the automatic outcome of perfect markets is efficient behaviour – consumer satisfaction maximised at least cost to society. This is obviously a highly desirable outcome. The question that follows is, given the imperfections of the health care market, can social efficiency be achieved within a given health care system? The short answer is probably no, and the question then becomes how close can systems get to this outcome. In principle, social efficiency is an uncontentious objective of any health care system because the objective seeks the greatest improvements in health from available resources. This is synonymous with what economists term minimising 'opportunity cost', i.e. minimising the cost to society of achieving these health benefits.

Minimising opportunity cost is derived from the notion of scarcity and the need to make choices between competing claims on resources. In economic terms, the decision to commit resources to tackling a health problem denies society the opportunity of using these resources to tackle other health problems. Therefore, some opportunities for improving health remain unfunded. The gains forgone are called opportunity costs. It follows that costs are inextricably linked with benefits. The optimum, social goal in any health care market – regulated market – can be defined as: maximise benefits and minimise costs. To have resources deployed inefficiently would mean that these resources could be reallocated to increase output and thereby social welfare.

Achieving efficiency is therefore about comparing the costs (or resources spent) and benefits (or well-being produced) of competing health care interventions and ensuring that resources are allocated in such a way as to maximise health gains to society.

There are two levels of efficiency: 'operational' efficiency and 'allocative' efficiency. Each of these is based on 'effectiveness'. These two types of efficiency and effectiveness represent different breadths of perspective—effectiveness being the narrowest and allocative efficiency the broadest. It is easier to talk about these levels, because they apply to health care provision, but it should be noted that, in the context of this book, they are important for evaluating changes in financing arrangements.

Effectiveness

Effective health care does not necessarily imply efficiency. It simply means that production or consumption of something will yield satisfaction (or utility). Thus, effective health care is about improving health status. Both operational and allocative efficiency, however, are necessarily conditional upon effectiveness. An example of effectiveness would be a drug with a proven beneficial impact on a health condition. The focus is limited to the production of health gains.

Operational Efficiency

Operational efficiency asks the question, 'Given that some activity is worth doing, what is the best way of providing it?' This perspective brings costs into the calculus alongside effectiveness. Operational efficiency involves the selection between alternative means of achieving the same ends, and may therefore be interpreted as the pursuit of maximum output for a given level of resources or minimum cost for a given level of output.

An example of operational efficiency would be if there was a choice between an effective drug therapy and a surgical operation to treat a given condition. Assessment of the costs and effectiveness of each option determines which is the more operationally efficient. If drug therapy is both less costly and more effective then it is clearly to be preferred. The difficult judgement is if one treatment modality is both less costly and less effective than the other. In such a situation, the cost–effectiveness ratios of the alternatives determine which is most efficient; the lower ratio indicates greater operational efficiency.

The 'rules' for achieving operational efficiency are thus:

–   If one means of achieving a given end is less (more) costly and produces the same amount of output then this option should (should not) be preferred;
–   If one means of achieving a given end is less costly and produces more output then this should be preferred;
–   If one means of achieving a given end is less costly and produces less output then cost-effectiveness ratios should be computed, the lower ratio indicating greater efficiency.

These rules are pursued through the techniques known as cost–effectiveness analysis (CEA) and cost–utility analysis (CUA). The former technique is more limited because the measure of output used is a uni-dimensional measure of health (e.g. lives saved, life years gained or reduction in disability days). Comparisons therefore have to be between alternatives with a similar single output. CUA enables a wider comparison of more disparate health care activities because the measure of output used is a unit known as the quality adjusted life year (QALY). This can capture aspects of both quantity and quality of life in a single index. Therefore, health care programmes which save lives, those which improve quality of life and those which do both may all be compared. CUA is still limited to the comparison of health-producing alternatives because costs and benefits are not measured in the same unit of account. The question of whether the activity should be pursued in the first place cannot be addressed by either technique.

Allocative Efficiency

Allocative efficiency judges whether an activity is worth doing. Also, given that much health policy is about the scale at which programmes should operate, allocative efficiency may also address the question of scale, or as economists term it, marginal analysis. Just as operational efficiency infers effective health care, so allocative efficiency infers operational efficiency. If something is deemed worth doing then it must be carried out in a way which ensures the optimum use of scarce resources. The social perspective is fundamental to allocative efficiency. This perspective ensures that due account is taken of all costs and benefits of interventions, regardless of whether they fall within or outside the health care sector (e.g. on families and patients or on the productive capacity of the economy).

The appropriate 'rules' to follow are those of the cost-benefit technique and are as follows:

– Undertake activities where benefits outweigh the costs;
– Stop doing activities where the costs outweigh the benefits;
– In deciding to alter the size of a programme apply the above rules to the change being considered.

As cost–benefit analysis (CBA) uses the same unit to measure costs and benefits (usually monetary units) this means that a comparison can be made between any alternatives however disparate (e.g. comparing an increase on spending on health care with a similar increase on education); indeed, evaluation of a single programme can be made (see for example Donaldson, 1990). Table 5.1 sets out the rules for pursuing efficient behaviour.

Table 5.1 Operational definitions of efficiency

Allocative efficiency	Pursuing health care programmes that are worth while (benefits exceed costs)
	For programmes that are worth while, expand up to the point where marginal benefits equal marginal costs
Operational efficiency	For worth-while programmes, ensure that the best use is made of scarce resources to meet the programme's objective

Note: Following these criteria will automatically eliminate ineffective health care programmes.

The rules of allocative efficiency capture the utilitarian ethic, the maximisation of satisfaction for the greatest number of individuals who collectively form society. It is important, however, to recognise the harm that over-zealous pursuit of allocative efficiency may lead to. It may create a pattern of resource and benefit distribution which discriminates against certain members of society; maximising health, or utility, from health care resources may not be conducive with a 'fair' distribution of health. It is to notions of 'fairness', or 'equity', to which we now turn.

EQUITY

Within most societies there exists, in some form or another, a concern that health care resources and benefits should be distributed in some fair or just way. McLachlan and Maynard (1982) have gone as far as to suggest this concern is of utmost importance:

'the vast majority [of people] . . . would elect for equity to be a prime consideration [of a health service].'

The guiding principles underlying each health care system give an indication of the relative concern for equity. There are two basic types of health care system, libertarian and egalitarian (Culyer *et al.*, 1981). The former values consumer sovereignty and market forces while the latter is committed to the pursuit of community health.

However, it is more often the case that a health care system is a mix of libertarian and egalitarian values and hence, depending upon the balance of this mix, the importance of equity will vary between health care systems. Even the US health care system recognises the shortcomings of a total reliance upon market forces. The main form of government regulation there is in the form of the insurance schemes for elderly people (Medicare) and indigent people (Medicaid).

Usually, the concern for equity is interpreted generally as providing a basic level of health services to all. Unfortunately, this succinct definition is insufficient to stand up to careful scrutiny (Pereira, 1989). Searching for more specific interpretations requires that a number of sources of confusion surrounding the term equity are confronted.

By working through these issues we should be better placed to judge whether it is feasible to get a grip on some usable equity criteria. The remaining aims of this chapter are therefore fourfold: to highlight where the confusion surrounding equity exists; to demonstrate how policy pronouncements add to, rather than clear up, this confusion; to introduce some philosophical and economic theories on equity; and to bring all this together by producing some operational equity objectives for health care.

CONFRONTING THE CONFUSION: WHAT DO WE MEAN BY 'EQUITY'?

Equity and Externalities

First, an important distinction needs to be made between the caring externality and equity. The latter brings us into territory which is much more extensive than that covered by externalities. In Chapter 3, the caring externality was described as the spillover effect individuals get from others' production or consumption of a commodity. Thus, individuals care about seeing or knowing that others within their society receive timely, needed health care. This, however, is an individually based concern. Conventionally, the concern is expressed by richer members of society, as they are more likely to be the ones with resources to give in backing up their preferences. Because these members care and are able and willing to pay for some of the poor's health care consumption, a sub-optimal consumption pattern can be mitigated; rich people feel better than they would if they could not contribute to other people's consumption of health care. Hence, the caring externality and other positive externalities relate to the notion of efficiency and are based upon underlying distributions of income and health and preferences for altruism within a society.

Equity is a broader concept, capturing the notion of fairness as an independent, external view. Reliance is not placed on the benevolence felt by the rich towards the poor but on the democratic process. Indeed, it is possible that the poor members of society, representing the majority view, might vote in favour of an equity objective discriminating against rich members' access to health care (e.g. cosmetic surgery not to be routinely offered as part of the public system). This would have to be accepted as fair.

Equity or Equality?

The second, and simplest, point to clear up is that the terms 'equity' and 'equality' are not always interchangeable. Consider some dictionary definitions: equity is 'a system of justice based on conscience and fairness'; equality is 'the state of being equal' (*Longman New Universal Dictionary*, 1982). Equality is, thus, a particular interpretation of equity. It is concerned only with equal shares. Equity, however, is about fairness, and it may be judged fair to be unequal. In health care it may be judged equitable to have unequal access to services; groups more likely to be ill should perhaps be given greater access.

Equity of Health Care or Health?

Does equity set out to achieve fair health or fair health care? At a cursory glance both ideas seem reasonable.

In practice, however, most health care systems are not expected to set about the enormous task of achieving a fair distribution of health. This is in part at least because there are many other influences on health as well as health care.

More realistically, health care systems are in the business of pursuing a fair distribution of health care, because this reflects their locus of control. However, equality of health within the sphere of health care activities is often still upheld as the 'gold standard'. In our view it is misleading to set such an unobtainable standard, for four (to us) compelling reasons:

— Equality of health is not a viable choice for an equity goal for a health service because it cannot be guaranteed as a basic human right. Genetically inherited conditions or natural deterioration in health over time inevitably conflict with this objective.
— It is still not known exactly what is meant by the term 'good' health.
— Attempting to achieve good health may be seen as élitist in the sense that informed individuals are prevented from choosing their own level of health which may be somewhere below 'good' health (e.g. a person may choose not to give up smoking). Such a goal would necessarily impose the level of quality of life on a community. The objective should be provision of opportunity which is about health care rather than health itself (Note 17).
— Mooney (1987a) argues that the pursuit of equality of health will inevitably lead to equal health at a level which is less than current best health (Note 18). It would not be possible to raise society's health towards the higher level, as this would prove too costly, so pursuit of health would inevitably mean reducing the health of some groups in society.

Some may argue that credence can be given to a more limited interpretation of reduced health inequality: 'equality of outcome given the uptake of services by individuals in equal need'. This objective seeks to ensure that once individuals with similar conditions present to the health service they are treated with the same effective health care (thus two individuals diagnosed with breast cancer should be given the same treatment, which will ensure that their survival chances are similar). However, similar outcomes for individuals infers there may be no differences in preferences either for compliance or for other commodities which may influence health and thereby generate actual differences in final health status. So, once again, this form of expression can be criticised for its élitist perspective, once more leading towards the conclusion that objectives should be focused on health care rather than on health.

Horizontal Equity

Table 5.2 summarises possible dimensions of health care equity in terms of either horizontal or vertical equity. Horizontal equity is concerned with equal treatment of equals. To make sense of the term we follow the advice of Mooney (1987b). Equal treatment for equals is about equal treatment for equal need. The term could not mean equality of treatment regardless of need, because those in good health would not want to be treated the same as those with an ill-health condition, however mild! It was also argued in Chapter 3 that 'need' is the appropriate concept to focus on as the denominator variable. Horizontal equity can be expressed at any stage of health care production; input, process or output (Cullis and West, 1979; West, 1981). As shown in Table 5.2, the usual expressions are equality of expenditure (or resources), of utilisation, of access and of health, the last of which has already been rejected as a realistic objective of health care financing.

Table 5.2 Operational definitions of equity

Horizontal-equity criteria

(1) Equal expenditure for equal need; e.g. equal nurse cost per bed ratios in all acute hospitals

(2) Equal utilisation for equal need; e.g. equal length of stay per health condition

(3) Equal access for equal need; e.g. equal waiting time for treatment for patients with similar conditions

(4) Equal health/reduced inequalities in health; e.g. equal age- and sex-adjusted standardised mortality ratios across health regions

Vertical-equity criteria

(5) Unequal treatment for unequal need; e.g. unequal treatment of those with treatable trivial versus serious conditions

(6) Progressive financing based on ability to pay; e.g. progressive income tax rates and mainly income-tax financed

Equality of expenditure (or resources) says something about provision of health care resources, but little about the services received or how that care affects health. Thus, equity defined in this way is quite limited. The main advantage, and reason for its prolific use, is the relative ease with which inputs can be measured and monitored.

There is an important distinction to be made between utilisation and access. 'Equal utilisation for equal need' requires both standardising medical practices for given conditions and equal compliance (e.g. two individuals living in different areas of the country receive the same treatment regime for their hip operations and both comply equally with postperative physiotherapy). 'Equal access for equal need' provides individuals simply with the opportunity to use needed health services. This term may legitimately lead to different patterns of utilisation for equal need because individuals may choose to comply with treatment to different extents. It does not rely on any element of coercion, as equal utilisation might, or give different preferences, and therefore it is not élitist. As a result, we would argue that equality of access is the superior form of expression. In addition, equality of expenditure and of utilisation implies that medical practice is standardised for each type of need. The literature on medical practice variations shows this not to be the case (Andersen and Mooney, 1990).

Equality of access becomes problematical if a price has to be paid for an equity-efficiency trade-off. For example, pursuit of equal geographical access to health services could mean that resource-intensive coronary care units should be provided equally in both sparsely and densely populated areas; clearly this is not an efficient strategy. The price of equity can be measured in terms of the loss of life and quality of life that could otherwise be achieved if resources were spent on their most productive uses. However, this is also a problem of the other concepts of horizontal equity in Table 5.2 and not just of equal access for equal need.

Equality of access cannot be measured in absolute terms, but it can be compared and assessed in relative terms (i.e. whether or not access in one area is more or less equitable than in another). This is because it is 'extremely difficult to state what equity is in any positive sense, but barriers to equity are readily identifiable' (Hall, 1991). For two communities to face equality of access of health care the following barriers need to be the same: geographical factors, e.g. travel distances to health care facilities; availability of transportation resources and communication services; waiting times for appointments and treatments; and equally informed patients (i.e. about ill-health and the effectiveness of health care treatments). Some of these barriers have natural units of measurement, and are therefore relatively straightforward to measure and monitor; for example, operating waiting times and appointments to see general practitioners or specialists. However, measuring and monitoring the extent to which patients have 'full information' (however that is defined) is more complex and open to differing interpretation. Indirect measurement is possible (e.g. schedules analysing patient knowledge), but it will usually fall short of capturing the concept comprehensively. Measurement difficulties inevitably mean that equality of access can often be only partially or inadequately measured, or at best approximated. For instance, as will be seen in Chapter 9, it is common to find equality of utilisation being used as a proxy measure.

Vertical Equity

Vertical equity addresses the question of the extent to which individuals who are unequal in society should be treated differently. In principle, unequal treatment of unequals is a sensible concept in the context of health care delivery. It may seem too obvious to be worth mentioning, but it is, however, difficult to put into operation (Wagstaff *et al.*, 1989). For example, the treatment needs for short-sightedness and obstetric care are clearly different. The harder question is that of assessing how unequally these conditions should be treated in pursuit of equity. Should one condition enjoy a higher standard of care because it is judged to be more important? And, if so, how much higher should it be?

The objective of financial equity is usually concerned with establishing a payment system based on ability to pay. McClelland (1991) explains the rationale for this concern. First, because ill-health can be unpredictable and uncertain, the impact of health care costs can be adverse, especially for poorer members of society. Protection against financial hardship owing to catastrophic illness is therefore desirable. Secondly, the consumption of goods and services which have an impact on health is regarded as important because health is regarded as being so important. Thus removal of financial barriers which impede consumption is, again, desirable. The concept of financial equity thus needs to be considered in two stages. The first is this broad achievement of vertical equity (payment based on ability to pay), the second that within groups of equal financial status (or however else vertical equity is to be defined) there is actual payment on fair terms, i.e. regard is paid also to horizontal equity.

The horizontal perspective has been defined by Wagstaff *et al.* (1989) as 'the extent to which those of equal ability to pay actually end up making equal payments, regardless of, for example gender, marital status ...' They suggest that it is conceivable that, in the UK NHS for example, anomalies in the personal income tax system may create a situation of inequity because some individuals with the same income may contribute different amounts to health care. This, unfortunately, is an area of equity that has been left relatively unattended in the literature, important though it may be. For this reason it is beyond the scope of this book to investigate the issue further.

The broader question of the pursuit of vertical equity in health care finance raises the following questions:

– How should ability to pay be defined?
– What should the relationship be between ability to pay and payments?

Surprisingly, as there is obviously an implicit regard for financial equity in those health care systems that have a large element of public finance, this has been given little attention in the literature. Thus, although we recognise the importance of vertical financial equity as a plausible health care objective, there are, at present, large gaps in knowledge as to how best this can be achieved.

The most comprehensive analysis has been described by Gottschalk *et al.* (1989). They describe four simultaneous goals of health care: to induce a socially efficient level of health care utilisation; to spread risk across people; to spread risk across a person's life; and to distribute resources according to need, where need reflects both income and health status. There are, obviously, efficiency–equity trade-offs to be made between these goals. For example, a society could be interested in achieving the first and third goals. If this were the case, then a possible financing strategy would be to use market prices at the point of consumption but allow for long payback periods. On the other hand, if the latter three goals were to be pursued at the expense of the first, then general tax revenue could be used to finance health care and the extent of redistribution would be determined by the progressiveness of the underlying income tax system.

In practice, in devising a scheme of fair contributions it is necessary to take account of the different forms of payment that can be made (i.e. out-of-pocket expenses, insurance premiums and tax revenues). A progressive system is usually most effectively achieved through taxation. Appropriate tax allowances, increasing tax-incidence with increasing income, and exemption categories for certain groups all enable the pursuit of vertical equity.

There are, however, a variety of taxes (e.g. general income tax, local income taxes, payroll taxes, indirect taxes) and some will be more progressive than others. It is important, therefore, to establish not only the contribution of taxation to health care financing but also the source of taxation. Maxwell (1981) has shown that income-conditioned taxation is the most progressive.

A tax-financed health care system or a social insurance system would normally be expected to achieve some degree of vertical equity. Those health care systems that rely heavily on large out-of-pocket payments for finance are more likely to require additional regulation (e.g. means testing) to protect low-income and high-user groups satisfactorily.

Muddying the Waters: Equity Policies and Pronouncements

Confronting some of the confusion over operational definitions of equity may be best served by examining policy statements and pronouncements made by the World Health Organization (WHO), along with some selected health systems. Examination of the documentation covering the WHO's 'target of health for all by the year 2000' reveals inconsistent interpretations of equity objectives (Mooney, 1987b). This goes to prove the complexities and confusions surrounding the equity objective-setting task. For example:

> 'The target on health inequalities presents a challenge: to change the trend by improving the health opportunities of disadvantaged nations and groups so as to enable them to catch up with their privileged counterparts.' (WHO, 1985)

'The existing gross inequality in the health status of people ... must be drastically reduced.' (WHO, 1982)'

From these statements it would appear that equal good health and reduced inequalities in health are being sought. Besides the arguments presented earlier, it seems that without clearer definitions these objectives could be contradictory. The first objective is definitely about raising everyone to the highest health level, but the second is less clear about how the health gap is to be reduced.

Lack of clearly expressed equity objectives has not, however, stopped individual countries expressing their own desires for health equity and reduced health inequality to be obtained from their health care systems. For example, Portugal (Constitucao da Republica Portuguesa, 1982), Spain (Rodriguez *et al.*, 1990), Sweden (Borgenhammer, 1987) and the USSR (Chazou, 1988) all aspire to the protection of health for every member of their respective populations.

In the UK (Black Report, 1980; Whitehead, 1988), Australia (Leeder, 1987; McClelland, 1991), China (Prescott and Jamison, 1985) and many Western European countries (Fox, 1989) there is substantial evidence on the existence and maintenance of health inequalities. These are either measured across geographical regions or between socioeconomic groups. In many instances, health care policy solutions have been either proposed or implemented. In China, for example, preventive strategies, barefoot doctors and community resource mobilisation have been implemented but have done little to reduce survival differentials (Prescott and Jamison, 1984). In the UK, there has been concern that health inequalities between social classes have increased since the 1930s and can be expected to continue (Davey Smith *et al.*, 1990). In Australia, five priority areas have been targeted for reduction of health inequalities (Health Targets and Inequalities Committee, 1988). In the case of most Western European countries there is a paucity of evidence about the role of health services in relation to mitigating health inequalities (Macintyre, 1989). Hungarians cannot agree about the extent to which their health care system should be held accountable for reducing health inequalities (Orosz, 1990).

WHO also recognises the importance of equality of access to health services. Primary health care is seen to be the crucial component of health care that should be equitably distributed (WHO, 1985). Indeed, this objective is taken up by many less-developed nations.

Many countries have expressed support for equality of access regardless of ability to pay. As Jörgensen and Kristiansen (1991) observe from various Danish policy statements, the health care goal is for equal access for equal need and should be independent of ability to pay. 'Access to the NHS is guaranteed to all citizens independently of their economic or social status' in Portugal (Pereira, 1990). Similar positions exist in the UK (Secretaries of

State, 1990), Sweden (Dahlgren and Diderichen, 1986), Denmark (Dans-kernes Sundhand, 1985), The Netherlands (Leenen, 1984), the USSR (Hakansson *et al.*, 1988), Poland (Tymowska, 1987), Bulgaria (Minev *et al.*, 1990) and Australia (Grant and Lapsley, 1989). Clearly, the foundations of the USA Medicare and Medicaid schemes rest on concern over incomplete private insurance coverage and unfair access to health care.

The UK (DHSS, 1976), Australia (NSW Department of Health, 1990) and Finland (Haro, 1987) are examples of countries which have also been concerned with geographical access, i.e. ensuring that where one lives within a country does not affect access to health services.

Concern for equality of utilisation was one of the factors influencing the change to a public insurance system in Canada, because it was felt that health care utilisation was becoming too dependent upon income (Evans, 1987). Carrin and Vereecke (1992) suggest that equity objectives in sub-Saharan Africa relate to equality of utilisation, with improvements achieved by redistribution of public health resources from urban to rural areas.

From this brief glance at how systems define their equity objectives, we find them to be widely varying. Indeed, as we have documented, health care systems may strive for both equality of health and of access without addressing the potential for conflict and how any such conflict should be resolved. The lack of clarity that can surround the notion of equity can be summarised by a statement written by an adviser to the Pan American Health Organization:

> 'The fundamental idea of equity is that of equal treatment for all the population. . . . The crucial notion is that whatever the level of access, it should be the same for all. Inequity results from the differences in the ability to obtain health care. . . . Treatment and resources should go where they are most needed.' (Musgrove, 1986)

This statement gives rise to three potentially conflicting health care equity objectives; equal treatment for all the population; equal access for all; and allocation on the basis of greatest need. Equal treatment for all is, as argued earlier, simply untenable. It should be equal treatment for equal need. However, equal treatment for equal need does not necessarily coincide with equal access for equal need, particularly if patients' preferences to comply with treatment differ. Resources allocated on the basis of greatest need may also be incompatible with equal access, particularly if access is defined in terms of geographical access.

So, although the discussion so far has attempted to confront some of the confusion surrounding the term equity, there are clearly issues that remain to be resolved. A logical next step is to ask the question, 'Can anything useful be gleaned from economic and philosophic theories or concepts?'

THE ECONOMICS AND PHILOSOPHY INTERFACE – THEORIES OF EQUITY

Fairness and justice are phenomena deeply embodied within philosophy and economics. In economics these phenomena form part of the area known as normative economics. A range of concepts have been offered by economists to explain these phenomena. Where these concepts relate directly to health care, the theories stem largely from the experience of the UK NHS. Table 5.3 briefly sets out some of these concepts. In the main, it appears that economists converge on the notion of equal access for equal need.

Table 5.3   Some economists' concepts of equity

Economist/Theory	Concept
Musgrave (1959) Merit Good Theory	Individuals will choose to consume less health care than they 'should'. Government intervention aims to ensure appropriate consumption by increasing availability, and is thus concerned with equality of consumption.
Lees (1962)	The crux of the UK NHS was the provision of free health care at the point of use to ensure equal consumption of health care.
Titmuss (1970)	Social duty meant the UK NHS was concerned with providing the *opportunity* to promote health and altruism; thus the closest interpretation is equal opportunity to use health services (i.e. access) because this enables the promotion of both health and altruism.
Sen (1977)	Individuals are committed to the idea that others' opportunity to consume health care may be just as, if not more, important than their own; thus the appropriate definition is equal access for equal need.
Margolis (1982)	Individuals are interested in doing their fair share for the community, which leads them to want to contribute to making services available; thus the appropriate definition is equal access for equal need.

The philosophy debate is less helpful for explanations of health care equity. Table 5.4 outlines some of the main theories of justice. Theories either of entitlement or of utilitarianism are too limited for the sort of concern that stems from an imperfect health care market. Rawlsian theory

Table 5.4 Some philosophers' concepts of equity

Philosopher/Theory	Concept
Nozick (1974) Entitlement Theory	Limited theory of justice. Market mechanism is considered fair.
Utilitarianism	Misplaced theory of justice. Maximising greatest happiness for the greatest number, but ignores distributional aspects.
Rawls (1971)	A basic set of primary social Rawlsian theory goods are distributed (behind a 'veil of ignorance') so that the position of the least well off in society is maximised. Health care is not one of these goods but may be seen as a primary institution to achieve fair distribution of basic liberties, etc. (Daniels, 1981). Even so, it is not clear if equity is about maximising consumption of primary social goods or health care. Therefore, it is possible that equality of utilisation is desirable.
Egalitarianism	Equal shares of a distribution of a commodity. Could be taken to mean equality of health or equality of health care.

(Rawls, 1971) appears promising. However, the crucial question about what should be the prime concern, primary social goods (these are things like basic freedoms and liberties) or primary institutions (which include health services), remains unclear. So it seems that egalitarianism provides the most promising theory of health care justice. Although, at its grandest, egalitarianism is about the concern for social, political and economic equality, in the context of health care it may be taken to mean equality of health or health care. Bearing in mind earlier arguments, the notion of equal access for equal need is to be preferred.

TOWARDS SOME OPERATIONAL EQUITY GOALS

In summary, it is clear that there are is no one universal equity measure. Each health care system has to decide upon its own equity objective(s), decide how to operationalise the objective(s), confront and resolve any potential conflict between equity objectives and then proceed to monitor performance accordingly. Despite an array of operational definitions, support for 'equality of access' seems very common. Another common equity objective, implicit within the organisation of health care systems, is the desire that financial contributions should be based on ability to pay.

Ideally, therefore, we advocate these definitions. Given the practical problems associated with measuring 'access', it seems that operational definitions will inevitably focus more narrowly on the notions of equality of utilisation and of inputs. It is therefore important to bear their short-comings in mind when attempting to assess performance of health care systems or changes to financial arrangements.

It has been argued that 'equality of health' is inherently wrong as a health care equity objective. As a constrained interpretation of 'reducing health inequalities', however, the goal of achieving 'equal outcome given the uptake of effective services by those in equal need' may be considered desirable.

INTERACTION BETWEEN EQUITY AND EFFICIENCY

It is inevitable that the ideal level of equity cannot be achieved. Some will have to be forgone to achieve efficiency. Likewise, ideal efficiency will not be achieved. This trade-off is inevitable because of the notion of scarcity. If scarcity did not exist, there would be no need to consider equity (who gets and who pays what and how much) or efficiency (what are the costs and benefits of different arrangements). Equity must therefore come at a price. To redistribute an efficient allocation of health care resources according to some just criteria means that the pursuit of health care equity may result in an unnecessary loss of life or of quality of life. This is a strong argument for seeking to make equity objectives as explicit as can be. By so doing, the trade-off between efficiency and equity can be measured and societies placed in a position to judge for themselves whether such trade-offs are acceptable or not.

CONCLUSIONS

In setting the economic objectives of health care systems, both efficiency and equity notions must be taken into account. Efficiency is easy and undisputed. It is sought at two levels; allocative efficiency determines the 'worthwhileness' of programmes and operational efficiency the best ways of producing worthwhile programmes.

Equity is a less straightforward notion, but we have argued in this chapter that there are two important dimensions: financial equity and equity of opportunity to use health care resources. Financial equity is assessed by the burden of financial contributions extracted from different socioeconomic groups. It is deemed fair that payment is based on ability to pay.

The opportunity to use resources is a more difficult notion to measure and monitor, because 'access' is a relative term. In the ideal, therefore, equal access for equal need is the most desirable horizontal equity objective, but in the light of practical difficulties we recognise that proxy measures are sometimes inevitable, particularly equal utilisation for equal need. Part 3 will judge the performance of some health care systems in relation to these economic objectives.

PART 3

A Review of Empirical Findings

CHAPTER 6

Countering Consumer Moral Hazard

INTRODUCTION

The problem of moral hazard, and possible solutions to it, is one of the most researched areas in the economics of health care, as witnessed by the content of the following three chapters. Let us briefly review the concept of moral hazard introduced in Chapter 3. Inefficiency in health care arises because insurance-based systems, in common with tax-financed systems, face the problem of potential excess demand: that is, a demand in excess of what it is felt the system ought to provide as a result of the benefits of this excess demand being exceeded by benefits forgone (or opportunity cost). The reasons for the existence and persistence of such excess demand are basically twofold: the problem arises from the absence (or the lowering) of a financial barrier to care on the side of demand; and, on the side of supply, financial arrangements enable (even encourage) providers to supply wasteful amounts. Supply-side effects are often exacerbated by a legal environment that encourages what has become known as 'defensive' medicine, a style of practice that minimises the probability of legal action for malpractice – but often only at considerable cost. The problem of changing attitudes of consumers and suppliers of care in response to such 'perverse' financial arrangements has become known in the literature as the problem of 'moral hazard', and it is moral hazard which leads to potential excess utilisation of health care.

Remember, from Chapter 3, that the above concept of moral hazard is very neoclassical. We have already questioned whether excess demand can be measured as a result of consumers not being fully informed, and, because of externalities, overprovision on the supply side is also difficult to measure. Despite these, policy makers and economists have come up with many 'solutions' to moral hazard on the parts of consumers and suppliers.

Initiatives aimed at countering moral hazard on the part of doctors and hospitals are reviewed in the following two chapters. The aim of this chapter is to review the evidence from research on the effect of different methods of dealing with consumer moral hazard that have arisen in both publicly and privately financed health care systems. In keeping with the objectives of health care outlined in Chapter 5, the effect of these methods is examined in terms of three criteria: patient utilisation of health care in general; utilisation by different groups of patients; and health status.

In the following section, a list of possible counters to consumer moral hazard is introduced. The evidence of the effect of these counters on moral hazard on the part of the consumer is then reviewed. Finally, some conclusions are offered on whether the evidence demonstrates that some funding mechanisms reviewed are more likely than others to achieve broad health service objectives.

Since so much evidence comes from insurance-based systems and analyses of the ways they have struggled with the problem of moral hazard, much evidence is cited on insured consumers' reactions to charges. It should be noted, however, that this evidence is also relevant to health care systems which are currently publicly financed, because some insurance plans provide care 'free' (in the financial sense) at the point of delivery as is often the case in such publicly financed systems.

POLICY RESPONSES TO CONSUMER MORAL HAZARD

Policy responses to moral hazard do not have to be financial. Traditional organisational responses to preventing overuse of expensive hospital services in many developed countries have involved the use of primary-care doctors as the 'gateway' to such services. Likewise, in less-developed countries a similar policy is to use 'barefoot doctors', as for example in Papua New Guinea and of course China. Such organisational considerations are, unfortunately, beyond the scope of this book.

In Chapter 3, a list of possible financial counters to consumer moral hazard was provided. On repeating this list, it can be seen that consumer moral hazard has typically been countered in the following ways, the first four of which have been implemented, mainly in private insurance-based systems, such as those in the USA, with the fifth being characteristic of publicly provided and financed health care, such as in the UK NHS:

- Use of copayments, whereby the insured person pays some fraction of the supplier's charge.
- Fixed periodic per-capita prepayment by consumers directly to the provider of comprehensive health care, such as a Health Maintenance Organisation (HMO), with a fixed subsidy towards payment or a fixed percentage of the premium contributed by employers or government (Petchey, 1987).
- Provision of incentives for consumers to demand care from selected providers, offering low cost packages of care, as in the case of Preferred Provider Organisations (PPOs).
- Placing financial limits on indemnity.

– Non-price rationing by doctors according to judgements of need, usually resulting in consumers incurring waiting 'costs' for elective treatment.

EVIDENCE ON COUNTERING CONSUMER MORAL HAZARD

Copayments

Copayments have been introduced in a number of countries to put some financial burden on the consumer to discourage 'unnecessary' use of health care or doctors' time. Individual schemes differ according to the nature of the financial arrangement but take four main forms: a flat-rate charge for each unit of service; coinsurance (the insured individual has to pay a certain proportion of each unit of health care consumed); a deductible akin to the 'excess' in some motor vehicle insurance policies (the individual pays 100 per cent of all bills in a given period, up to some maximum amount beyond which insurance benefits are paid in full); or a combination of the last two.

Most evidence on the effect of copayments on the demand for medical care has come from the Health Insurance Experiment (HIE) conducted by the RAND Corporation (Newhouse, 1974). Families participating in the experiment were randomly assigned to one of 14 different fee-for-service (FFS) insurance plans or to a prepaid group practice. The FFS plans had different levels of cost-sharing, which varied in two dimensions: first, the coinsurance rates were zero (viz. free care), 25, 50 or 95 per cent; and second, each plan had a maximum dollar expenditure limit (or MDE) on annual out-of-pocket expenses of 5, 10 or 15 per cent of family income, up to a maximum of $1000, beyond which the insurance plan reimbursed all covered expenses in full. Covered expenses included most medical services. In one additional plan, the families had free access to inpatient services but faced a 95 per cent coinsurance rate for outpatient services, subject to an annual limit of $150 out-of-pocket expenses per person ($450 per family). This, for practical purposes, is equivalent to a $150 individual deductible for outpatient care. Those randomised to the prepaid group practice were given a plan of benefits identical to the zero cost-sharing insurance plan (the 'free plan'). In all, 5809 persons were involved in the free plan and cost-sharing part of the experiment, and 1982 in the prepaid group practice part of the experiment.

The most recent results from the HIE were reported by Manning *et al.* (1987). They clearly showed that utilisation responds to amounts paid out-of-pocket. Per-capita total expenses on the free plan were 45 per cent higher than those on the plan with a 95 per cent coinsurance rate. Spending rates on the other plans lay between these two extremes. Outpatient expenses in the free plan were 67 per cent higher than those on the 95 per cent coinsurance plan, while outpatient visit rates were 63 per cent higher. The largest, and statistically significant, decrease in use of outpatient services occurred between the free and 25 per cent coinsurance plans with outpatient expenses 37 per cent higher in the free plan. There were no statistically significant differences between plans for inpatient expenses, because of the $1000 MDE. The outpatient deductible plan resulted in a reduction in outpatient expenses similar to that from the 50 to 95 per cent plans and also showed no significant differences in terms of inpatient expenses compared with the other plans. Generally, these results do not differ from the previously published analysis of the HIE data (Newhouse *et al.*, 1981).

Manning *et al.* (1987) showed that price elasticities for all health care are in the -0.1 to -0.2 range, that is, a 10 per cent increase in user price will cause demand to fall by 1 to 2 per cent. These values are consistent with those elsewhere in the literature (Davis and Russell, 1972; Newhouse and Phelps, 1974; Phelps and Newhouse, 1974). Analysis of the RAND data by individual episodes of care, rather than by plan, lend further support to the previous RAND results, reporting a price elasticity of -0.2 (Keeler and Rolph, 1988). Effects observed by Keeler and Rolph were limited to presentation for each episode of care rather than the amount of treatment carried out per episode. This highlights, unsurprisingly, the effect of copayments on patients' initial demands for treatment rather than the content of treatment for each episode. Content of treatment is an area over which doctors can have more influence, indicating that charging for care does not necessarily cope with the problem of provider moral hazard.

Therefore, it is possible that one result of implementing charges would be that doctors would then concentrate more of their demand-inducing abilities on those who can afford to pay. The same amount would be spent on health care, but probably to less effect, as those more in need would have less access to services. This is a problem of the conventional neoclassical approach taken by the RAND study. Because of the influence of doctors, the response of aggregate utilisation to charges is likely to be less than is suggested by the RAND results. It may be that, in aggregate, those less in need but more able to pay for care simply replace those more in need but less able to pay. The 'influence of doctors' on utilisation is assumed away in the design of RAND.

Thus, despite the small proportionate overall response of demand for health care to changes in its price, it is important to know whether the size of the response is different for different groups in society and whether reductions in demand are for care which would otherwise have made no difference to people's health status. Lohr *et al.* (1986) compared those HIE families on all cost sharing insurance plans (that is, 25, 50 and 95 per cent coinsurance) with those families on the free care plan in terms of the probability of occurrence of episodes of care for specific diseases. They found that the effect of cost sharing was often greater among low-income than higher-income persons. Low-income persons were defined as those whose family incomes were in the lower third of the income distribution (that is, below $20 200 per annum, with a mean of $11 000 per annum). The probability that a low-income adult would obtain care for acute pharyngitis if he or she was on the cost sharing plan was 54 per cent of the probability for low-income adults having free care. For non-poor adults there was little difference between these probabilities. Differences were even greater among children (that is, people under 14 years of age). For the eight acute conditions examined, probabilities of use of services for poor children on cost-sharing plans were between 33 and 68 per cent of those for poor children on the free plan. For non-poor children, probabilities of use of services on the cost-sharing plans were 65–219 per cent of those on the free plan. The figure of 219 per cent is an outlier which, according to Lohr *et al.* (1986), may be explained by a lack of precision in the estimate because the particular diagnosis concerned (trauma from acute sprains and strains) occurs less frequently in higher-income groups, hence yielding a small sample.

The results of the HIE for differential effects of charges on poor and non-poor confirm the results from previous studies of the effect of copayments. Beck (1974) analysed the introduction of charges of $1.50 (Canadian) per office visit and $2.00 per house visit and for use of emergency or hospital outpatient services in Saskatchewan in 1968. He estimated the consequent reduction in use of these services to be from 6 to 7 per cent for the whole population but 18 per cent for the poor. Helms *et al.* (1978) assessed the impact of the introduction of a small payment (one dollar each for the first two consultations and 50 cents for the first two prescriptions per month) for (previously free) out-of-hospital services for some Medicaid beneficiaries in California. This group was compared with another group of Medicaid beneficiaries in California who were exempt from the charge. The result was that the copayment reduced doctor visit demand by 8 per cent but increased hospital demand by 17 per cent, thus increasing overall programme cost.

Lohr *et al.* (1986) also examined whether reductions in utilisation were for inappropriate or unnecessary medical use. They found significant differences between poor and non-poor children. For example, the probability of at least one episode of highly effective (as judged by several doctors at the RAND Corporation) ambulatory care for poor children in cost-sharing plans was 56 per cent of the level for those with free care compared with a figure of 85 per cent for non-poor children. Foxman *et al.* (1987) demonstrated that cost sharing reduced appropriate as well as inappropriate antibiotic use to similar degrees.

Despite these results, the HIE studies of health outcomes have shown negligible effects of cost-sharing on general measures of health for both adults and children (Brook *et al.*, 1983; Valdez, 1986). The conflict between these findings and those of Lohr *et al.* could be due to one or more of at least three effects. First, although some people on the free plan received benefits (in improved health status) from care for which medicine has effective interventions to offer, others in the same group may have suffered compensating adverse effects from their care (Lohr *et al.*, 1986). Such adverse effects may result either from more consumption by free care enrollees of treatments for conditions for which medical care has relatively little effectiveness (thus prompting 'sick role' behaviour such as staying home from school or work which might not otherwise have happened), or from iatrogenic exposure to antibiotics or minor tranquillisers or other psychotropic agents, leading to adverse effects not experienced by those on cost-sharing plans.

Second, the measures of health used were very limited. The actual indicators were general health, health habits, psychological health, and risk of dying from any cause related to measured risk-factors such as high blood pressure. The number of deaths in the experimental groups was too small to permit any meaningful analysis of survival. Most of the observations were made on a population of healthy adults under the age of 65. This population is less likely to require or benefit from health care than other groups, like elderly people, who were excluded from the study. Some condition-specific measures were used. For instance, it was demonstrated that the free-care plan was associated with improved visual activity (for those with poor vision) (Brook *et al.*, 1983). Also, the free-care plan resulted in improved control of blood pressure, particularly among high-risk groups. The cause of the difference, it has been claimed, was additional contact with doctors in the free-care group, resulting in better detection and treatment (Keeler *et al.*, 1985). Similarly, adverse effects of cost sharing on health status have been found for oral health, particularly in younger age groups (under 35 years of age) (Baillit *et al.*, 1985).

The third effect could be that the total duration of observations (three years for 10 per cent of enrollees and five years for the rest) was too short to reveal possible long-term cumulative effects of reduced consumption of medical services (Relman, 1983a). The measures excluded potential benefits from medical consultations in the form of reassurance and information, and so have a bias towards underestimation of the welfare losses brought about by cost sharing.

In the UK, charges have been levied on non-exempt groups for prescriptions and dental care. Groups exempt from such charges include children under 16 years of age, retired pensioners, pregnant women and nursing mothers, and those on low incomes. Birch (1986) has shown that real increases in prescription charges for non-exempt people has led them to reduce their per capita consumption of prescriptions by 7.5 per cent over the period 1979 to 1982 compared with a per-capita increase in consumption by the exempt group of 1 per cent over the same period. It has also been demonstrated that elderly consumers of dental care who are not exempt from payment of charges are four times more likely to receive emergency care only than elderly people who are exempt from such charges. The former group is also 340 times more likely to receive a check-up only, and, when receiving treatment, receive 40 per cent less treatment than exempt patients (Birch, 1989). Such effects could be due not only to charges but also to differences in health status between groups compared which can justify the differences in consumption, or, in the latter example, to greater abilities of dentists to induce demand for services to exempt groups.

The emphasis on charging for care in LDCs is more on revenue raising than is the case in developed countries. This is because many of these countries lack the depth in infrastructure required to raise and distribute taxes. There is, however, an element of prevention of moral hazard involved, with charges deterring frivolous use in situations where scarcity of resources is at its most stark. Charges can also be used to pursue equity objectives; by charging 'urban rich' people more for services and transferring the proceeds to the 'rural poor'. In all, however, charges account for only about 7 per cent of health care revenues in LDCs (Griffin, 1988).

Studies have demonstrated that increased prices for outpatient care have little impact on use of services in Indonesia, Malaysia, Mali, the Philippines, Peru and Rwanda (Heller, 1982; Griffin, 1988). The price changes tested represented a doubling or trebling of a price which was initially close to zero. But this does demonstrate the potential for revenue raising in such countries. Inadvertently, charging for care may also improve quality of care. Using simulated data, it has been shown that an increased charge for attendance at government rural health clinics in Kenya would result in an initial fall in use: for example an increase from 1 Kenyan shilling to 2 Kenyan shillings resulted in a fall in use of 9 per cent. However, if the extra revenue generated by the increased charge was used to improve facilities, then, subsequently, use of the service would rise past its previous level (Mwabu and Mwangi, 1986). This is a useful finding, as government clinics in Kenya tend to be used by lower-income groups. Another important aspect of this finding is that the extra revenue was seen to be fed back into improving local services. Incentives to collect charges (in many cases this is done by volunteers) are diminished if such feedback does not take place.

More worrying is evidence that such charging can affect more vulnerable groups in LDCs. Yoder (1989) analysed the imposition of a 300–400 per cent increase in the price of government curative services in Swaziland while mission sector fees remained the same. The aim was to equalise charges across sectors. Fees for preventive services increased from zero to E0.50 (E1 = $US 0.90). There was little effect on curative services while demand for services to protect against childhood diseases (BCG and DPT immunisations) and against dehydration in children decreased by 16, 19 and 24 per cent respectively. About a third of those who stopped using government or mission services were from low-income groups. Therefore, one has to be careful about the notion that charging is good for revenue raising in LDCs. It may not be good for people's health! Which outweighs the other in terms of magnitude and importance?

A methodological problem with many of these studies is that they may not have lasted long enough to detect changes in consumption patterns over time, as consumers may lag in their responses to increased prices. However, they do demonstrate a role for pricing which does not have the same level of importance in developed countries. If, over time, consumers do adjust their consumption patterns more drastically in response to a price increase, this simply highlights the importance of using the short-term gains in revenue in an effective way.

Fixed, Periodic, Per-capita Payment

The second way of countering consumer moral hazard is the use of fixed periodic per-capita prepayments paid by consumers directly to a provider of comprehensive health care, such as an HMO. Consumers receive a fixed subsidy towards payment, or a fixed percentage of the premium, from employers or government agencies, and so have an incentive to be cost-conscious. Enthoven (1980) has suggested that 60 per cent of a family's actuarial premium be deducted from the family's taxable income, giving them an incentive to 'shop around'. Results from the RAND HIE demonstrate that outpatient visit rates from HMO enrollees were similar to those for people on the free care insurance plan. However, expenditures per person in the HMO group were 72 per cent of those on the free care FFS plan. This difference is a result of a markedly less hospital-intensive style of care in the HMO plan (Manning *et al.*, 1984; 1987). An additional result, from Dowd *et al.* (1986), demonstrates that HMO cover also led to reduced lengths of hospital stays as well as reduced admissions. For the seven diagnosis-related groups Dowd and his colleagues studied, patients in prepaid group practices exhibited significantly shorter lengths of stay than similar patients in FFS plans. This result was obtained after controlling for the effects of patients' age, sex, medical condition and severity of illness. Although lengths of stay were analysed, effects on outpatient treatment (which may have been greater in prepaid group practice) were not.

These results confirm those of earlier studies reviewed by Luft (1978) and have been confirmed by a recent study which demonstrated that Californian legislation allowing public and private third-party payers to negotiate contractual agreements with individual hospitals led to a significant reduction in total hospital costs (Zwanziger and Melnick, 1988). Contrasting such results in looking at care for rheumatoid arthritis, Yelin *et al.*

(1986) found that those receiving care in prepaid group practice consumed services similar in amounts and kinds to those consumed by patients in an FFS setting. Both groups achieved similar outcomes in terms of symptoms, functional status and work disability. Baseline data, however, did show the prepaid group to be more educated than the FFS group, thus introducing a bias likely to favour the former (given similar educational levels, the prepaid group practice population may have fared worse than the FFS population). A recent comparison of US metropolitan areas with and without HMOs showed no differences in hospital expenses per-capita, thus indicating that while hospital expenditure per-capita for HMO enrollees may be falling, those of non-HMO groups may be increasing by offsetting amounts (McLaughlin, 1988).

The most conclusive evidence on the effect of prepaid group practice on people's health is once again provided by part of the RAND HIE, in which 1673 individuals were randomly assigned to one HMO or to an FFS plan in which care was provided free at the point of delivery (Ware *et al.*, 1986). On average those people assigned to the HMO suffered no adverse effects when compared with those in the 'free' FFS plan. However, health outcomes in the two systems of care differed for those individuals in both high and low-income groups who began the experiment with health problems. For those in the high-income group who were initially sick, the HMO produced significant improvements in cholesterol levels and in general health ratings by comparison with the free FFS plan. For those in the low-income group (i.e. those in the lower fifth of the income distribution) who were initially sick, HMO care resulted in significantly more bed-days per year due to poor health, more serious symptoms and a greater risk of dying compared with free FFS care. This evidence has recently been disputed by Wagner and Bledsoe (1990), who claim that such differences may be due to chance, because analyses of results by income group were based on small sample sizes and large standard deviations.

This suggests that HMOs may have to select risks in order to achieve such cost savings without adversely affecting health, which confirms both recent and past work on risk selection in HMOs (Berki *et al.* 1977; Buchanan and Cretin, 1986; Juba *et al.*, 1980; Moser, 1987; Porell and Turner, 1990). Whether HMOs select good risks or good risks select HMOs is not clear. Potentially sicker people may prefer to stay in an FFS system. It should be noted, however, that such selection (or 'cream skimming') is consistent with what one would expect in competitive environments (see the discussion in Chapter 3 above).

One suggested way of overcoming such problems is a 'community-rated' voucher system, which would give poor risks more purchasing power than good risks (Goldsmith, 1988). It has been asserted in public discussion of this strategy that the administration of such a system may be very costly relative to many existing systems, and if consumers are free to 'top up' their contributions then access to better-quality care may be restricted to higher income groups, thus resulting in a two-tier system. We do not know of any evidence, however, on either of these points.

Although included in this chapter as an instrument aimed at reducing consumer moral hazard, HMOs also rely on providers of care to change their behaviour, as a response to being faced with a fixed budget per annum. Thus HMOs act simultaneously on both consumer and provider moral hazard. Because HMOs vertically integrate financial arrangements, making the HMO financially responsible for primary and hospital care, they affect both primary and hospital doctors and so will enter into reviews of evidence on paying doctors and hospitals which are presented in the following two chapters.

Indeed, the evidence presented above indicates that savings are made as a result of less referrals to hospitals and shorter lengths of stay, two areas over which doctors have considerable influence. Therefore, it may be that HMOs have more of an effect on the behaviour of providers than on that of consumers, if they have an effect at all. Once again, this highlights the special nature of the health care market and the importance of influencing providers of care rather than consumers. Similar experiments with vertical integration have taken place in, or are proposed for, countries with publicly orientated financial arrangements, such as the (former) USSR and the UK (Hakansson *et al.*, 1988; Secretaries of State, 1989a and b). These experiments, discussed earlier in Chapter 4, are deliberately aimed at the supply side of the market with consumers observing no apparent change in the financial organisation of the system (i.e. care is still 'free' at the point of delivery). Again, therefore, evidence on such reforms will be reported in the following two chapters.

Preferred Provider Organisations

Preferred provider organisations (PPOs), the third USA mechanism for control of consumer moral hazard, are too new to have a track record regarding evidence on cost and quality. PPOs contract with lower-cost doctors and hospitals and offer themselves to company employees at a lower cost than competing alternatives. Consumers may choose between the contractors and remain free to use other providers of care, but on less favourable terms. Diehr *et al.* (1987) examined the use of ambulatory health care services in a PPO, an HMO, an independent practice association (IPA, similar to an HMO) and a Blue Cross/Blue Shield FFS plan. The study was badly flawed because of a difference in patient mix between the groups. As with the HMO and IPA, the PPO had a higher percentage of patients making use of ambulatory services (90 per cent) compared with the Blue Cross/Blue Shield group (69 per cent). Cost per enrollee was no different between the PPO and Blue Cross/Blue Shield but was higher in the IPA and lower in the HMO.

Attempting to control for case-mix in comparing PPO and non-PPO users with one of seven primary care diagnoses in a Californian health care plan, Wouters (1990) found that outpatient expenditures were likely to increase as a result of PPO use. This may be consistent with less inpatient use. Drug costs were also higher, while diagnostic costs were lower for PPO users. Again attempting to control for case-mix, Garnick *et al.* (1990) analysed non-PPO and PPO claims data by episode of care for patients. For PPO patients, charges per doctor were lower but charges per episode of care were higher. The authors concluded that the increased frequency of visits may have been doctor-induced, to offset discounts, or patient-generated, since there were no copayments in the PPO. However, it is the doctor who is likely to have more of an influence on the content of the episode once the patient has made initial contact. Zwanziger and Auerbach (1991) found that PPO enrollees incurred increased expenditures as a result of expanded outpatient use and ineffective utilisation management which swamped the effects of reductions in inpatient use and discounted fees.

The effect of PPO provision on hospital inpatient use and on health status has not yet been analysed. There is limited evidence linking PPO enrolment to individuals requiring relatively little medical care (Wouters and Hester, 1988; Zwanziger and Auerbach, 1991). This limits the potential for overall cost savings, as higher-risk users remain with more-costly, non-PPO, FFS primary-care providers. Somehow, such providers would have to be brought into the PPO system in order to test whether real cost savings can be made.

Fixed Indemnity

Another potential method of controlling consumer moral hazard is by placing a limit on the financial obligations of the insurer – a maximum financial benefit to the insured person contingent on the nature of the health problem suffered. Thus, for example, if the policy pays £x per hospital inpatient day or £y per GP surgery visit (with the premium being related to the sizes of x and y) then the consumer who uses a more expensive hospital or doctor will bear the full extra cost themselves. If, in addition, there is a fixed upper limit on the indemnity (for example, £z per hospital inpatient spell) then the consumer has a further incentive to moderate demand, once the limit has been reached. We have come across no empirical evaluation of indemnity insurance for health care and it is plain that, to work, it requires the consumer to have access to a considerable amount of fairly detailed cost (price) information, which may once again be administratively costly to provide.

Non-price Rationing

There is also little evidence about the effect of waiting time on use of services for which there is no monetary cost. Lindsay and Feigenbaum (1984) estimated that a 10 per cent increase in waiting time leads to a 5.5 to 7 per cent decrease in use of NHS inpatient care. The effect of waiting time on the use and effect of services on the poor and on health status in general have not been analysed. Schwartz and Aaron (1984) reported that 31 per cent of those on UK NHS waiting lists for surgery had been waiting for more than a year. Seven per cent of those on the lists were classified as urgent. Bloom and Fendrick (1987), analysing 1984 UK data, estimated that, for one quarter of patients in England who had been placed on a waiting list, the total wait was 96 days. This was for non-emergency care leading to hospitalisation, including primary care and specialty ambulatory care. Of the remaining 75 per cent, half were admitted immediately and a quarter were booked or transferred from other hospitals. They concluded that the widely accepted notion that a large majority of hospitalised patients wait a long time for care in the UK is mistaken, and that the emphasis on primary ambulatory care means that essentially no one has to wait for general practitioner care. Most diagnoses for which there is a wait have a fair degree of electivity for patient and doctor, and the wait, therefore, probably has little effect on outcome in a clinical sense. However, reduced functional capacity and quality of life for such people is evidently a feature not to be ignored in assessing the 'costs' of using waiting as a rationing device.

Further evidence on waiting time for general practitioner care has been cited by Potter and Porter (1989). Using data from the RAND HIE and the University of Minnesota Center for Health Services Research (1987) and from Bloom and Fendrick's work, they estimated that mean waiting times in the UK and the USA were one day and three days respectively. They also concluded that outpatient waiting times were about the same for both countries, but that access to specialists in the USA was, in general, greater. Despite this latter result, the longest waits for specialists in the UK were for elective procedures (e.g. 80 days for plastic surgery), with those treatments requiring more urgent attention receiving such attention (e.g. pulmonology).

It should be pointed out that the analogy between a price and waiting is not exact (Lindsay, 1980). There is a 'cost' of waiting imposed on patients, but in the NHS it is not one that is avoided by not joining a waiting list, unless one moves into the private sector (Culyer and Cullis, 1976; Cullis and Jones, 1985). As a means of rationing resources *within* the NHS, therefore, waiting time provides no 'deterrent effect' on the demand for care (unless one dies while waiting). It is important to distinguish between the sort of time-cost that *does* operate like a price (for example, travel time, waiting in a surgery), which is avoidable by not demanding care, and waiting for an appointment or for admission, the 'costs' of which are not avoided by not being put on a waiting list, except by incurring further expense (through private insurance or direct out-of-pocket payment) in 'going private'.

CONCLUSIONS

The evidence suggests that introducing cost sharing does result in reduced utilisation of health care relative to free care at the point of delivery. Further, there is evidence to show that most of this reduction in utilisation is by people in lower-income groups and, more specifically, children. The evidence additionally suggests that it is effective treatments for which demand is reduced as well as trivial or placebo care. On its own, charging patients for care in developed countries may not reduce moral hazard overall if doctors still remain free to concentrate their demand-inducing abilities on those who can afford to pay. This could result in the same amount of money being spent on health care but to less effect on the health of the community, as those more in need of care would have less access to it. Thus, naive neoclassical solutions to consumer moral hazard may have serious unintended consequences which will not be picked up by neoclassical analysis of their implementation. Charging (small amounts) for care in LDCs, however, should not be dismissed to the same extent, although the claims that they have equity-inducing effects should be treated with great caution; vulnerable groups can be adversely affected.

In response to proponents (whom he sees as medical associations and private insurance companies in Canada) of charges, Evans (1990) has summed up the evidence as follows:

'There is an occasional nod in the direction of the conventional rhetoric of economics, that charging "consumers" of health care will result in reduced utilization and costs, but it is quite obvious that no one really believes this. If medical associations thought that there was any risk of a reduction in their members' workloads and incomes, they would not be such staunch advocates of charging patients. In fact, however, medical associations are quite familiar with the American experience, showing that utilisation rates continue to climb even at very high rates of direct patient payment.'

Through less hospital use, HMOs result in less costly modes of care compared with insurance plans with effectively free care at the point of delivery, although, once again, this seems to be at the expense of people in low-income groups. Little is known about the effect of waiting time on patient demand, though theory suggests it will be negligible.

Keeler *et al.* (1985) noted that, although free care resulted in better control of hypertension than charging, effects in both charged and free-care groups were greater in those who had an initial screening examination, after which personal doctors were notified of patients' hypertension status. Once again, as with the HMO results reported above, and suggestions that charges do not deal adequately with provider moral hazard, such results highlight the importance of influencing providers of care as well as, and perhaps to a greater extent than, consumers.

It is difficult to determine whether, in particular instances, reduced utilisation is for inefficient care, even if that care is effective. A useful indicator of this is to examine how different health services achieve the objectives outlined in Chapter 5.

The most comprehensive sets of results presented in this paper are on cost sharing and finance of care through HMOs, and the evidence is equivocal on how these methods meet efficiency objectives. Costs are reduced, but at what, if any, harm to patients? Neither of these alternatives appears favourable relative to 'free' care in the light of equity objectives.

The evidence is that free care at the point of delivery does not necessarily result in higher health care costs through increased moral hazard anyway, as in Canada and the UK. This is because of initiatives to control costs on the supply side of the market which are examined in parts of the following two chapters. The percentages of GNP spent on health care in Canada and the UK in 1982 were approximately 8 and 6 per cent respectively, as opposed to approximately 10.5 per cent in the USA. Health care costs are also rising at a faster rate in the latter country. Thus, the key to controlling cost while achieving objectives seems to lie in public finance, though not necessarily public provision, of health care (Donaldson and Gerard, 1989b).

The implication seems to be that some method of non-price rationing with public finance will achieve health care objectives at least cost. However, more evidence from controlled trials of the effect of other modes of finance is required. Also, because of the dynamics of the health care market, initiatives aimed at consumers cannot be considered in isolation from those aimed at suppliers of care. It is this side of the market to which we now turn.

CHAPTER 7

Countering Doctor Moral Hazard

INTRODUCTION

Provider moral hazard can take one of two forms: specifically, that which occurs within identifiable actors in the health care system, for the most part doctors; and, more generally, that which occurs within institutions, without being narrowed down to the behaviour of identifiable individuals or groups of people. In this chapter, we are concerned with the former of these. In the next chapter, the latter issue will be addressed within the context of different financial arrangements for payment of hospitals for the care they provide.

Moral hazard on the part of doctors occurs for two related reasons. First, on the supply side, a third party (such as an insurance company or a government agency) often pays for care which is provided by doctors. With this third party bearing the costs of care, doctors will have few incentives to moderate the amount of care they supply. They do not have to bear the full costs of their decision making and are often not even aware of the costs they have incurred. Secondly, on the demand side, there is asymmetry of information between patients and doctors regarding the technological relationship between health care and its effects on health. In such situations, the patient seeks advice on what services to demand from the very person who is supplying these services, the doctor. Thus, the doctor is placed in the unusual position of being both a demander and a supplier of a service for which they bear little, if any, financial burden. Such a situation will almost inevitably lead to overutilisation of services.

This latter type of doctor moral hazard is most often associated with systems of payment based on fee-for-service (FFS) in which the doctor receives a fee for each item of work performed (for example, an operation or a consultation). More work done leads to more income for the doctor. It is often claimed that much of this work results in 'overuse'; that is, for services which are of little or no therapeutic value *vis-à-vis* the cost of providing them. In a perfect market, with fully knowledgeable consumers, provision would be less. But it should be remembered that such markets still fail to account for certain factors, such as externalities. Thus, some 'overuse' of services may be warranted, implying that *some* doctor moral hazard is efficient. So, certain types of doctor behaviour, such as supplier-induced demand, should not be seen as all 'bad'.

Thus, an important part of the health care funding debate relates to the method of payment of doctors; different payment systems have different financial incentives for doctors which in turn have different implications for the cost and quality of care provided. For example, some methods of payment may restrict costs but have more adverse effects than other methods on the use of services by the population as a whole, on the use of services by different groups within the population and on the population's health status. It is the aim of this chapter to summarise the available evidence (mostly from the USA) on the effect of different methods of paying doctors in terms of these three criteria. Once again, the importance of this evidence depends on health service objectives. Therefore, the chapter will conclude by considering the results in the light of some of these objectives.

METHODS OF PAYING DOCTORS

In two comprehensive reviews of methods of remunerating doctors, Maynard *et al.* (1986) and Donaldson and Gerard (1989a) outlined six main ways of paying doctors: (1) FFS remuneration; (2) salaries; (3) reorganisation of allowances in order to permit payment for 'good practice', assessment being based on standards, which may be set by professionals themselves; (4) capitation payments, including those which could be made to health maintenance organisations (HMOs); (5) charges to patients for a part or the full cost of care; and (6) private practice, allowing market forces to determine both quality and rewards. An additional form of payment, recently implemented by the UK government, is budgets for some general practitioners from which the full cost of a restricted range of services must be met. This is a similar concept to the HMO, the UK policy being that general practitioners receive a budget from which payments are made for diagnostic tests and elective surgery in hospitals (Secretaries of State, 1989a and b). Another form of influence on doctors' activities, though not strictly financial, is direct government regulation of what they can and cannot do. This can have a financial element in that if doctors do not behave accordingly, they could be subjected to financial penalties. Governments in, for example, Australia, Norway and the UK use this type of control to limit the range of drugs which general practitioners can prescribe. It is also common in developing countries.

The first three and the last two of the above forms of payment/control mainly affect doctor behaviour, as does the fourth as usually defined. However, capitation payments within HMOs aim to give both doctor and patient incentives to provide, and look for, low cost care of acceptable quality. Therefore, it is important to examine evidence on the effect of HMOs on doctor behaviour when reviewing methods of remuneration. The fifth method, charges, is clearly aimed at patients rather than doctors and has been discussed in detail in the previous chapter. Charges to patients will not be discussed any further in this chapter, but as we have pointed out in Chapter 6, it would be naive to assume that they will affect only patient behaviour. Charges may reduce (or control) use of services by some groups of patients, but, if this is the case, then doctors remain free to switch their demand-inducing abilities to those willing and able to pay for care.

The sixth method of payment, through market forces, is not reviewed here because, in its present form, it would open up the market to non-qualified practitioners, which could affect the quality of service unacceptably. Not since the commencement of registration for doctors allowing the exclusion of non-qualified practitioners (in the early twentieth century in countries such as Australia and the UK) has such a situation existed (Peterson, 1978; Allen 1982) (Note 19). Thus, market prices beyond the elements of competition which exist in the seven other alternatives are unlikely to appear on the shortlist of options in a review of the payment of doctors.

FEE FOR SERVICE: DOES SUPPLIER INDUCEMENT REALLY EXIST?

Supplier-induced Demand: Evidence and Explanations

Remunerating doctors by fees for each item of service provided rewards doctors according to the amount of work carried out. The conventional wisdom is that this encourages the use of services by patients on the recommendation of their doctors, thus inflating health care costs with possibly little or no effect on health itself. This power of doctors to recommend, or induce, demand for their services is known as 'supplier-induced demand'. In line with our definition of provider moral hazard, supplier-induced demand is the amount of demand, induced by doctors, which exists beyond what would have occurred in a market in which consumers are fully informed.

The phenomenon is thought to be more likely to exist in systems of remuneration based on FFS rather than under alternative reimbursement mechanisms. However, despite the many indications from empirical work as to the existence of supplier inducement in FFS environments, neoclassical economists remain convinced that observed increases in health care utilisation which can be 'explained' by the inducement hypothesis can also be 'explained' by the straightforward market forces outlined in Chapter 2. This point is explored in more detail below.

Another dilemma in this field is that 'true competitive prices' for doctors' services are not known. In FFS systems, problems of how much care is provided arise only if fees actually depart from these true competitive prices. Thus, in accordance with the conventional wisdom of the supplier-induced-demand school, if the fee is greater than its true competitive price, there will be an incentive to overprovide. But, contrary to this conventional wisdom, if the fee is below its true competitive price, there will be an incentive to underprovide care. Therefore, although supplier inducement may be shown to exist for some types of care, this may not be the case across the board. This argument is further complicated, however, by the hypothesis that doctors have in mind some 'target income' which they seek to achieve (Evans, 1974). In such a case, general underpricing of fee levels may lead to greater provision of services than if fees were, in general, higher. By providing more services, doctors maintain their target income.

Adding to this the argument that some utilisation above the truly competitive level may be justified anyway (because of externalities), one is left to judge how much of each type of care provided is appropriate. So-called 'overutilisation' may be appropriate in that it is still cost-effective. We have already seen, in Chapter 6, how charges for care lead to reductions in utilisation by certain groups for some well-proven therapies. The basic problem is that so little is known about what represents best medical practice in the sense of being either effective or efficient (Loft and Mooney, 1989).

Therefore, much of the evidence cited in the remainder of this subsection may appear ambiguous, depending on which way one looks at it. This evidence is of three types: cross-country comparisons of health care utilisation and doctor payment; tests of the effects of changes in doctor to population ratios on utilisation and on doctors' fees; and quasi-experimental.

There is a considerable body of evidence from cross-country comparisons that (after controlling for differences in age, sex and population) the higher rates of common surgical procedures in Canada and the USA compared with those in the UK are due to factors such as lack of agreement about indications for surgery, variations in use of technology, national priorities and values, and payment of a fee for service in Canada and the USA, and not to differences in the incidence or prevalence of disorders. The different rates appear to have little effect on outcome; although the latter have been measured only crudely (Vayda, 1973; McPherson *et al.*, 1981; Vayda *et al.*, 1982; McPherson *et al.*, 1982; Vayda *et al.*, 1984).

Some studies have examined the effect of increases in doctor-to-population ratios within specified geographical areas in health care systems based on FFS remuneration. For example, in response to an increase in the supply of doctors, doctors may encourage patients to use more services in order to maintain their income. This is supposed to explain the noted correlation between increased numbers of doctors within a geographical area and increased use of services (Fuchs, 1978; Cromwell and Mitchell, 1986; Phelps, 1986).

However, there are other possible explanations. The neoclassical interpretation would be that greater numbers of doctors increase their availability to patients, other access costs are reduced or the increase in use as supply increases may simply be meeting previously unmet needs. With supply increasing, fees and non-monetary costs (related to waiting time and access) go down and, naturally, the amount of care demanded by patients will increase (i.e. there is a movement along the demand curve as 'price' falls). Increased utilisation is compatible with both hypotheses and can be interpreted as either a demand shift initiated by doctors or as a normal market response by consumers to lower costs to them.

Thus, it seems that studies employing doctor-to-population ratios as an independent variable provide ambiguous results. However, as Reinhardt (1978) has argued there is still one unambiguous test of supplier inducement using such ratios: that is, a test of the effect of doctor supply on doctors' fees. Neoclassical theory predicts a negative effect on fees of an increase in supply (i.e. if supply goes up, price, or fees, should go down). Fees could also fall in an inducement world, but only in an inducement world could fees either rise or be kept steady. With fees as the dependent variable in an econometric model, then, assuming other variables are adequately controlled for, a zero or positive coefficient for the doctor–population ratio independent variable is not compatible with neoclassical theory; supplier-induced demand exists.

Despite doctors' fees being the definitive test in the use of doctor-to-population ratios to determine supplier-induced demand, there is little evidence of how fees are affected by such ratios. Wilensky and Rossiter (1983) found the effect of such ratios to be insignificant in each of five model specifications, a finding which Rice and Labelle (1989) consider to be 'most readily consistent with the demand-inducement model'. Cromwell and Mitchell (1986) found a strong, positive influence of surgeon density on surgeon fees.

Despite argument in favour of effects on fees being the unambiguous test, it is possible that non-financial demand-side factors (such as access and waiting costs) are reduced by an increase in the supply of doctors to a level whereby so much demand is forthcoming that fees are pushed up beyond their previous levels. So, once again, the evidence is ambiguous.

One Irish study of general practitioners used doctor-to-population ratios as an independent variable, but with more detailed survey data which discriminated between patient- and doctor-initiated return visits (Tussing and Wojtowycz, 1986). They found a positive relationship between doctor-to-population ratios and the proportion of return visits arranged by the doctor.

Using a quasi-experimental, before-and-after type of design, an examination of the effect of increasing reimbursement rates for some services and decreasing the rates for others in Colorado's Medicare system found that a 1 per cent decrease in the reimbursement rate for medical services resulted in a 0.61 per cent increase in medical service intensity (measured by numbers of standard units of quantity provided) and that a 1 per cent decrease in the reimbursement rate for surgical services resulted in a 0.15 per cent increase in the intensity of the surgical services provided (Rice, 1983). Similar results were shown for auxiliary services, such as laboratory tests. Changes in practice and doctor characteristics over time were controlled for, and these results appear to be consistent with doctors adjusting patient use so as to maintain a target income (Evans, 1974).

Two recent analyses lend further support to the 'target income' hypothesis. The first was of USA and Canadian data on doctor services per capita and doctor fees (Fuchs and Hahn, 1990). Using 1985 data, fees for procedures were about three times higher in the USA than in Canada, while those for evaluation and management were about 80 per cent higher. However, per-capita use of services is higher in Canada, the authors suggesting that this may result from universal insurance and 'from encouragement of use by the larger number of doctors who are paid lower fees'.

The second study, in Copenhagen, investigated the effects of changing general practitioners' remuneration from a capitation-based system to a mixed FFS and capitation system (Krasnik *et al.*, 1990). The behaviour of practitioners in Copenhagen city, where the change took place, was compared with that of practitioners in Copenhagen county, where remuneration remained the same; the latter group were already on the mixed-remuneration system. Patient contacts did not increase significantly, despite payment of a fee for service. However, rates of examinations and treatments that attracted specific additional remuneration rose significantly. Referral rates to secondary care and hospital fell.

All of the above evidence supports the existence of supplier inducement. But, as Phelps (1986) points out, the empirical work has reached the limit of its ability to inform us on this issue, particularly on the extent of supplier-induced demand. There remains the question of what level of supplier-induced demand is optimal. The Copenhagen study suggested that it is possible to encourage general practitioners to carry out some procedures on an FFS basis, thereby resulting in more of these procedures being conducted in general practice and less in hospital. Whether this is more efficient is not answered in the study – or in any other that we know. The existence of externalities also suggests that some level of supplier-induced demand (rather than none) is optimal. Thus, according to the Copenhagen group, 'research is now required on what constitutes "optimal inducement"'.

Intervening to Set Fees

If it is thought necessary to control the powers of doctors to manipulate demand and fee setting, health policy makers would appear to have two options as regards remuneration:

(1) Intervene heavily in fee setting, as many governments (Canada and Australia) and other third-party payers (as in Germany) have done.
(2) Move to a different form of payment altogether.

The latter course of action is discussed in the following section, while examples of the former course are the subject matter of the remainder of this subsection.

In Chapter 3 we discussed the roles of the Australian and Canadian governments in fee setting. The reason for such intervention is that it is recognised that for public or private insurers to guarantee full payment of medical fees which are set by the medical profession itself would simply result in a climate of continual fee increases being met by private and public payers. This would substantially increase health care costs at possibly little or no benefit to patients.

What the experience of these countries demonstrates is that the responses of governments to such a problem could vary. In Australia, the government sets its own fee schedule and reimburses only a fixed percentage of the fee (85 per cent for general practitioner care and 75 per cent for hospital care, while for the latter the 'gap' between 75 and 100 per cent can be privately insured against). In general practice, doctors can accept the 85 per cent coverage as full payment, thus waiving the patient's obligation to make up the other 15 per cent of the fee. Doctors are free to charge at a rate above the government's set fee, but the amount above the government's fee cannot be privately insured against. Thus, there is a tendency for doctors to compete for patients by minimising patients' out-of-pocket contributions. Although there is the appearance of doctors being given 'freedom' to charge what they want, this competition drives fees down to the amounts funded by government, thus giving the government effective control over fee levels. In Canada, the approach is more direct. Each Province produces a schedule of fees to which doctors must adhere.

Both systems lead to much conflict between the medical profession and government. However, a positive way of looking at this conflict is simply as a situation in which a strong supplier of services (the medical profession) meets a strong demander of services on the community's behalf (the government). The result is some kind of compromise in fee levels which works in the interest of the greater good, much as does the 'invisible hand' of Adam Smith (see Chapter 2), when fragmented suppliers are faced with fragmented demanders. The worst scenario is one in which one side or the other is fragmented while the other is united.

Another problem is that although such regulation gives governments control over fee levels, they do not have direct control over the volume of services provided. Indeed there is evidence from Canada that services per-capita have continually risen since the introduction of public insurance (Barer *et al.*, 1988). However, this growth has been at no greater a rate than in the USA despite maintenance of lower fees in Canada over the same period. In addition, presumably institutional constraints, such as hospital capacity, help to check the volume of services provided, particularly if governments have a large element of control over investment in such institutions (as is the case in Canada or Australia). It does seem that continual negotiation between the medical profession (as the suppliers of the care) and governmental bodies (as the negotiators of the price on the patients' behalf) can be successful in preventing cost escalation.

It also seems that, although tight control may be required when fees are used as part of a remuneration package, fees may still represent a useful form of payment for certain services. There could be areas to which a degree of importance is attached and for which targets have to be reached. For instance, the target may be one hundred per cent coverage for vaccination rates, where an obvious financial incentive wiil be to offer a fee for each vaccination. In certain circumstances, FFS may result in improved effectiveness and less overall cost.

ALTERNATIVES TO FEE FOR SERVICE

Salaries

Maynard *et al.* (1986) claimed that the advantages of a salaried system are that it would make health care planning easier, as doctors' salaries would be known in advance, and that promotion could be related to performance. They also noted some disadvantages. General practitioners and hospitals would have little incentive to compete for patients. Indeed, they might have an incentive to please superiors rather than meet the health care needs of patients. Continuity of care might suffer as primary-care doctors, without a financial stake in their practice, would be more likely to move away from their original locality. There might also be problems in motivating doctors who had reached the top of the promotion ladder. Non-financial considerations (such as ethics and caring) – which of course might be powerful – aside, why should a doctor, with a guaranteed salary, and no prospect of it increasing, do their best for the patient in front of them? The incentive might be for doctors to refer patients inappropriately to other departments or to other doctors in order to minimise time spent with them. Merit awards, if related to some index of performance, could be used to overcome this problem – current UK NHS merits awards for consultants vary from £790 to £20,550 per annum for life. However, the system of awards is not related to performance and tends to favour those in more 'glamorous' specialties (Fallon, 1988).

One USA study of doctors serving as residents in a single clinic compared utilisation patterns under salaried and FFS payment regimes (Hickson *et al.*, 1987). Doctors were randomly assigned to receive a salary or FFS reimbursement: the latter group scheduled more visits per patient. No results were reported on diagnostic testing or on health status. Apart from this study, we know of no evidence of the effects of salaries on overall use of services by patients, on use by different groups or on health status to corroborate any of the above claims or expectations.

Special Payments for 'Good Practice'

Under this method of payment, general practitioners would receive a combination of capitation fees, fees for items of service and some allowances, and hospital doctors would receive a basic salary with additional merit awards, as in the existing situation in the UK. The difference would be that allowances and merit awards would be based on 'good practice'.

There is evidence that doctors will respond to incentives to earn 'bonuses'. Health Stop, a major chain of for-profit ambulatory care centres in the USA, paid its doctors a flat hourly wage until mid-1985, after which a system of bonuses was introduced whereby the doctor's bonus depended on the gross income individually generated (Hemenway *et al.*, 1990). Not surprisingly, in one year from the period under the waged system to that under the bonus scheme, the number of laboratory tests and X-rays performed per visit rose by 23 and 16 per cent respectively. Real revenue from charges grew by 20 per cent, mostly as a result of a 12 per cent increase in the average number of patient visits per month.

Of course, such changes may not be desirable, but do demonstrate that doctors will respond to performance incentives placed in front of them. It is obviously important to tailor allowances and merit wards to the achievement of 'good practice' rather than to simply doing more for patients. This would encourage more standard setting and review. Of course, there are problems in defining 'good practice'. A study analysing the costs and effects of standard setting in general practice for five common conditions of childhood in the North of England has recently been completed (Russell *et al.*, 1986; North of England Study, 1990). This controlled before-and-after study demonstrated the following for one condition, recurrent wheezy chest:

- reduced prescribing of antibodies but increased prescribing of therapeutic drugs (mainly bronchodilators and oral steroids), an overall small
  cost increase;
- increased follow-up and better compliance with drugs;
- substantially improved outcome relative to cost (outcome measured by
  the reduced numbers of days spent wheezing, breathless, coughing or
  awake at night).

Thus, addressing standards can result in improved outcome, and may
result in a more efficient, if more costly, health service. For the four other
conditions no outcome effects were detected. Drug costs were reduced for
bedwetting, increased for acute vomiting and itchy rash, while antibiotic
costs for acute cough fell along with an increase in the cost of bronchodilators.

There is also limited evidence of the effect of peer review on the use of
specific services, although peer review is a common activity within HMOs
and PPOs. Two studies have shown that providing clinicians with information on their own use of laboratory tests as well as that of their colleagues
had no effect on laboratory use (Grivell *et al.*, 1981). Myers and Schroeder
(1981), however, reported that such schemes could be successful if accompanied by an educational programme.

The introduction of formulae for antibiotics in general medical practice
has been shown to reduce antibiotic costs without increasing the number of
patient consultations, home visits or referrals to hospital (Needham *et al.*,
1988). In addition to this, it has been demonstrated that examinations of
general medical practitioners by trained assessors resulted in their prescribing fewer drugs than before examination, while a control group prescribed
more (Grol *et al.*, 1988). The effects of such changes in practice on health
status, however, have not been examined.

Capitation

Capitation is often used as a method of payment in primary care. Doctors
receive an annual payment in advance to care for each individual who elects
to join their list. The main advantage claimed for this method is that it
motivates doctors in the primary care sector to practise in a way that
encourages patients to join their lists, although it would be to the doctor's
advantage to attract only low-cost people. Prior to recent policy changes,
capitation accounted for approximately 47 per cent of general practitioners'
income in the UK. The recent changes include an increase in this percentage
to 60 per cent, so as to give general practitioners more encouragement to
compete to attract patients (Secretaries of State, 1989a and b). Thus,

practices which, according to patients, are more 'attractive', will be financially rewarded. The problem with this proposal is that very little is known about what patients take into account when assessing their general practitioner or, indeed, whether this is something which patients actively wish to do. Recent studies have shown a distinct lack of behaviour of the sort one would expect from the fully-informed consumer described in Chapter 2 in the way people choose their doctor (Leavy *et al.*, 1989; Salisbury, 1989; Donaldson *et al.*, 1991; Lupton *et al.*, 1991).

Another advantage of such per-capita payments is that they sever the link between amount of service provided and financial reward and hence involve minimal distortion of purely professional medical judgement. Relative to FFS payment, capitation may encourage more preventive activities because the doctor's future income does not depend on further consultations resulting when the patient is ill. However, guaranteed payment may encourage some general practitioners to cut their financial and personal costs by curtailing consultation time, by prescribing more, or by increased referral to hospitals. We know of no evidence of the effect of competition for patients to join lists on the use of services by the population as a whole or by different groups, on the outcomes of such services, or on the characteristics which patients look for when deciding whether or not to register with a general practice or general practitioner. Although it is known that in European countries other than the UK general practitioners are more likely to refer public insurance patients (for whom they receive capitation) to hospital than privately insured patients (who pay on a FFS basis), it is not clear whether such differences in referral rates are due to the payment systems or to the different health status of people in the public and private systems (Donaldson and Gerard, 1989a). The UK government has attempted to mitigate some of the problems of capitation by proposing a system of budgets for general practitioners from which payments may be made for diagnostic tests and surgery provided in hospital. Again, however, we know of no evidence as yet of the effects of this specific innovation, although some results from hospital budgeting experiments are reviewed below. The Copenhagen study, however, has demonstrated that it is possible to encourage general practitioners to carry out some procedures on an FFS basis, thereby resulting in more of these procedures being conducted in general practice and fewer in hospital. Whether this represents a more efficient use of resources is not known.

One other way of avoiding inappropriate referrals is to extend the UK government proposals and integrate totally payment for primary and hospital care, as in HMOs. Under this system, the providers (for example, a group of primary-care doctors) receive an annual per-capita payment in advance and have to provide comprehensive health care in return, buying in hospital care when needed. Thus the temptation to refer on or to prescribe inefficiently is reduced.

HMOs (and other health care intermediaries in the USA) have an annual 'open season' during which they compete to retain existing customers and to attract new customers. This gives the organisation the incentive to provide comprehensive care at minimum cost; otherwise patients will look for another health care plan, because they receive only a fixed subsidy from employers towards payment of the premium.

Most evidence on HMOs has come from the RAND HIE in the USA, much of which was cited in the previous chapter. Results from this experiment demonstrate that use of outpatient services, including general practitioners, was similar among HMO patients and people on the 'free' care insurance plan. However, expenditure in the HMO group was 72 per cent of that in the free-care insurance group, the difference being a result of a markedly less hospital-intensive style of care in the HMO (Manning *et al.*, 1984; 1987). This result has been confirmed by a later study of seven conditions treated in hospital, in which HMO patients had significantly shorter lengths of stay than similar patients in FFS plans (Dowd *et al.*, 1987). A study of the chronic condition rheumatoid arthritis, however, showed no difference in services used or in outcome measures (functional status, work disability and systems) when comparing similar groups receiving HMO and FFS care (Yelin *et al.*, 1986). The problems with HMOs may be that they achieve some, or all, of their cost savings, either by selection of good risks (or by being selected by good risks) or to the detriment of the health of ill people in lower-income groups (Ware *et al.*, 1986; Buchanan and Cretin, 1986; Moser, 1987; Wagner and Bledsoe, 1990).

The Leningrad experiment, in which hospital budgets have been transferred to polyclinics for 37 specialties, appears to have resulted in shorter lengths of stay (from 18 to 12 days), although it is not clear what the trend in length of stay was before the experiment was implemented (Hakansson *et al.*, 1988). No effects on use by different groups or on health status have been measured.

Clinicians as Budget Holders

There is no evidence on how general practitioners would respond to being allocated fixed budgets for providing and purchasing services for their patients, including hospital care. However, there is limited evidence on the effects of budgeting in the hospital sector.

In proposing to make clinicians budget holders, the UK experiment with clinical budgeting attempted to increase the awareness of and provide incentives for clinicians to be more efficient. Information on costs and clinical activity was provided to each budget holder (e.g. a group of clinicians working in a particular specialty). Planning agreements with clinical teams (PACTs), based on previous workloads, prospectively determined activity levels and declared the nature of the incentive structure for participants, i.e. some fixed percentage of any savings made could be given back to budget holders and spent on improving patient care. The results demonstrated that PACTs led to little or no change in resource use in five categories of revenue expenditure which were analysed (Wickings *et al.*, 1985). The five categories were drugs, X-ray films, X-ray chemicals and equipment, equipment for medical and surgical purposes, and laboratory instruments. However, these results were not surprising, because only to a very limited extent to could clinicians determine how the budget was allocated and choose between different factor mixes in determining their production function. Also, it is difficult to separate the possible effects of PACTs from others, such as the introduction at around the same time of performance indicators and of general management, since the experiment was not controlled.

It is encouraging, however, that a recent (but also uncontrolled) before-and-after study has demonstrated that, in response to information produced by clinical budgeting, it was possible to reduce drug costs on long-stay wards for elderly people by 34 per cent, with no adverse effects on patients' physical and mental states (Gibbens *et al.*, 1988).

Government Regulation

Direct government regulation of health care providers is not necessarily solely through financial control. But it can be, in the sense that if such providers do not comply with the regulation, then they can be subjected to financial penalties. There is some evidence on the effect of government regulation to control providers. Irwin *et al.* (1986) examined the effect on prescribing of the limited list in a computerised UK general practice of 3000 patients. Such a list indicates those drugs which cannot be prescribed for a patient to obtain free of charge or at preferential rates in the UK NHS. For drugs 'on the list' Irwin *et al.* found significant decreases in the amounts of cough and cold remedies, vitamins and antacids prescribed, whereas no change occurred in the prescribing of laxatives, benzodiazipines or analgesics. Much of the decrease was for prescriptions issued for 'non-essential' reasons (especially vitamins). However, the prescribing of irons and penicillins (which were not on the list) increased, the former probably being a result of substitution for decreased vitamin prescriptions.

Yule *et al.* (1988) analysed the prescribing habits of 17 doctors in the north-east of Scotland after the introduction of a limited list, asking them what they would have prescribed in each situation had the list not existed. For the drugs listed, NHS expenditure was reduced, but not by as much as expected. In many cases, costs to patients increased as a result of more private prescribing and over-the-counter purchases.

Many other countries operate a 'limited list' of sorts (Smith, 1985), and some impressionistic evidence is available on their cost-effectiveness. At first sight, the Norwegian system appears to be quite strict; before any drug is registered for use, manufacturers must produce evidence on its quality, safety, efficacy, cost and need. However, despite this, there is a special licensing clause whereby a doctor can prescribe a drug which is not currently available. Such licences are commonly issued. A recent study compared anti-inflammatory use in the Netherlands, where 22 products were available, with that in Norway, where only 7 were on the market (Dukes and Lunde, 1981). The average Dutch rheumatologist prescribed 12–13 of the 22 drugs, using only 7 regularly. In Norway, the average rheumatologist used 4 to 6 of the 7 drugs available. But, 40 per cent made use of the licensing system to prescribe drugs not on the national list. No outcome effects were tested.

In Australia, a two-stage regulatory procedure exists. A company wishing to introduce a new drug to Australia submits it first to the Drug Evaluation Committee, which decides on safety. Quality and cost are then considered by the Pharmaceutical Benefits Advisory Committee. The scheme is strongly supported by doctors and patients and has kept prescribing costs below those in Britain (Smith, 1985).

In countries like Norway and Australia, the only disenchanted party seems to be the pharmaceutical industry; it tends not to locate manufacturing plant in these and other highly regulated countries, Canada being another example. All of these countries are sparsely populated, which may be another factor; demand is not sufficient to warrant a manufacturing presence there. Presumably communities lose out from such absences, though this has never been quantified.

The results of all of these studies do demonstrate, however, that regulation can change behaviour. More regulation to encourage generic prescribing and local formularies could lead to more efficient changes in prescribing habits from the point of view of health services, although the effects on the costs and benefits to the community at large are not known.

CONCLUSIONS

There is little evidence about the effect of different methods of payment on doctors' performance. One of the best-documented areas concerns the effect of payment by FFS on supplier-induced demand. Despite doubts about the adequacy of the data, most evidence tends to support the view that FFS remuneration leads to induced demands for fee-yielding services by patients on the recommendation of their doctors. However, the effects of supplier-induced demand on service use by different groups and on health status are not known. Thus, it does seem that if fees are to be used as part of a remuneration package, tight control of fee schedules is required, that is, fees must be targeted in line with priorities in order to maintain effectiveness at least cost.

Salaried payments probably lead to less utilisation relative to FFS. But apart from this result, from one study, little is known about effects of salary or capitation payments (as the latter currently exist in the UK) on utilisation or outcome. However, the effect of receiving a fixed per-capita payment in advance, such as in HMOs in the USA, results in a less hospital-intensive style of care. Despite this, lower-income groups fare worse in this system than in an insurance system with free care at the point of delivery. Evidence on payment of another type which can be fixed prospectively, budgets, is equivocal, though its potential has been demonstrated. From the previous chapter, another method of payment of doctors, charges to patients, appears to deter utilisation but, like HMOs, at the possible expense of lower-income groups.

The importance of such results depends on the objectives of health care provision. Once again, it seems that charges and HMOs can be ruled out in terms of achievement of these objectives when compared with free care at the point of delivery. More evidence is required from other countries on all methods of payment in order to determine the most efficient remuneration package for doctors. Although evidence from the USA is valuable, initiatives in health care financing have been dominated by the need to reduce costs. In 1982, health care costs in the USA amounted to approximately 11 per cent of gross national product, and were rising, whereas in the UK costs were a fairly stable 6 per cent of gross national product. Other developed countries lie between these two extremes (OECD, 1987).

The potential for cost savings in such countries, therefore, may be likely to be less than in the USA system, their concerns being more on the quality of care achieved for the resources spent. Thus, research results from within countries' own health care environments are essential. Much evidence will be provided by current and, hopefully, future research, but, without such evidence, change resulting from any current review of funding health care is likely to lead to moves from one unproven system to another.

CHAPTER 8

Countering Moral Hazard in the Hospital Sector

INTRODUCTION

Financial incentives operate on institutions as well as on individual actors within any health system. Therefore, it is important to review the effect of different methods of financing on hospital behaviour. This is not only because there is a large, though incomplete, volume of literature on the subject of hospital financing but also because hospitals are the single most identifiable group of users of health care resources in any economy. For instance, in 1982, the hospital sector accounted for approximately 42 per cent of health care expenditures in the USA and Australia, 41 per cent in Canada and 62 per cent in the UK (OECD, 1987). Obviously, then, the nature of reimbursement of the hospital sector will play an important role in determining not only the level and nature of hospital activity itself but also the extent of control over total health service costs.

Variations in methods of hospital funding exist both within and between public and private health care systems. During the 1980s, several countries introduced or proposed new methods of hospital reimbursement. Well-known innovations in the USA are the Medicare Prospective Payment System (PPS) based on diagnosis-related groups (DRGs), and the introduction of more competition in the health care market as reflected in the California selective contracting system and the growth of health maintenance organisations (HMOs). Both HMOs and DRG-type systems have recently been discussed in the context of the Australian health care system, although it is not clear if DRGs are ultimately intended for the purposes of strict reimbursement or for more general planning (such as the setting of budgets) (Commonwealth Department of Health, 1986; Australia, Budget Statements, 1989). Many European countries (for example, Denmark, Hungary and Norway) are experimenting, or considering experimenting, with DRGs, as are countries such as Brazil, in South America. In the UK and the Netherlands it is not yet clear what the exact nature of reimbursement of the hospital sectors will be under the recently proposed systems of 'competition', save for references in the UK to 'block funding' for a specified number of cases, with additional cases being funded on a 'cost per case basis' (presumably allowing the price of care for these additional cases to be determined by market forces) (Secretaries of State, 1989a and b). Canada has maintained a stable method of hospital reimbursement, global budgeting, throughout the 1980s (Evans *et al.*, 1989). It is important, therefore, to reflect on the evidence which now exists on the effects of different methods of payment on hospital efficiency and to highlight areas for further research. These are the aims of this chapter.

One problem in devising optimal financial incentive mechanisms for hospitals has been the lack of development of theoretical models of hospital behaviour. This problem is discussed in more detail in the following section. Thereafter, three main methods of hospital reimbursement are introduced and their possible effects on the price and quantity of hospital care are discussed. In section four, evidence of the effect of each payment system on hospital costs, throughput and patient outcome is summarised. The effects of hospital ownership on efficiency are briefly examined in a separate section, because it is often assumed that private ownership represents greater competition and is, therefore, positively associated with efficiency. This last issue is not strictly one of finance, but is related to financing and is of importance given the 'public versus private' debate which often takes place in political circles. Before concluding, we summarise the evidence to date and propose a possible solution to the problem of hospital funding.

THEORETICAL PERSPECTIVES

Problems of traditional economic models of hospital behaviour have been reviewed in Evans (1984), McGuire *et al.* (1988) and Donaldson and Gerard (1991). The lack of a satisfactory theory (economic or otherwise) of hospital behaviour makes it difficult to predict how hospitals are expected to react to different methods of hospital reimbursement and to determine performance criteria for assessing these reimbursement methods.

Regarding prediction, it is difficult to derive hypotheses from traditional competitive market models. In the classic model of economic behaviour, hospitals would act as profit-maximising 'firms', responding to the preferences of fully informed and knowledgeable consumers. In this model, each 'firm' is regarded as being so small, and one of so many, that it cannot exercise control over any aspect of market behaviour, except its own cost structure. Without the possibility for collusion, 'firms' are forced to compete on the basis of price, as fully knowledgeable consumers will seek out those 'firms' with the lowest prices. 'Firms' therefore have an incentive to operate at minimum cost in order to enable prices to be set low enough to attract as many consumers as possible. Those not operating at least cost would have this reflected in higher prices, to which consumers would respond by switching their consumption to other 'firms' within the health care industry or within other industries.

As described in Chapter 2, but concentrating more specifically on the hospital sector, consumers' preferences would play a crucial role in deciding on the amount of resources to be allocated to hospital care in general and, more specifically, to each type of hospital care. The result would be an efficient allocation of resources to hospital care (allocative efficiency). At the same time, hospitals, being profit maximisers, would seek to produce consumers' most highly valued types of hospital care at least cost, so acting in a technically efficient manner. This combination of allocative and technical efficiency ensures that consumers' utility is maximised at least cost to society.

However, because of market failure, described in Chapter 3, the hospital market does not operate like this. Consumers' preferences do not have much of a role in the allocation of resources to hospital care because of the existence of externalities and consumer ignorance in a market where the principal adviser on the consumer's behalf is also a supplier of care (Evans, 1984).

On the supply side, hospitals are not profit maximisers, simply responding to the well informed demands of consumers. Given their size, and lack of competition, hospitals will inevitably exert a degree of discretion over their activities, even if consumers were well-informed. In addition, ownership and management are separated in hospitals, as in many large companies. Management objectives are unlikely to be as profit-driven as those of owners, thus relaxing the incentive to produce the most highly valued care at least cost. Analyses of hospital behaviour are further complicated by yet another division of responsibilities: those of the doctor and the administrator. In many countries, doctors are not even employed by the hospitals in which they work: without responsibility to administrators, doctors make decisions regarding admission and, treatment of patients. Doctors, taking on a role of advocacy, and administrators, with more of a global view of hospital activity and costs, may even respond differently to the same method of hospital reimbursement. Such complicated structures make it difficult to determine exactly who, if anyone in particular, within the hospital reacts to the financial incentives associated with different reimbursement schemes.

All of these factors contribute to the difficulty of generalising about hospital conduct. Who reacts to incentives, how they react, and whether different people within the same hospital react independently or together, will depend on physical structures, power structures and relationships within the hospital and wider health care environment. Such factors are better analysed using sociological and behavioural techniques. Through the use of such techniques, it may be possible to build up a more general model of hospital behaviour at a later date. But until then, the role of more general predictive economic models of hospital behaviour will be severely limited.

This current lack of theory highlights the need to learn from experience with different reimbursement mechanisms. Despite this it is reasonable to conclude that hospitals will respond differently to different funding mechanisms. Some attempt at predicting such responses will be made in the next section, although the relationship of the predictions to some prior economic theory is not always entirely clear.

On performance criteria, the diminished role of the consumer leads to decisions affecting both allocative efficiency (i.e. what types of health care to provide) and technical efficiency (i.e. how best to provide each type of health care) resting largely with suppliers of care operating in a regulated system: policy decisions are made at various levels (national, regional and local) and tend to blur the notions of allocative and technical efficiency. In addition to the diminished role of the consumer, much health care remains unevaluated. This makes it difficult to determine what, and how much, health care should be provided by hospitals. Suppliers do not seem to be able to get this right, as witnessed by variations in surgical rates within countries and by evidence on inappropriateness of care (McPherson *et al.*, 1982; Vayda *et al.*, 1982; Morgan *et al.*, 1987; Lowry, 1987; Greenspan *et al.*, 1988; Winslow *et al.*, 1988a and b). Thus, the allocative question 'Should hospitals be doing what they are doing and to the extent that they are doing it?' remains, for the most part, largely unaddressed.

In the hospital sector it is easier to focus on technical efficiency in answering the question, 'How well are hospitals doing what they are doing?'. It is mainly the question of technical efficiency which is to be addressed in presenting evidence on different methods of hospital reimbursement (e.g. whether hospitals behave in a technically efficient manner), although questions relating to allocative efficiency will be raised. If, for example, hospitals cut costs at the expense of health outcomes, is this desirable? For the most part, alternative funding mechanisms will be compared in terms of cost per day, cost per case (mainly as reflected in length of stay) and effects on total hospital costs (mainly as reflected in hospital throughput), and less often (because of lack of data) in terms of effects on outcome, equity of outcome and equity of access. Once these later pieces of data are introduced, questions relating to allocative efficiency can be asked (but not necessarily answered).

METHODS OF REIMBURSING HOSPITALS: A CASE OF MINDING OUR P's AND Q's?

Hospitals supply care to patients and are reimbursed by the patients directly or, more likely, by a private insurance company or government agency. The total amount expended by these payers on any hospital during any time period is made up of the price of each medical/surgical treatment offered by the hospital multiplied by the number (or quantity) of times each treatment is carried out, summed over all treatments. More formally, for any hospital:

$$TE = \sum_{i=1}^{n} P_i Q_i, \tag{1}$$

where TE is total expenditure on hospital care, P_i is the price of treatment i and Q_i is the quantity of treatment i carried out by the hospital. The number of treatments available in the hospital is n. Therefore, in attempting to control total expenditure on hospital care, reimbursement schemes can act on the variable P_i, the variable Q_i or on a combination of the two $(P_i Q_i)$. This can be done at the level of different treatments (setting different fixed prices for different treatments, so constraining P_i; setting budgets at departmental levels, so constraining $P_i Q_i$) or at the level of the whole hospital (setting a global hospital budget without regard to individual departments, so constraining $\sum P_i Q_i$).

The amount of operating surplus (or profit) per unit of treatment offered by a hospital will depend on the cost of inputs to treatment relative to price, and total surplus for the period will further depend on the number of treatments carried out. Thus:

$$\Pi = \sum_{i=1}^{n} P_i Q_i - \sum_{i=1}^{n} C_i Q_i, \tag{2}$$

where C_i represents the cost of inputs to treatment i and Π represents operating surplus. The quality of care provided by any hospital will be reflected in C_i which can be varied up to, but not beyond, the level of P_i. According to this simple model, a hospital will break even where $\sum P_i = \sum C_i$.

A more generalised form of $\sum C_i Q_i$ is

$$TC = CQ, \tag{3}$$

where C is equal to the average cost per admission to a hospital, Q is the number of admissions and TC is the total cost of hospital care. It is necessary to specify this latter form of the total cost equation, because, although different reimbursement schemes focus on prices and quantities as expressed in equation (1), results of studies of their effects are often reported in the form of the variables in equation (3); reporting effects on average hospital costs per admission or discharge and numbers of cases admitted to or discharged from hospitals. For the remainder of this section, reimbursement schemes will be described in terms of equation (1), although many of the results reported in the following section are reported in the more general form of equation (3).

Given the inevitability of government intervention, there are three main methods by which hospitals may be reimbursed: retrospective reimbursement at full cost; prospective reimbursement per type of case or level of workload; and competition (regulating on the supply side to allow market mechanisms to decide on level of payment and amounts of care provided). Each method has important implications for hospital activity through the inherent incentives they offer to hospital budget holders and hospital doctors. How each of these systems impacts on P_i, Q_i and P_iQ_i is discussed in the remainder of this section.

Retrospective Reimbursement at Full Cost (Minding Neither P_i Nor Q_i)

Under a system of retrospective reimbursement at full cost, a hospital receives payment in full from financial intermediaries for all 'reasonable' expenditure incurred during the previous year. Such a system encourages hospital budget holders to maximise hospital income by encouraging either as much work as possible or long lengths of hospital stay, with patients being subjected to many (perhaps excessive) diagnostic tests and procedures as well as being provided with care of possibly unproven value. As well as a lack of incentive to control the quantity of care delivered, this system offers no obvious incentive to control the price of such care. Since retrospective reimbursement is usually linked with paying hospital doctors by fee-for-service (FFS), the two mutually reinforce one another. Such a payment system provides no incentive for hospital budget holders to be cost-conscious, indeed full-cost retrospective payment encourages the escalation of costs through its inherent inflationary bias.

Prospective Reimbursement (Minding P_i, P_iQ_i or $\sum P_iQ_i$)

Under a prospective reimbursement system, hospitals contract with financial intermediaries to work within a predefined budget. This may be very tight, on the basis of general population or utilisation criteria usually integrated into a system of hospitals and services, as in Canada, the UK, Denmark and the Australian public hospital sector, or much less tight but also direct in the linking of the hospital to the reimbursing agency, as in the USA and the Australian private hospital sector.

Under the former, hospital workload is usually estimated by funding agencies from historical hospital activity data. This estimated workload is then given a fixed price per type of case and combined with estimates of levels of workload to determine a hospital's budget for the forthcoming financial year. Budgets can be administered at the global level of the whole hospital or at a departmental level with teams of clinicians (sometimes known as clinical budgeting). Control is exercised over P_iQ_i or $\sum P_iQ_i$, which permits control over the cost and quantity of care as long as the department or hospital remains within the overall budget. Incentives can be offered whereby the hospital or department is permitted to retain at least part of budget surpluses on the condition that such surpluses are spent on patient care.

One prospective payment system (PPS) in the USA makes particular use of diagnosis-related group (DRG) information to categorise hospital inpatient activity and set prices per case. DRGs group inpatients according to diagnosis and resource use, and the reimbursement rate per case is set prospectively for each DRG category according to the average cost for that DRG. Thus price per case is constrained by the funding body, and the hospital is free to decide on quality and quantity, in terms of length of stay, procedures administered or number of cases admitted.

The introduction of a PPS based on DRGs in the USA Medicare programme was seen as a means of controlling hospital costs. A budget holder under this system is encouraged to minimise hospital costs per case in order to maximise hospital net income. It may be expected, therefore, that PPS encourages hospital efficiency by keeping costs as close as possible to, or below, average costs. In particular, costs per admission and per case may be expected to fall. Minimising costs could, however, be achieved through one of several routes: shorter hospital stays, substitution of less expensive inputs for costlier ones, reduction in the quality of hospital care or a combination of all three. It is important to know exactly what factors have contributed to reduced costs if claims that hospital efficiency improves with a PPS are to be substantiated. Indeed, efficiency may be sacrificed if cost savings are achieved at the expense of quality of care and hence the health status of patients. In developing a theory of doctor behaviour under prospective reimbursement, Ellis and McGuire (1986) predict this response if (as is likely) hospital doctors do not act as perfect agents when treating patients (Note 20). Moreover, the effect may be, through lowering inpatient stays, to lower costs per case while at the same time raising overall costs through a knock-on effect on throughput, similar to the effect of fee-for-service payment to doctors on supplier-induced demand as described in Chapters 3 and 7 (Note 21).

Further effects of a PPS of this nature are known as 'cost shifting', 'patient shifting' and 'DRG creep'. At present, the USA Medicare PPS applies only to Medicare inpatient services. Hospital costs can thus be reduced by shifting costs and/or patients into other sectors of the health care system not under the jurisdiction of PPS. Other patients may include private patients and other sectors may include outpatient departments, day hospitals, long-term care facilities or primary care. 'DRG creep' results from deliberate or inadvertent misclassification of cases into DRGs which make cases appear more complicated than they actually are, thereby attracting a higher prospective payment than if 'correctly' classified (Note 22).

As well as price per case, price per day could also be constrained. Under this mechanism of reimbursement, one would expect to observe much the same effects as under a price-per-case system, except – and it is an important exception – that there is no incentive to moderate length of stay.

Competition (Minding P_i, Q_i or P_i and Q_i Together)

Hospital care in the USA in the past has been dominated by large institutions, principally of three types: privately owned for-profit; voluntary not-for-profit; or publicly owned. More recently, however, competition in the USA health care market has grown rapidly with the introduction of HMOs. As outlined in Chapter 4, HMOs are competitive organisations that must attract customers who enrol each year for a fixed fee in return for a guaranteed health care package. The 'health care package' includes both primary and secondary care to be provided by the HMO or other suppliers who are paid by the HMO.

Advocates claim that HMOs are efficient organisations for two reasons. Firstly, they are paid a fixed capitation sum, and the doctors in them have their pay linked to the performance of the HMO in generating (net) income, so there is no incentive for HMOs to 'overtreat' patients. Secondly, HMOs must compete for their per-capita payments, no automatic residual component to income being received unless HMOs can attract custom; this leads to claims that quality is maintained at least cost. Thus, one can expect P_i or Q_i to be moderated under such competitive systems.

Owing to the absence of market mechanisms in health care systems which are provided and/or financed by government monopolies, such as the UK National Health Service (NHS), there exists no natural pricing mechanism through which the supply of health care resources can be efficiently matched to demands. In theory this must be overcome by introducing 'quasi-markets' or 'internal markets'. Such artificial markets may be created through rules and regulations. According to the nature of these rules and regulations, incentive structures may be set up to reward producers and/or consumers for efficient behaviour.

For example, the basic content of the reforms of the UK NHS were published in the White paper on 'working for patients' (Secretaries of State, 1989b). District Health Authorities (DHAs) remain responsible for purchasing comprehensive care on behalf of their catchment populations. However, it was proposed that major acute hospitals (i.e. those with more than 250 beds) could volunteer to become self-governing, offering services to DHAs in return for block funding for a specified number of cases (on a three-year rolling basis), with additional cases funded on a cost-per-case basis. The first wave of fifty-seven self-governing trusts came into being in April 1991. The board of directors of such hospitals are ultimately responsible to the Secretary of State and are free to acquire and dispose of assets, raise funds, retain operating surpluses and build up reserves, employ whatever staff they consider necessary and determine pay and conditions of staff. The trusts will compete with directly managed DHA units and the private sector for funding from DHAs.

In this way, responsibility for finance and provision of services is separated, a DHA being faced with its own hospitals, self-governing hospitals and the private sector competing for contracts and cases. The DHA, it is claimed, would choose between providers on the basis of cost, outcome, availability, convenience, etc. It is responsible for ensuring provision of core services (such as accident and emergency departments), which must be provided locally and for monitoring quality of services (e.g. through patient surveys). Funding for training, research and specialised services will be provided centrally for whatever hospitals happen to provide such services.

An additional proposal was that some general practices (those responsible for the care of more than 11 000 people – subsequently reduced to 9000 people), if they so wish, may be given more responsibility (through holding a budget) for the purchase of elective inpatient services, outpatient services and diagnostic tests on behalf of their patients, similar to HMO arrangements in the USA. The aim is that general practitioners too will choose care for patients on the basis of both cost and quality. Patients will remain free to change practice, budget allocations being suitably adjusted. DHAs containing general practices which opt for budgets will have their own budgets reduced by the amount allocated to these general practices for 'buying in' hospital services.

This represents only a brief description of the recent UK government reforms, but it is hoped that the general principles have been conveyed. The 'Dekker' reforms for the Dutch health care system also include proposals for an 'internal market' whereby insurers will purchase services from suppliers of health and social services on the bases of cost and quality (van de Ven, 1989). Internal markets of the sort canvassed by the UK government are largely a priori in nature and there is only limited evidence to date to report concerning their impact. Again, as is probably now clear, one would expect this impact to be on both P_i and Q_i.

One recently implemented system which has parallels to those in the UK and Netherlands governments' reforms is the selective contracting scheme in California. Introduced in July 1982, this scheme permits Medicaid and private insurers to contract selectively with hospitals and other providers of care, the aim being to stimulate price competition among these providers. Both Medicaid and private insurers can negotiate terms and conditions with each specific provider, whom they will reimburse for services to their subscribers. Previously, this could not be done because of the threat of antitrust prosecution of funders by providers. The California state Medicaid programme has used the system to negotiate discounts with hospitals, as have private payers (Melnick and Zwanziger, 1988). Likewise, the Leningrad experiment, mentioned earlier in Chapter 4, was a forerunner of the UK proposals. In this experiment, polyclinics, the main provider of primary care, have been given budgets to purchase hospital care for thirty seven conditions (Hakannson *et al.*, 1988).

EMPIRICAL EVIDENCE ON REIMBURSING HOSPITALS

The empirical evidence on reimbursing hospitals relates largely to comparisons between prospective and retrospective reimbursement systems in the USA. Limited evidence is available on clinical and global budgeting. Regarding competition, much recent evidence has emerged from the advent of HMOs, and this has already been reviewed in Chapters 6 and 7. Evidence from more publicly orientated systems, such as that of the UK NHS, is much more limited, while evidence is emerging on the Californian initiative on competition.

Retrospective Versus Prospective Reimbursement

The studies referred to in reviewing comparisons of retrospective and prospective payment systems in the USA are listed in Tables 8.1 and 8.2. These examine the effect of regulatory controls on the price (P_i) of care only, hospitals being free to decide on quality and quantity.

Studies of effects on length of stay and cost are listed in Table 8.1. First, Rosko and Broyles (1987) analysed the short-term effects of an early experiment with DRG prospective pricing mechanism on hospitals in New Jersey. Effects on cost per admission, cost per day, length of stay and cases treated were examined under two PPSs relative to a comparison group of hospitals in Eastern Pennsylvania where reimbursement took place under a cost-based retrospective method. The initial PPS was known as the SHARE (standard hospital accounting and rate evaluation) programme and replaced retrospective payment in the state of New Jersey in 1974. This programme used a formula to calculate a prospective patient *per-diem* payment for Blue Cross and Medicare patients. After 1978 the *per-diem* rate was replaced by charges based on DRG categories and the system extended to cover all patients. Both PPSs reduced costs per day and costs per admission relative to the comparison group. The SHARE programme reduced costs per day by 9.1 per cent and cost per admission by 9.6 per cent. The DRG programme reduced costs per day by 9.8 per cent and costs per admission by 14.1

Table 8.1   Retrospective versus prospective reimbursement: effects on length of stay and costs

Authors	Description of study	Results
Rosko and Broyles (1987)	84 hospitals in New Jersey subjected to PPS compared concurrently with 76 hospitals in another geographic area. Two PPSs, one operated on a per-day basis (SHARE system) and one using DRGs	Length of stay relative to retrospective reimbursement SHARE PPS – no change DRG PPS – 6.5% less Cost per admission relative to retrospective reimbursement: SHARE PPS – 9.6% less DRG PPS – 14.1% less Admissions relative to retrospective reimbursement: SHARE PPS – 8.8% more DRG PPS – 11.7% more
Guterman and Dobson (1986)	Before-and-after study of Medicare claims data including only hospitals subjected to Medicare PPS (which commenced in 1983)	Length of stay fell by 9% from 1981 to 1984
Sloan et al. (1988)	Before-and-after study of US national cohort of hospitals, using 34 hospitals in non-PPS states and non-Medicare patients as controls	Post PPS: Length of stay in ICUs constant. CAT scanning increased at slower rate. Use of non-surgical techniques declined. Use of routine tests declined.
Newhouse and Byrne (1988)	Before-and-after study of all Medicare patients including all hospitals so as to control for patient shifting	1981–4: Length of stay increased by 9% 1981–5: Length of stay fell slightly (by 3%)
Kahn et al. (1990a)	Uncontrolled before-and-after study comparing multiple time points pre-Medicare PPS (in 1981–2) in five US states. Various factors, such as hospital size and case-mix, were controlled for. Five conditions were examined (congestive heart failure, myocardial infarction, pneumonia, cerebrovascular accident and hip fracture)	Length of stay post-PPS declined by 24%

Table 8.2 Retrospective versus prospective reimbursement:
effects on outcome/quality of care

Authors	Description of study	Results
Fitzgerald *et al.* (1987)	Comparison of two cohorts of patients hospitalised with newly diagnosed hip fracture before-and-after the introduction of Medicare PPS. Controlled for age, sex, ethnic group, marital status and home support	Length of stay fell post-PPS (from 16.6 to 10.3 days) Number of physical therapy sessions fell post-PPS (from 9.7 to 4.9) Proportion of patients in nursing homes after discharge rose post-PPS (from 13% to 39%)
Weinberger *et al.* (1988)	Comparison of two cohorts of non-insulin diabetics admitted to hospital for glycaemic control before-and-after the introduction of Medicare PPS. Controlled for age, sex, ethnic group, staff availability, length of stay and admitting glucose levels	Less laboratory tests post-PPS (9 out of 16 tests showed statistically significant differences) Less education and consultation post-PPS (e.g. dietician seen by 96% of patients pre-PPS and 71% post-PPS) More general medical and clinic visits post-PPS Worse post-discharge glycaemic control post-PPS
Draper *et al.* (1990) Kahn *et al.* (1990a) Kahn *et al.* (1990b) Kosecoff *et al.* (1990) Rubenstein *et al.* (1990)	See Kahn *et al.* (1990a) in Table 8.1	Implicit review judged improvements in quality of care: reduction from 25% to 12% receiving 'very poor care'. But increase from 4% to 7% in patients discharged early and in unstable condition Measures of stability showed increase from 10% to 15% in patients discharged unstable Mortality: – in hospital fell 3.5% – 30-day mortality fell 1.1% – 180-day mortality unchanged

per cent. However, both programmes increased admissions, the SHARE programme by 8.8 per cent and the DRG programme by 11.7 per cent, thus supporting the hypothesis that these particular types of PPS encourage more episodes of care despite reducing the cost of each episode. Hospital average lengths of stay were shortened by 6.5 per cent under the DRG programme, but were unaffected by the SHARE programme.

The difference between the two systems, i.e. payment on the basis of case-mix treated versus a *per-diem* rate, seems to have led to a divergence in average lengths of stay – the DRG programme encouraged shorter stays. Neither payment system was monitored for the impact that shorter lengths of stay or lower costs per admission and per day had on the quality of care or health status of patients.

Further evidence on the effect of DRGs on hospital costs is conflicting. Guterman and Dobson (1986) presented results showing that length of stay had fallen by 9 per cent, which was more than in any previous year since Medicare's inception, but that admissions had also fallen by 3.5 per cent. The authors emphasised that this counter-intuitive result should be treated with caution, because other factors were not controlled for, the possibility being that hospitals could still react to the increase in empty beds by raising admission rates. Interestingly, total expenditure on inpatients still increased, owing partly to an ageing population and partly also to 'DRG creep'. Ginsburg and Carter (1986) found that the case-mix (an index reflecting the proportion of patients in high cost weighted DRGs relative to low cost weighted DRGs) was 9.2 per cent higher in 1984 than in 1981, mainly owing to changes in documentation and coding which were largely brought about by the Medicare PPS programme. Whether this 'DRG creep' is a once-and-for-all effect is not yet known.

In a controlled before-and-after study aimed at assessing the effect of Medicare prospective payment on the use of medical technologies in hospitals, Sloan *et al.* (1988) found that length of stay within intensive care units does not change as a result of introducing prospective payment, while the use of many non-surgical procedures either continued to increase at a slower rate (e.g. CAT scans) or actually decreased (e.g. occupational and physical therapy). Use of routine tests also declined. In this study, results for the non-Medicare control population mirrored those of the Medicare population, the most plausible explanation for this being that PPS influenced treatment patterns of the former group in addition to the latter, for which it was intended. Effects on use of outpatient services and patient outcome were not estimated.

Newhouse and Byrne (1988) suggest that a fall in length of stay as a result of the Medicare PPS is simply an artefact of limiting analysis to only hospitals included in the PPS. When looking at all Medicare patients in all hospitals in forty-six US states, Newhouse and Byrne found average length of stay rose slightly between 1981 and 1984 before falling, in 1985, to just below the 1981 average. One factor contributing to the doubt about PPS leading to reduced lengths of stay is reckoned to be patient shifting to modes of care not included in the PPS, a factor partly controlled for by analysing changes in length of stay in all hospitals.

More recently, the RAND study of the effects of the USA Medicare PPS (see below) demonstrated a 24-per-cent fall in length of stay for Medicare patients over the period 1981–2 to 1985–6 (Kahn *et al.*, 1990a). Despite its complexity, this study was uncontrolled and did not account for the criticisms of Newhouse and Byrne (1988).

Studies of the effect of such innovations on quality of care and outcome are limited. Only two had been published up to the end of 1989 (Fitzgerald *et al.*, 1987; Weinberger *et al.* 1988), and in 1990 the RAND Corporation published several papers from its nationally representative study in a single issue of the *Journal of the American Medical Association* (Draper *et al.*, 1990; Kahn *et al.*, 1990a, b; Kosecoff *et al.*, 1990; Rubenstein *et al.*, 1990).

These studies are listed in Table 8.2. The first of these was a before-and-after analysis of the effect of the Medicare PPS on patterns of hip fracture care (Fitzgerald *et al.*, 1987). Although mean length of hospitalisation fell (from 16.6 to 10.3 days) after the introduction of PPS, the number of physical therapy sessions received also decreased (from 9.7 to 4.9) and the proportion of patients discharged to nursing home care increased (from 21 per cent to 48 per cent). More revealing about effects on patient well-being is that, after six months, 39 per cent of patients remained in nursing homes under PPS as opposed to 13 per cent pre-PPS. According to the authors, these results suggest deteriorating care and an overall cost increase. The study by Weinberger *et al.* showed DRGs for non-insulin dependent diabetics hospitalised for glycaemic control resulted in the realisation of short-term goals (i.e. shorter hospital stays and fewer tests) but led to adverse long-term effects in terms of care (i.e. less patient education, more emergency room visits and more hospital admissions) and in terms of medical outcomes (i.e. worse glycaemic control). Although these studies were based on small samples, they do demonstrate that too much focus on cost reduction may have adverse effects on the health production function in which cooperation between doctors and patients may be very important, and that overall costs may in any case not be reduced.

Results from the RAND papers demonstrated reductions in inpatient and 30-day mortality over the study period, while 180-day mortality remained unchanged. Implicit review judged improvements in quality of care. However, there were substantial increases in the numbers of patients discharged in an unstable condition. The main problem with these results is that it is not totally clear what would have happened to such measures in the absence of the PPS over the same period of time.

Evidence on cost shifting from inpatients to outpatients is also contradictory (see Table 8.3). The national survey in the USA by Guterman and

Table 8.3   Effects of prospective payments on cost-shifting

Authors	Description of study	Results
Guterman and Dobson (1986)	Before-and-after study of Medicare claims data	Outpatient expenditures post-PPS increased but no more than past trends would imply
Fisher (1987)	Before-and-after study of distribution of allowed physician charges under Medicare, comparing pre-PPS (1982) with post-PPS (1985)	1982: 61% of charges for inpatient services 5% of charges related to outpatient services 30% of charges related to office visits 1985: 50% of charges related to inpatient services 12% of charges related to outpatient services 32% of charges related to office visits
Dranove (1988)	Changes in prices charged to private patients regressed with profits from government-funded (Medicaid) patients in 79 hospitals in Illinois while accounting for case mix and occupancy	Hospitals responded to reductions in Medicaid payments by increasing prices to private patients
Russell and Manning (1989)	Compared hospital and outpatient expenditure projections for Medicare beneficiaries made before Medicare PPS with those made after, adjusted for inflation and admission rates	Hospital expenditure in 1990 US$18 billion less (in 1990 dollars) than expected before PPS went into effect. Little effect on outpatient expenditure projections

Dobson (1986) found outpatient expenditure to be increasing, but no more than past trends would have suggested, while Russell and Manning (1989), after examining Medicare expenditure projections to 1990 as estimated in ten successive years, concluded that the PPS is having a major impact on Medicare's hospital expenses and that the savings are only partly offset by an increase in outpatient expenditures. Evidence on the changing distributions of doctor charges under Medicare found, on the other hand, large shifts from inpatients to outpatients (Fisher, 1987). Between 1982 and 1985 the proportion of doctor charges for inpatient activities fell from just over three-fifths to just under a half, mostly offset by increases in the share of services in outpatients. Clear evidence of shifting costs from patient groups subjected to prospective payment to groups not subjected to such payments (i.e. private paying patients) has also been demonstrated. This was achieved by regressing changes in prices charged to private patients against profits from government-funded patients in 79 hospitals in Illinois after attempting to control for case-mix and occupancy (Dranove, 1988).

Carroll and Erwin (1987) addressed the issue of patient shifting under competing reimbursement systems (see Table 8.4). This was a before-and-after study which investigated the impact of introducing prospective payments on the health state of inpatients upon discharge to long-term care facilities. On the belief that prospective payments would induce shorter hospital stays, a significant increase in the disabilities and health problems of patients admitted to long-term care facilities upon hospital discharge was predicted. The data for 353 patients admitted to ten long-term care facilities in Georgia were examined. The results showed significant statistical differences for three treatment and health status variables. Patients in the post-PPS group were more likely to be incontinent of bladder, to have nasogastric tubes and to be on dietary supplements, suggesting a shift of the more dependent patients into long-term care facilities. However, catheterisation and ambulatory status did not show any significant differences between the groups. It was concluded, therefore, that minimal patient-shifting from hospital to long-term care facilities took place. However, only Medicare beneficiaries were considered. No forms of shifting other than to long-term care facilities were considered. Moreover, the PPS occurred early in the transition period towards total implementation of the DRG system. As a result, only initial responses of hospitals and long-term care facilities to the PPS were measured. The study design thus had clear defects.

More recent (and more rigorous) studies, however, do support the hypothesis that prospective payment has led to increased transfers to sub-acute care. Morrisey *et al.* (1988) found that the introduction of the Medicare PPS increased the likelihood of early discharge from hospital to sub-acute care and reduced length of stay for five common DRGs. Sagar *et al.* (1989) examined changes in location of death of elderly people after the introduction of the Medicare PPS, the increase in nursing homes being greater than expected and accompanied by a decline in the percentage of deaths in hospitals. Resulting effects on quality of life for the clients concerned and, therefore, the efficiency of such transfers is not known.

As regards regulatory control over price times quantity, some quasi-experimental work has been carried out on clinical and global budgeting (see Table 8.5). In proposing to make clinicians budget holders, the UK experiment with clinical budgeting attempted to increase the awareness of, and provide incentives for, clinicians to be more efficient. The evidence on the effects of clinical budgeting on costs and outcomes has already been reviewed in Chapter 7. It is equivocal (Wickings *et al.*, 1985; Gibbens *et al.*, 1988).

Table 8.4   Effects of prospective payment on patient-shifting

Authors	Description of study	Results
Carroll and Erwin (1987)	Before-and-after study of impact of Medicare PPS on health state of patients on transfer to long-term care	Post-PPS, patients more likely to be incontinent of bladder, have naso-gastric tubes and be on dietary supplements. No more likely to be catheterised or less ambulant
Morrisey *et al.* (1988)	Before-and-after study of PPS on probability of transfer of Medicare beneficiaries from hospital to subacute care and on length of stay for five DRGs. Hospital and patient characteristics controlled for	Length of stay declined but not statistically significant at conventional levels Probability of transfer increased, in particular for stroke, pneumonia and major joint and hip procedures
Sagar *et al.* (1989)	Before-and-after study of Medicare PPS on location of elderly people at death using national mortality data specific for age and location of death. Controlled for overall mortality and changes in number of nursing home beds	1981–2 (pre-PPS): little change in proportion of deaths occurring in hospitals or nursing homes 1983–5 (post-PPS): progressive decline in proportion of deaths in hospital and increases in deaths in nursing homes

In the UK, it is now intended, through what is called 'resource management', to use information on costs from budgeting as part of an information package for clinicians which also includes information on effectiveness and standard of quality achieved (Department of Health and Social Security, 1986a; Bowden, 1987). With none of the previous financial incentives, the aim is simply to analyse the effects of providing the information. Also, as it has turned out, the resource management initiative has acted as a forerunner to the UK government's recent proposals for broader reform, providing useful information on costs of care for use in the 'internal market' mechanism.

A similar experiment with global prospective hospital budgeting in the USA resulted in appropriately reduced inpatient admissions for some conditions (e.g. less elective inpatient surgery for which more care was

Table 8.5   Effects of budgeting on costs and outcome

	Effects on cost	
Authors	*Description of study*	*Results*
Wickings *et al.* (1985)	Uncontrolled before-and-after study of effect of budgeting on change in five categories of expenditure—drugs, X-ray film, X-ray chemicals and equipment, equipment for medical and surgical purposes, and laboratory experiments	Little or no change in resource use
Gibbens *et al.* (1988)	Uncontrolled before-and-after study of effect of surveillance of prescribing in response to information produced by clinical budgeting. The before phase consisted of monthly assessments for three months and the after phase of monthly assessments for six months	Cost of drugs reduced by 34%
Mushlin *et al.* (1988)	Uncontrolled before-and-after study of effect of prospective payment at hospital level on quality of care, availability and outcomes	Less elective surgery More admissions for maternal problems associated with pregnancy and acute myocardial infarction
	Effects on outcome	
Authors	*Description of study*	*Results*
Gibbens *et al.* (1988)	As above	No effects on patients' physical and mental states
Mushlin *et al.* (1988)	As above	Rate of neonatal deaths declined

provided on an ambulatory basis) and stable community-wide outcomes, along with increased admissions for apparently more serious problems associated with the management of maternal illness and acute myocardial infarction. The authors concluded that such results demonstrate that community-wide prospective payment can be financially and clinically successful (Mushlin *et al.*, 1988)

It has also been claimed that annual global prospective hospital budgeting has resulted in a significantly less rapid rise in hospital expenditures in Canada than in the United States (Evans *et al.*, 1989). Despite this, the system of hospital financing is similar in Sweden, which has one of the highest-cost health services in the world. Therefore, it is not necessarily the ability to cap costs which counts, but actually exercising that ability.

Table 8.6 Effects of competition on costs

Authors	Description of study	Results
Manning *et al.* (1984)	Randomised controlled trial of prepaid group practice HMO versus fee-for-service care	Expenditure on HMO group 72% of that in fee-for-service group due to less hospital-intensive care
Zwanziger and Melnick (1988)	Controlled before-and-after study of effect of preferred provider organisations (PPOs) using econometric analysis to account for other factors affecting hospital costs	Differences in costs between hospitals subjected to high level of PPO competition and those subjected to low level reduced from 9% in 1982 to 2% in 1985
McLaughlin (1988)	Compared US metropolitan areas with and without prepaid group practices after controlling for non-random selection processes of PGPs into the areas in which they were located	No significant effects of PGPs on hospital expenses
Melnick and Zwanziger (1988)	Uncontrolled before-and-after study of selective contracting versus retrospective reimbursement in California. Other factors affecting hospital costs, such as case mix, the introduction of Medicare PPS and degree of competition in local markets were accounted for	In areas of 'high' relative to 'low' competition over the period 1983–5: – cost inflation per discharge reduced by 3.5% – total inpatient costs reduced by 4.72% – total inpatient discharges reduced by 1.62%
Robinson and Luft (1988)	Controlled before-and-after study of California's selective contracting experiment. Other factors, such as case-mix, mix of payers, teaching roles, ownership status and numbers of local physicians were controlled for. Controlled comparison was with 43 states in USA	1982–6: Cost inflation down 10.1% Effects concentrated in areas of high competition

Competition

Studies used to examine the effects of competition on costs and outcome are listed in Tables 8.6 and 8.7. In these tables, the results of the RAND HIE are cited, as they provide the most comprehensive evidence on the effects of HMOs relative to the traditional mode of financing (i.e. a fee-for-service insurance plan, with retrospective full cost reimbursement for hospitals). As reviewed in Chapters 6 and 7, HMOs led to reduced costs as a result of the practice of a less-hospital-intensive style of care (Manning *et al.*, 1984). Reduced lengths of stay appear to have arisen as a result of the Leningrad experiment in which polyclinics now pay for hospital care for some conditions (Hakannson *et al.*, 1991). The US evidence has been contested (McLaughlin, 1988), and there is some evidence that cost savings may be a result of risk selection or, if risk status does not differ between HMO and 'free' care groups, at the expense of patients' (or some patients') health outcomes.

Regarding internal competition, no evidence is yet available from the experiments in the Netherlands and the UK. Limited evidence on effects on price and quantity of care is available from the Californian selective-

Table 8.7   Effects of competition on outcome

Authors	Description of study	Results
Ware *et al.* (1986)	Randomised controlled trial of prepaid group practice HMO versus fee-for-service (FFS) care	On average: – no differences between HMO and FFS in terms of health habits, psychological health, risk of dying and general health Low income, initially sick: – more bed days and more serious symptoms in HMO than in 'free' FFS Low income, high risk: – greater risk of dying in HMO High income, initially sick: – general health rating better in HMO than 'free' FFS High income, high risk: – risk of dying less in HMO

contracting system. Melnick and Zwanziger (1988) carried out a before-and-after study of the effect of selective contracting on total hospital costs, cost per discharge, and the number of discharges. As can be seen from Table 8.6, selective contracting reduced all of these in areas of higher competition (Note 23). This evidence is supported by that of Robinson and Luft (1988), which demonstrated that the Californian strategy reduced hospital cost inflation by 10 per cent over the period 1982 to 1986 compared with forty three control states, but that the effects were almost entirely confined to areas of high competition. (Such areas were defined as those served by local markets with more than ten competitors. A local market was defined by the number of neighbouring non-federal, short-term general hospitals within a 24-kilometre radius of the hospital of interest.)

DOES OWNERSHIP MAKE A DIFFERENCE?

Given the extent of private ownership of hospitals in a number of countries, it is useful in this context to address the question of whether hospital ownership makes any difference to efficiency. This can be done by examining, for like groups of patients, whether one type of hospital care costs less than another with no detrimental effects on patient outcome, or, in studies where case mix is not controlled, whether there is evidence that the less costly type of care achieves this gain as a result of treating less complicated cases, or, more accurately, through avoiding treating more complicated cases (i.e. 'cream skimming'). Such comparisons are important, as it is often assumed implicitly that private ownership leads to greater efficiency.

If we turn to the experiences of for-profit and not-for-profit hospitals in the USA, evidence on the relative efficiency of for-profit, not-for-profit and public hospitals has been reviewed in some detail by Stoddart and Labelle (1985) and the Institute of Medicine (1986). Early studies by Clarkson (1972) and Rushing (1974) found that non-proprietary, not-for-profit hospitals employed more internal constraining rules for managers than for-profit hospitals, and, which is of less ambiguous significance for efficiency, that they also exhibited a greater variability in their ratios of inputs. However, case-mix and case complexity were not controlled for in these studies and the level of statistical significance was not high. Actual costs and actual outcomes (and their quality) were also not reported. These results have been supported by other work, but again without robust measures of costs and outcomes (Rushing, 1974).

More recent US studies, listed in Table 8.8, have compared investor-owned chain hospitals with not-for-profit community hospitals (Lewin *et al.*, 1982; Pattison and Katz, 1983; Sloan and Vraciu, 1983; Becker and Sloan, 1985; Watt *et al.*, 1986). The former generated greater net income (revenue minus operating costs) but also higher operating costs per admission and per day in four out of the five studies reviewed. Costs per admission ranged from being 4 per cent lower to 8 per cent higher in investor-owned hospitals. However, adjusting for occupancy still does not make up the cost difference (Institute of Medicine, 1986). The greater net income of the for-profit hospitals, despite their higher costs, was explained by their larger mark-up over costs and greater use of high-profit activities such as laboratory tests (Lewin *et al.*, 1981; Pattison and Katz, 1983; Watt *et al.*, 1986). It has been suggested that, unless it is assumed that for-profit hospitals treat patients in greater need, or produce a higher outcome, then the greater use of high-profit tests and other procedures indicates the discretionary use of these services – a species of supplier-induced demand

Table 8.8 Studies of effect of ownership on costs

Authors	Description of study	Results
Lewin *et al.* (1978)	Compared 53 matched pairs of for-profit chain and independent not-for-profit hospitals in California, Florida and Texas	Cost per inpatient-day: For-profit 8% higher Cost per admission: No difference
Sloan and Vraciu (1983)	Comparison of for-profit chain and not-for-profit hospitals under 400 beds in Florida	Cost per adjusted day: For-profit 3% lower Cost per adjusted admission: For-profit 4% lower
Pattison and Katz (1983)	Comparison of for-profit chain and not-for-profit private hospitals in California, excluding large teaching, Kaiser, rural, speciality and tertiary	Cost per patient-day: For-profit 6% higher Cost per admission: For-profit 2% higher
Becker and Sloan (1983)	Regression analysis of national sample of for-profit chain and not-for-profit hospitals, adjusting for case-mix, teaching status, size, and area characteristics	Cost per adjusted patient day: For-profit 10% higher Cost per adjusted admission For-profit 8% higher
Watt *et al.* (1986)	Comparison of national samples of 80 matched pairs of for-profit chain and not-for-profit hospitals adjusted for case-mix differences	Cost per adjusted admission and per adjusted day: For-profit higher but not significantly different

(Relman, 1983b). The only available data on outcome show no consistent pattern of mortality rates across types of hospital ownership for Medicare patients who had undergone elective surgery between 1974 and 1981 (Gaumer, 1986).

Stoddart and Labelle (1985) concluded that their review 'does not substantiate (indeed it refutes) claims that privately owned for-profit hospitals operate more efficiently (i.e. at lower costs of production) than do non-profit hospitals. In fact, the success of the investor–owners in generating above average sales and revenues appears to have relieved the need to minimise the production costs'.

The Institute of Medicine (1986) concluded that 'studies of hospital costs that control for size (and in some cases case mix and other factors) show for-profit hospitals to have slightly higher expenses than not-for-profit institutions – ranging from a statistically insignificant level to 8–10 per cent higher – when payment is based on costs incurred. Second, . . . for-profit institutions charge more per stay than not-for-profit institutions – ranging from 8 per cent for cost payers to 24 per cent for charge payers. . . . Third, . . . for-profit chains have achieved higher levels of profitability before and after taxes. . . . On most quality-related measures differences between investor-owned and not-for-profit institutions are small, and the direction of differences varies'.

Evidence has been found to support a 'cream-skimming' hypothesis. In a survey of forty one general non-teaching hospitals in California it was found that the for-profit hospitals specialised in the less complicated case mixes (Bays, 1977). In Australia, private hospitals took less severe cases than public hospitals and concentrated more on routine and non-urgent surgery, although two of the four private hospitals examined remained less costly than their public counterparts after controlling for case mix (Butler, 1984).

Finally on ownership, Richardson (1987) has said that at least 'private hospitals did achieve their main objective, namely an increase in profits. The hospitals responded to the incentives provided by the US health care market. It is not their concern that revenue to them is a cost to the remainder of society. It is possible that in another market with a different set of incentives a more favourable social result would be achieved'. Perhaps this is what the UK government is trying to achieve by incorporating private hospitals into an 'internal market' where finance and contractual arrangements remain publicly controlled (for the most part) and heavily regulated.

TOWARDS A SOLUTION: BACK TO BUDGETING?

The most depressing conclusion from this review is that despite much work, the relative efficiency of most reimbursement mechanisms has yet to be determined. This is mainly because of a dearth of data on patient outcomes. Competitive initiatives in the form of HMOs seem to achieve cost savings, mainly through reductions in the quantity (i.e. number of hospital admissions) rather than in the price of services used. However, such effects may be achieved through 'cream skimming', or at the possible expense of patient outcome. Internal markets seem to be able to reduce hospital cost inflation by affecting both price and quantity, but their effects on quality of care and patient outcome are unknown. What is more, the effects of internal markets in California were achieved only in local markets containing several competitors. There may be little potential for such competition in hospital markets in other countries, such as the UK, where the degree of competition in many geographical areas is likely to be low, and where general practitioners are likely to have established relationships with hospital doctors. In addition, given previous research demonstrating that US citizens are two to three times more likely to be admitted for common hospital procedures than their UK counterparts (McPherson *et al.*, 1982), the 40 per cent reductions in admissions achieved by the HMO in the RAND HIE would still leave US admission rates higher than in the UK. This suggests that the scope for such cost savings in health care systems like the UK NHS is much less than in the US and may be non-existent. This argument also highlights the danger of unthinkingly transferring results of valuable US studies of interesting US initiatives to non-US contexts.

Initiatives regulating solely on the price of hospital care have the fundamental weakness of a lack of control over quality and quantity of care provided. This has been demonstrated by the evidence highlighting the indeterminate effects of PPSs using DRGs. Indeed, the study by Newhouse and Byrne (1988) means that evidence on whether PPSs reduce the length of hospital inpatient stays at all, and hence reduce cost per case, must be treated as equivocal. As a means of controlling total expenditures PPS also remains vulnerable to any compensating increases in patient throughput. Although more research is necessary on this subject, there is limited evidence that achievement of short-term goals of shorter lengths of stay and fewer tests through the use of DRGs may have adverse long-term effects in terms of greater hospital admissions and worse medical outcomes. Current evidence is unclear about the extent of cost shifting and patient shifting under PPS. A safeguard in any one hospital is obviously for all beneficiaries to be contracted under the same payment system, but how this would affect other non-hospital sectors is not clear. It would prevent cost shifting but not patient shifting and would still leave the system vulnerable to knock-on effects on throughput. The question of whether patient shifting, and knock-on effects represent efficient practice would still need to be answered.

The usefulness of such results on PPSs for health care policy depends on the intended use of case-mix classification systems. Evidence points to the conclusion that DRGs are useful as a planning tool (e.g. to standardise care provided for particular conditions) within a system of global prospective budgeting rather than using DRGs themselves as the principal mechanism for financing care. However, even using DRGs as a standardisation tool can be called into question at this moment in time. The problem is that DRG standardisation cannot be useful as a planning tool until more is known about what represents efficient clinical practice. The current implication is that reducing variations around the prevailing average cost of treating people in any DRG will result in increased efficiency. However, small variation around the mean is not necessarily any better than large variation if we have no idea what efficient practice is. Instead, we need to focus on establishing efficient practice criteria before introducing the planning and incentive mechanisms to achieve it. In this process, DRGs should ideally be used as an end point and not a starting point.

The need to establish efficient practice criteria has been highlighted by the wealth of data on variations in health care. This literature, comprehensively reviewed in Andersen and Mooney (1990), has focused on both innappropriate use of procedures and variations in practice of procedures which are nevertheless still appropriate to carry out. International comparisons of surgical rates for common procedures have demonstrated that such rates tend to be higher in North America than in the UK (Vayda, 1973; McPherson *et al.*, 1981; Vayda *et al.*, 1982; McPherson *et al.*, 1982; Vayda *et al.*, 1984). Swedish rates have been shown to be as high as in the USA for some conditions, but lower than in the UK for others (Pearson *et al.*, 1968). Indications are that variations in such rates have little effect on patient outcome. The lack of a demonstrable effect on outcome may be simply because outcome was not measured, or the measures used were not sensitive enough.

Focusing on individual procedures, explicit and independent reviews of hospital records and claims data have demonstrated rates of inappropriate surgery ranging from 13 to 32 per cent for carotid endarterectomy (Merrick *et al.*, 1986; Chassin *et al.*, 1987; Winslow *et al.*, 1988b), 86 per cent for tonsillectomy (Roos *et al.*, 1977), 20 per cent for pacemaker implantation (Greenspan *et al.*, 1988) and 14 per cent for coronary artery bypass surgery (Winslow *et al.*, 1988a). Sui *et al.* (1986) found that 23 per cent of hospital admissions in the RAND HIE were inappropriate. Individual practice style has been found to be a determinant of caesarean section birth rates among obstetricians, with no obvious difference in neonatal outcomes associated with differences in the rate (Goyert *et al.*, 1989). The term 'inappropriate' in the above studies is usually taken to mean 'ineffective'. This is an extreme definition of inappropriate; much care may be slightly or moderately effective but still inappropriate. Therefore, for the most part, studies beg the question of what 'inappropriate' and 'appropriate' actually mean. This brings us back to the issue of what represents 'best medical practice' raised in Chapters 3 and 7 (Loft and Mooney, 1989; Andersen and Mooney, 1990).

Most of the evidence cited above comes from either the USA or Canada. In the UK, studies have shown variations in the use of acute hospital services to be partly due to practice style (Logan *et al.*, 1972), variations within regions in the treatment of childhood asthma by paediatricians (Lowry, 1987) and variations within regions in the use of hospital beds for common surgical procedures (Morgan *et al.*, 1987). Rates of admission to psychiatric institutions have been shown to vary substantially between Scandinavian countries (Hoyer, 1985). The rate of hysterectomy in a county in Denmark has been shown to be close to the national average, while market areas within that county showed variations by a factor of 5–6 (Andersen *et al.*, 1987). Obviously, such variations are of economic importance. For instance, in the treatment of asthma, some doctors use expensive drugs which others see as of little value (Lowry, 1987). Likewise, some doctors may be using unnecessary bed space which could be utilised by patients waiting for care. Obviously, in this last case, reductions in length of stay could be accompanied by more admissions, thus putting more demands on hospital resources. However, this should not prevent consideration of appropriate resource use relative to patient outcomes in trying to achieve an optimal use of such resources. In this respect, the limited evidence presented in this chapter is supportive of this approach. Control of total costs (i.e. price times quantity) through clinical and global budgeting has been seen to be effective in cost control without being harmful to patients.

Therefore, we propose that the starting point for hospital funding (which has already been reached in the UK) should involve clinicians being given budgets based on historical costs. In working with such budgets, it would be possible to examine current uses of factor inputs as well as outcomes achieved. Once current uses and outcomes are known, it should be possible to examine whether clinicians can achieve either the same levels of outcome at less cost or improved outcome for the same cost. Then funding (possibly DRGs) could be based on efficient health care practice, and standardisation would be according to efficiency rather than to current average cost.

Of course, this is why the results of the clinical budgeting and (more recently) resource management experiments in the UK are so important. However, to use such results to standardise payments for care on the basis of average cost would inhibit the ability of an internal market to price spare capacity at marginal cost (Note 24). This is why DRGs do not have to be the end point – nor even, necessarily, an intermediate point.

CONCLUSIONS

One of the most striking messages to emerge from this review has been the indeterminate effects of attempts to control hospital costs by regulating prices only: more specifically, the US Medicare PPS, using diagnosis-related groups, remains vulnerable to compensatory increases in patient through-put, despite cost per case and cost per admission being reduced. Cost shifting and patient shifting under any PPS are potential problems. HMOs have achieved cost savings which could be a result of selection or of reductions in quality of care. Other competitive innovations, such as those in selective contracting in California, reduce costs, but only in areas with high concentrations of hospitals and with unknown effects on patient outcome. Thus the 'transferability' of selective contracting to countries with less concentration in facilities will not be great. Private ownership does not necessarily result in less costly hospital care.

To date, many innovations in hospital funding have focused too narrowly on cost minimisation as an objective. What is important is the identification of cost reductions which can be achieved with little or no effect on patient outcome. In this respect, we propose that the most fruitful way forward in this area is to use clinical budgeting to monitor both costs and outcomes, thus establishing efficient modes of practice in hospitals. From the limited evidence on outcome to date, it is regulatory controls of total costs (or price times quantity), at global and clinical levels, which appear to offer the greatest potential for maintaining patient outcomes at lesser cost.

CHAPTER 9

Achieving Equity

INTRODUCTION

Chapters 6, 7 and 8 have all been concerned with reviewing empirical evidence about different financial arrangements for health care and their effects on efficient consumer and producer behaviour. But, as indicated in Chapter 5, a system's health care objectives are not exclusively concerned with efficiency. Equity, too, is an important objective. The desire to achieve a fair allocation of health care resources prevails within any given society, although its precise meaning and importance depends on cultural beliefs and social attitudes.

The overall aim of this chapter is to determine how successful different methods of financing health care are at achieving a fair allocation of health care resources. Sometimes international comparisons can be made, but more often success will be judged according to a country's own equity objectives. Thus, where appropriate the equity objectives selected in Chapter 5 (Table 5.2) will be scrutinised: namely financial contributions according to ability to pay; and equality of access. In Chapter 5 we outlined the problems of defining and measuring access. Therefore, it will be seen in this chapter that evidence on equality of access is often proxied by evidence on equality of expenditure and equality of utilisation.

In pursuing this aim a number of areas of enquiry are explored. Is there evidence to suggest that population coverage of and access to health care insurance are sizeable problems? If so, do they seem to be getting larger? What policy recommendations and actions might countries use to mitigate such adverse effects? Do substantially publicly financed health care systems do better as regards coverage and access to health care than more privately financed systems?

In the following section the possible forms of government intervention in health care financing are discussed. This is followed by a review of the evidence on vertical equity; by examining the relationship between income and health care contributions and by examining the evidence on effects of patient charges and community financing on equity. Finally, the evidence on equity as equality of access is reviewed. We do this by drawing some broad international comparisons and then by examining more detailed evidence from four countries: the USA, Canada, the UK and Finland.

THE ROLE OF GOVERNMENT IN HEALTH CARE FINANCING

One aspect of health care equity may be considered by looking at how comprehensively health care systems cover their respective populations. However, comprehensive coverage is not a sufficient condition to guarantee the provision of adequate insurance protection. Protection must cover the risk of financial hardship and provide sufficient access (however defined) to health services.

The failure of voluntary health care insurance markets to provide comprehensive insurance cover gives government intervention legitimacy. Such intervention may be by helping the market to work or by taking greater control. There are potentially four ways that government intervention can ensure comprehensive cover: making subsidised insurance compulsory; using tax revenue to finance care that is mostly free at the point of use; using subsidies to offset experience-rated premiums; and requiring community-rating for catastrophic insurance. These options therefore represent a continuum of levels of government intervention.

Making health care insurance compulsory controls all the effects of adverse selection. A publicly financed insurance system purchasing health insurance through an agency of the state can purchase or provide insurance cover for the whole community on a community-rated basis. A public intermediary can also embody redistributive policies into health care financing in a way which a private market cannot. The purchase of insurance for the whole population enables the financial intermediary to separate the value of insurance contributions from the expected risk levels of each individual (i.e. community rating). Alternatively, the government can provide the insurance and charge 'social insurance' premiums on a community basis. Compulsory participation may be by consumers, by employers or by both.

Providing free health care is similar in effect to compulsory public insurance, in that competition between financial intermediaries is removed. The extent of progressivity of the taxation system used to extract contributions may provide the opportunity for payment according to community rating or according to a more pro-poor and pro-ill formulation. It is prudent to recognise that unless community rated systems are subsidised, community rating itself may cause people to be uninsured, since it raises prices for low risks above their expected value. However, compared with full experience rating, community rating probably causes more poor people to become insured but more good risks to become uninsured. How large these empirical effects are is not known.

Both these means of countering selection bias in the insurance market have been widely implemented in various forms. The remaining two methods require minimalist government intervention, but, to date, there has been no experience of how either solution might work in practice.

It is believed that experience-rated premiums with subsidies could check adverse selection in the voluntary health insurance market by introducing subsidies to individuals at high risk of needing health services. This would ensure access to health care by making higher premiums affordable. Subsidies could take many forms, either cash or kind. One method could be to use health vouchers enabling individuals to purchase health insurance.

The final possibility would be selective community rating which would divide the means of purchasing health care into health risks that impose 'large' financial losses and those that impose 'small' financial losses. Thus the first part would have a special, regulated insurance market for catastrophic coverage and a second part for regular care. Alternatively, the second part could be out-of-pocket payments. In this form the worst effects of adverse selection would be controlled, namely the lack of cover for major health care expenses. It may still be necessary to provide subsidies for low-income groups for whom the regular premiums or out-of-pocket expenses would take up too large a proportion of their income. Some theoretical foundation for this solution is given by Pauly (1986). The main benefit from insurance comes from cover against large financial losses, as occurs in the event of a catastrophic illness.

EVIDENCE ON VERTICAL EQUITY

Are health care systems successful in achieving an equitable basis for the financing of health care? Do richer members of society finance a dispro-portionately greater share of health care expenditure than poorer members, and is there adequate protection from catastrophic expenditure? For many health care systems vertical equity in financing is an overt objective (e.g. the UK, Portugal, Canada). For many others it is implied (e.g. Denmark) and for yet others it is seen as desirable (e.g. most LDCs). For the few health care systems which rely predominantly on private sources of finance (such as in the USA or the Philippines) vertical equity is much harder to recognise as an objective.

Income and Health Care Contributions

A number of studies in recent years have addressed the question of vertical equity. In these studies it has been usual to examine the distributions of health care finance in relation to post-tax (disposable) income distributions for each country. Gottschalk *et al.* (1989) compared the financial arrange-ments of the USA, UK and Dutch health care systems. The results (reproduced in Table 9.1) show the UK having the most progressive method of paying for health care (e.g. the lowest income decile receives

2.7 per cent of society's disposable income and contributes 1.7 per cent of health service finance, while the highest decile receives 23.7 per cent of society's disposable income and contributes 25.6 per cent of health service finance). Not only are tax rates progressive but in the UK 90 per cent of health care finance comes from general taxation. The Netherlands health care finance arrangements are proportional. For 7 of the 10 income deciles the proportion of medical care bill paid is similar to the proportion of income received. The US sources of health care finance on balance are extremely inequitable. The highest income decile is the only group which contributes less to health care financing. All other income deciles receive smaller shares of post-tax income, but greater shares of health care payments are extracted from them. Furthermore, this situation is greàter the lower the income decile.

Table 9.1   Comparison of distribution of total health care expenditures: USA, UK and Netherlands, 1981

	Distribution of post-tax income			*Distribution of health care financing*		
Decile	*USA*	*UK*	*Netherlands*	*USA*	*UK*	*Netherlands*
1	1.4	2.7	0.4	3.9	1.7	1.9
2	2.9	4.0	5.2	4.9	2.5	4.3
3	4.4	5.3	6.6	5.5	4.0	6.1
4	5.7	6.8	7.9	7.0	6.2	8.3
5	7.1	8.2	8.9	8.6	7.9	9.8
6	8.5	9.6	10.1	9.7	9.8	11.5
7	10.1	11.1	11.5	10.9	11.5	12.3
8	11.9	13.0	13.1	12.8	13.5	13.9
9	14.9	15.6	15.5	15.0	17.1	15.4
10	33.1	23.7	20.8	21.8	25.6	16.7

Source: Gottschalk *et al.* (1989).

A similar type of study conducted by Hurst (1985) showed both the UK and Canadian health care systems to be progressive and the US system to be regressive. Using the same methods as Gottschalk *et al.*, Wolfe and Gottschalk (1987) investigated the pattern of financial contribution among elderly people in the USA. They found an even starker regressivity than for the population taken as a whole. While elderly people in the lowest income decile contribute negligibly to health care financing through taxes, they contributed a total of 64.7 per cent of their pre-tax income to medical care expenses through direct payments and insurance premiums.

These studies are limited because the nature of the analyses is such that they compare distributions of disposable income with distributions of health care contributions. This means that while it is possible to determine whether or not each system is progressive, the relativities between health care systems cannot be examined, i.e. how much more progressive or regressive one health care system is compared with another. To do this a single measure of progressivity is required for each system. This question is currently being addressed by a European group of researchers (the COMAC project on Equity in the Finance and Delivery of Health Care) and their results will be published soon. Until then, comparable data exist only for the countries studied by Gottschalk *et al.* Wagstaff *et al.* (1989) have calculated progressivity indices using the Kalwani Index (KI; Note 25), which confirm the descriptive results reported above for the USA (KI = −0.15) and the UK (KI = 0.03); see Table 9.2. However, reanalysis of more recent data for the Netherlands showed a mildly regressive system (KI = −0.06) and, interestingly, when broken down by source, insurance premiums were found to be regressive (KI = −0.10) and direct payments progressive (KI = 0.12).

Table 9.2 Progressivity of health care finance in the USA, the UK (1981) and the Netherlands (1984) using the Kakwani index

Country	Total payments	Direct payment	Taxation	Insurance
USA	−0.15	−0.39	Income tax 0.15 Payroll tax −0.04	Private −0.19
UK	0.03	n.a.	General tax 0.02	Social 0.03
Netherlands	−0.06	0.12	n.a.	AWBZ 0.00 Private + sickness funds −0.10

Source: Wagstaff *et al.* (1989).

Examining the issue of access and financial hardship would seem to indicate more problems for the US system. Poor individuals are more exposed to the risk of financial hardship than are richer individuals and there are a significant number of hospitals and physicians threatened with bad debt because individuals do not have adequate protection. Farley (1985) estimated that 8 per cent of the privately insured population incurred out-of-pocket expenses for bills amounting to at least some 10 per cent of their family's income.

As there is no explicit definition of catastrophic medical expenditure, Wyszewianski (1986) defined three threshold levels of his own. Above these thresholds medical expenditure would be considered catastrophic. These were out-of-pocket medical expenditure accounting for 5, 10 and 20 per cent of family income. At most, 20 per cent of families bore the burden of total catastrophic expenditure. However, this expenditure accounted for a disproportionately large share of total health expenditure of all families. For example, 9.6 per cent of families had out-of-pocket expenditures exceeding 10 per cent of income, but this was 25.3 per cent of total health expenditures for all families. The most likely characteristics of these families included low income (below the poverty line), unemployment and being headed by someone 65 years or older. The conclusion reached was that although stop-loss coverage policies are generally needed and desirable (covering catastrophic expenditure that exceeds insurance coverage limits), these particular families need basic protection from high out-of-pocket expenditure in relation to income not covered by third parties.

The 1986 US Access to Health Care Survey reported that the poor were 5.2 times more likely to experience major financial problems because of chronic or major medical illness (Hayward *et al.*, 1988).

Evidence about financial equity from other countries is less explicit, if available at all. It seems reasonable to suggest that in those few LDCs where private finance is predominant (e.g. Burkino Faso, Haiti, Mali and The Philippines; see de Ferranti, 1985) financing will be inequitable.

Charges and Community Financing in LDCs

The importance of direct payments in LDCs varies. For example, it is 74 per cent of health spending in Mali, compared with some 50 per cent in the USA (Creese, 1990). An increasingly important component of these direct payments is user charges. In some LDCs, the public sector has opted to levy charges as a means of cost recovery (in Ghana 15 per cent of recurrent expenditure has been recouped in this way) and in others community financing has been tested (in Indonesia 22 per cent of finance for a large capital project was financed this way). Both mechanisms have been proposed for financing primary health care developments arising from WHO's health-for-all goals. The thinking behind public-sector charges is to improve access for the poor by driving richer individuals into the private sector. The poorest individuals and those of high risk remain exempt from the public-sector charges. The policy is targeted at the middle-income groups. Usually there is a marked difference in quality of service between the private and public sectors, the private sector providing the higher quality. With the introduction of charges into the public sector those middle-income groups previously opting out of the paying private sector can expect to increase their demand as it now looks more attractive. The empirical evidence cited below suggests a mixed reaction to this hypothesis.

A case study by Stanton and Clemens (1989) examined the likely impact of charges on public health services in Bangladesh. They found, first and foremost, that there was minimal ability to pay for health care. In 50 per cent of households surveyed, food expenditure accounted for 72 per cent of income and 53 per cent of families spent less than 1 per cent of their income on health expenditure. Secondly, there were two especially vulnerable groups, women and the poor, who would be most affected if user fees were introduced into the public sector. Examination of utilisation data for government hospitals showed that while under-utilised overall, they provided substantial health care to these vulnerable groups. So the conclusion reached was that raising additional finance from user charges in Bangladesh's public sector would be judged inequitable.

A similar kind of question was addressed in Kenya by Mwabu and Mwangi (1986). Can user charges imposed in the large government health care sector be used to raise finance to expand or improve health services in an equitable way? Mwabu and Mwangi simulated the effect using probabilistic demand schedules. These were estimated according to two scenarios: (1) the fee was a pure tax; (2) the fee was reinvested to improve the quality of (and thereby access to) government clinics. Improved quality meant better supply of drugs at the clinics and improved working conditions of health care workers. The results of the exercise indicated that under certain conditions user charges may improve equity. These conditions were that (a) fees were reinvested in government clinics and (b) fees were levied only on government clinic facilities and not across the board of public health services. Equity could improve because fees used to improve quality of care in government clinics would obviate the need to incur additional transportation expenses to seek quality treatment in the private sector. Overall, demand for government clinic services was forecast to increase. However, the richer individuals were more responsive to fee rises on this service because they curtailed demand by a greater amount as fees rose, preferring instead to seek their treatment privately. Thus, overall, poor and sick individuals could become better off under the imposition of selective user charges. To enhance equity further, the authors suggested that a selective charging policy across health areas could be introduced, depending on some index of a community's health status in different areas. This simulation exercise therefore pointed out how equity may be enhanced if user charges were selectively used in the public sector, and estimated that the amount of additional finance raised would be significant.

Although no evidence exists to support the hypothesis, it is thought that community financing will be inequitable (Abel-Smith and Dua, 1988; Carrin and Vereecke, 1992). This is because it relies on contributions (cash, kind or labour) from individuals, families or community groups to support some of the cost of health services, many of whom are poor or sick themselves.

Evidence from other countries about financial equity is hard to come by, although Abel-Smith (1986) suggests 'health insurance contributions levied as a proportion of earnings are much fairer than many other taxes imposed on developing countries'.

EVIDENCE ON EQUITY AS ACCESS

Comprehensive coverage, either by public programmes or by a mix of private and public finance, does not guarantee appropriate access to services. The extent of health care benefits provided by OECD countries has been summarised as follows:

> 'Hospital inpatient services, inpatient physician services, and outpatient physician and diagnostic services are covered under virtually all programmes. For drugs, eye glasses, hearing aids, nursing homes, home health, and health-related social services there is far more diversity. . . . there are numerous differences across countries in the conditions under which certain services are covered. . . . virtually all countries impose cost sharing on pharmaceuticals. . . . virtually all countries waive cost sharing for the poor.' OECD (1987)

Although this summary appears an encouraging one, it masks the details of how well health care systems perform according to specific operational definitions of equity in the delivery of health care. For example, there is a wide variation in the services offered under the US Medicaid programme across different states (Thorpe *et al.*, 1989).

How successful, therefore, are health care systems at meeting their horizontal equity objectives? The scope of such a question is very broad, because each health care system may have a number of equity objectives. In Chapter 5 we tried to document some of them. The evidence presented in this section cannot be comprehensive, because that would require a book in itself. What follows is a selection of some important empirical findings, using the interpretations of performance set out in Table 5.2.

First, we present evidence from several countries on access in the pursuit of equity. There are few systems for which comprehensive data on equity exist. We have identified four (the USA, Canada, the UK and Finland), and therefore feel a case study of each is important before going on to draw some conclusions.

Some Brief International Comparisons

As regards OECD countries, only the USA stands apart from the rest as having a problem of comprehensively covering its population for the risk of ill-health which requires health care. The most recent figures, shown in Table 9.3, reveal the extent of public coverage of health care in 1987. The percentage of population in each country with public health insurance cover for hospital care, ambulatory care and medical goods was in most cases close to a hundred per cent. Public coverage of medical goods in Canada, of medical goods and ambulatory care in Ireland and the Netherlands and of all forms of coverage in the USA fell substantially short of a hundred per cent. However, copayments are commonly used to contribute payment for ambulatory care and medical goods, which explains most of the lower rates of public coverage in these two areas of health care. Australia, Switzerland and the Netherlands along with the USA have a significant amount of private health care insurance, but unlike the USA achieve high rates of public coverage through universal public programmes. The USA, on the

Table 9.3   Public coverage of health care: percentage of total population in OECD countries, 1987

Country	Inpatient care costs	Ambulatory care costs	Medical goods
Australia	100.0	100.0	100.0
Austria	99.0	99.0	99.0
Belgium	98.0	93.0	93.0
Canada	100.0	100.0	34.0
Denmark	100.0	100.0	100.0
Finland	100.0	100.0	99.0
France	99.0	98.0	98.0
Germany	92.2	92.2	92.2
Greece	100.0	100.0	100.0
Iceland	100.0	100.0	100.0
Ireland	100.0	37.0	40.0
Italy	100.0	100.0	100.0
Japan	100.0	100.0	100.0
Luxemburg	100.0	100.0	100.0
Netherlands	73.0	67.0	61.0
New Zealand	100.0	100.0	100.0
Norway	100.0	100.0	100.0
Portugal	100.0	100.0	100.0
Spain	97.1	97.1	97.1
Sweden	100.0	100.0	100.0
Switzerland	98.7	98.7	98.7
Turkey	–	–	–
UK	100.0	100.0	100.0
USA	43.0	43.0	10.0

Source: Tables 15, 16 and 17 in Health Care Financing Administration (1989), Annual Supplement.

other hand, only achieved 40 per cent population coverage for hospital care and 25 per cent for ambulatory care under Medicare and Medicaid. This means that the extent of cover by the private sector (which includes the employer-sponsored, tax-subsidised health care insurance plans) is a crucial determinant of the system's universality. In the case of the USA, this issue is covered in more detail below.

The evidence from Australia, during periods in the 1970s and 1980s when no compulsory public insurance scheme was in place, provides further evidence of the shortcomings of predominantly privately financed health care. During these periods it was estimated that 15 per cent of the Australian population (usually Southern European migrants and those in low-income groups) had no insurance cover (Deeble, 1982; Palmer and Short, 1989).

Roemer (1987) considered the extent of population coverage of statutory health insurance schemes in LDCs:

'Except for Latin America, where eight countries have come to exceed 25% in population coverage . . . (Bolivia [26%], Venezuela [30%], Uruguay [50%], Panama [47%], Mexico [56%], Argentina [80%], Brazil [80%] and Chile [100%]) . . . the proportions of national population covered are small. The programme in India, while covering about 28 million people, reaches about 4% of the country's huge population. Coverage data are difficult to find for developing countries, but a fair estimate for the statutory health insurance systems as a whole outside Latin America would be well under 10% of the population.'

Slightly higher rates have been reported for China, at 30 per cent (Prescott and Jamison, 1984) and for Ethiopia, at 43 per cent (Ministry of Health, Ethiopia, 1984).

Although there is inadequate data from LDCs most have substantial problems of ensuring universal and adequate health care insurance. A large part of the explanation is because of high population growth and increasingly severe stringency placed on health care finance.

The performance of largely publicly financed systems in Eastern and Western Europe is also open to improvement. Borgenhammer (1987) suggests that important aspects of geographical equity are violated in Sweden's public health care system, e.g. the geographical distribution of medically trained personnel. Giraldes (1990) points to inequalities in Portugal between the rural North and the industrialised areas around Lisbon. Minev *et al.* (1990) suggests that in Bulgaria during the 1970s and 1980s access of health care to rural communities:

'continued to be more difficult . . . the structure and scale of the health system in the villages do not correspond well to the needs of the population.'

The WHO Regional Director for Europe, commenting on the proceedings of a 1987 WHO meeting held on Inequalities in Health states:

'In our continuous monitoring of . . . Health for All . . . it is revealed, rather worryingly, that progress is slow if there is any at all, in reducing prevailing inequalities in health. . . . Data . . . show considerable inequalities within (European) countries, regarding . . . health service provision or health man-power, uptake of perinatal care and provision of general practitioners in urban areas.' (Asvall, 1990)

In other regions of the world too there are equity problems. The longstanding Chinese health policy of strengthening primary health care (viz. barefoot doctors, prevention and mobilising community resources) has failed to achieve geographical equity. There remains unequal distributions of physical and financial resources both across provinces and within urban and rural areas of any given province (Prescott and Jamison, 1985).

Musgrove (1986) examined Peruvian data for 1984 and showed the inequality of medical attention: expensive resources, especially doctors, were heavily concentrated in the capital city, Lima.

In the remainder of the chapter we examine the evidence on horizontal equity in the USA, Canada, the UK and Finland. In doing so we also offer our own judgement of performance.

USA: No Explicit Equity Objective

What of horizontal equity within the USA health care system? The USA health care insurance market is extremely diversified. There are over 1500 private insurers offering fee-for-service plans, preferred provider plans, health maintainence plans and more besides (Himmelstein *et al.*, 1989). Collection and compilation of information about population coverage and adequacy of plans is thus messy and difficult. It is as difficult to determine the explicit definition of an equity objective in the USA as it is clear that consumer choice (and its consequent market base) is regarded as an important objective which may conflict with any equity goal. However, equal access for equal need may be a goal as attempts by government-sponsored programmes to help make the market work 'better' bear testimony. Not only are Medicare and Medicaid publicly financed pro-grammes, but the large, employer-sponsored insurance programmes are financed in part by payroll taxes.

The issue of access can be looked at in terms of several aspects: the extent of insurance coverage; its effect on access to services for those in equal need; geographical equity; and the effect of competitive innovations (like HMOs) on access.

Estimates of the numbers of Americans with no health insurance cover-age have been reported as significant by a number of researchers. Walden *et al.* (1985) estimated 9 per cent of those under 65 years in 1977, Davis (1989) estimated 15 per cent (or 37 million people) having no cover, many of these lacking any cover at all. More recently Frank *et al.* (1990) suggested 13.9 per cent in 1980, rising to 17.1 per cent in 1984 of non-elderly people. Trevino *et al.* (1991) found that over a third of Mexican Americans, a fifth of Puerto Ricans and a quarter of Cuban Americans did not have health insurance. Large proportions of these groups are employed, but live below the poverty line. These rates were anything up to three times higher than the white non-Hispanic population. The black non-Hispanic population had a non-coverage rate similar to Cuban Americans. Studies by Quam (1989) and Newacheck (1988) have also demonstrated how needed medical care for the uninsured is not received to the same extent as it is by those who have cover.

The performance of Medicaid in providing health care insurance for the indigent comes under serious attack in a number of studies. According to the analysis by Trevino *et al.* (1991) the extent of Medicaid coverage is not adequate for eligible ethnic Americans. The Hispanic Health and Nutrition Examination Survey examined the characteristics of the uninsured. Despite a half of Mexican Americans, two-thirds of Cuban Americans and just under a half of Puerto Ricans being employed, large proportions (50 per cent or more) of these populations lived below the poverty line. Newacheck (1988) found that the Medicaid programme covered less than half of the eligible US citizens (i.e. those on incomes below the official poverty level). This is supported by Thorpe *et al.* (1989), who estimate that, overall, 10.9 million of the 37 million uninsured are poor. However, performance varies across states, the eligible proportion covered ranging from 17 per cent to 83 per cent, and the range of benefits offered above the basic minimum is also variable.

From the provider perspective the problem of inadequate insurance protection may lead to unpaid medical bills and accumulated bad debts. This has in fact been happening generally throughout the USA (Sloan *et al.*, 1986). A multi-hospital study of patients' socioeconomic status and use of hospital resources has demonstrated higher costs of treatment for poor people. They have 3 to 30 per cent longer hospital stays and hospital charges are 1 to 18 per cent higher (Epstein *et al.*, 1990). These higher costs should be backed up with supplementary payments to counter claims of inadequate access to services by the poor.

Frank *et al.* (1990) examined the National Hospital Discharge Survey data to determine accessibility of hospital stays for patients without insurance cover. This was the first national analysis to have been completed, and showed a selection bias in the share of the burden of uncompensated hospital care by hospital ownership. Public hospitals bore the greatest share, church and non-profit hospitals treated more than for-profit hospitals. Controlling for case mix, the uninsured admitted to for-profit hospitals were discharged more quickly and were transferred (usually to nursing homes) at a higher rate than insured patients. This burden placed on public hospitals is of concern, given the continued shrinkage of the public hospital system. A similar burden was also found by Lewin *et al.* (1988) using regional data, but regional analyses by Herzlinger and Krasker (1987) and Pattison and Katz (1983) found no deficiency in the contribution made by investor-owned hospitals to uncompensated care.

Health care in the rural USA is subsidised for the poor to ensure some geographical equity. The performance of this policy has been monitored by Patrick *et al.* (1988) and is, on the whole, encouraging. They analysed the use of services by the poor and non-poor in rural areas and found availability of medical providers to be similar across these groups. The poor were more likely to be older, female, black and without insurance and to have poorer health. The poor reported more visits to providers and those of poorer health reported more visits except for the uninsured. The level of poverty was not a significant predictor of physician visits when need was controlled for. Persons at or below 150 per cent of the poverty level had a higher number of ambulatory visits.

However, access to health care across racial groups is variable, favouring young, white males. The Council on Ethical and Judicial Affairs (1990) have recently reviewed the evidence. The inequalities are stark. For instance, given the same severity of illness, black men are half as likely to undergo angiography and a third as likely to undergo bypass surgery; the likelihood of haemodialysis and transplant surgery for kidney disease is 5–15 per cent greater for white men aged 25–44; and the intensity of care for treating pneumonia after controlling for clinical characteristics and income is also greater. The situation is similar for other ethnic American groups (Hayward *et al.*, 1988).

The variety of health insurance plans that exist in the US system, with differing incentive structures for consumers and providers, allows tremendous scope for diverse health care access. Because it is not possible here to review these plans comprehensively, we choose to concentrate on the most important growth area, namely the impact of competition, through health maintenance organisations (HMOs), on access for disadvantaged groups.

Health maintenance organisations are a form of managed care. They offer comprehensive coverage for a predetermined premium. However, beyond that they take a variety of forms (e.g. prepaid group practices, independent practice associations, staff models or networks), depending on the contractual arrangements between the HMO and doctor(s). They have been more effective in controlling health care cost escalation and excessive utilisation than have traditional fee-for-service insurance plans (see Chapters 6 and 7). Why? Is this control due to more cost effective provision or to the squeezing out of high health risk individuals? If it is the latter then cost control will flounder in the long term. Given the increasing popularity of HMOs (21 million people were enrolled in HMOs in 1987), they need to be scrutinised for their effect on patient selection and access to health services.

It might be expected a priori that compared with regular FFS insurance plans, HMOs would be selected by individuals who perceive their health risks as high and who expect to make relatively high use of services, because this makes sense from the consumer's point of view. Furthermore, since HMO plans cover dependents and encourage preventive practices, such HMOs might expect to attract young, expanding families.

However, HMO providers may wish to behave in a way which is not in line with these expectations. Providers may attempt to select low-health-risk individuals with low expected use of health services into HMO plans. In this way, providers are acting in a way which is consistent with profit-maximising behaviour under competitive pressure, even if the members are committed to community rating. Thus, it is not clear, a priori, what, if any, contribution HMO care makes to the problem of adverse selection. Furthermore, as HMOs have been evolved from within a system of FFS insurance plans there is likely to be some consumer loyalty towards FFS plans regardless of health risk.

If HMOs do skim off the best risks then one would expect to see better health risks enrolled in HMO plans compared with FFS plans. Hellinger (1987) examined the current evidence and found that, overall, favourable selection (i.e. healthier enrollees) occurred in prepaid group practice HMOs for both non-elderly and elderly enrollees. It seems that prior use of services is a good indicator of selection to HMOs. A low previous use correlates strongly with HMO enrolment. There was less evidence to support favourable selection occurring in independent practice associations. Hellinger expressed concern about the potential impact of selection bias in Medicare risk-based HMOs, but his sample size was too small for any stronger inference.

Early studies and reviews were mixed in their conclusions. Berki and Ashcraft (1980) were sceptical about the charge of skimming under HMO care. Blumberg (1980) rejected it. Eggers's (1980) conclusions supported favourable selection in a study of Medicare beneficiaries, as did studies reported more recently by Buchanan and Cretin (1986), by Moser (1987) for non-elderly enrollees and by Porell and Turner (1990) for Medicare beneficiaries.

The Medicare Competition Demonstration Projects were set up to provide information on risk contracting with HMOs on behalf of Medicare beneficiaries. The results cannot be generalised, but include favourable selection during the evaluation period (Langwell and Hadley, 1989). The difference in use of health care was statistically highly significant when comparing Medicare beneficiaries selecting an HMO with those holding plans with local Medicare supplemental insurers. HMO enrollees used less in the two years prior to joining and were less likely to die during the two years following enrolment.

Judgement

The evidence presented suggests that in the USA there exist substantial obstacles to ensuring universal and adequate health care insurance. This is a growing problem, particularly for poor ethnic Americans. It leads to great difficulties in achieving equal access for equal need, and competitive reforms, such as HMOs, have done nothing to ameliorate this situation.

Canada: Objective – Equality of Utilisation

Data from the Canadian Health Survey have been used by Broyles *et al.* (1983) to examine the extent to which the use of physicians by beneficiaries insured under the Canadian Medicare programmes was determined by medical needs rather than by non-medical factors such as patients' financial status. Did comprehensive insurance coverage necessarily achieve access to physician care on the basis of medical need? They showed that medical needs, as measured by medical conditions, number of accidents, disability days and the use of prescription drugs, were the dominant determinants of both the decision to seek treatment and the volume of services consumed. An individual's ability to pay (as defined by economic status and occupational status) did not contribute to an explanation of this pattern of use.

A more recent study by Manga *et al.* (1987) confirmed the above finding, using a similar, but refined measure of need. Income failed to contribute significantly to the determination of the pattern of utilisation, after standardising for health needs.

Waiting for care in the Canadian system is an important indicator of equality. Morris *et al.* (1990) report the success of cardiovascular services in Manitoba in giving the highest priority to cases with greatest urgency. The study compared patient characteristics and indications for cardiac catheterisation as between the elective care list on the one hand and the immediate care list on the other. It was found that immediate care patients were sicker than those put on the elective list according to various indicators. They were also more likely to enter hospital via the emergency room (25.5 per cent of immediate care and 2.2 per cent of elective care were admitted for cardiac catheterisation, while 55.4 per cent and 96.4 per cent respectively had normal admissions). Elective patients stayed in hospital for shorter periods (e.g. 80.7 per cent of elective cases stayed 1 to 3 days compared with 75.2 per cent of immediate cases, who stayed 8 days or longer).

However, mortality among the two groups was similar: 92 per cent of immediate cases survived at least one year following admission compared with 94 per cent of elective cases who waited. The study concluded that those patients needing immediate care and those who could wait with a low probability of a poor outcome were being successfully identified in Manitoba.

Judgement

Equal utilisation for equal need is supported by the evidence. However, it should be noted that equality of utilisation is not as sound an equity objective as equality of access. Thus the evidence can be interpreted only as a tentative measure of equity.

UK: Objective – Equal Access for Equal Need

The UK equity objective can be looked at in terms of both social class and geographical equity.

Despite the absence of major financial barriers in the UK NHS there has been much evidence reported of unequal access and receipt of care (e.g. Cooper and Culyer, 1971; Maynard and Tingle, 1975; Le Grand, 1978; Black Report, 1980; Blaxter, 1984; Whitehead, 1987; Townsend *et al.*, 1987; Carstairs and Morris, 1989; Waller *et al.*, 1990; Davey Smith *et al.*, 1990). Moreover, much of this exhibits a social class gradient, with those in the lowest and poorest social groups experiencing at once both the worst health status and a lower than predicted rate of utilisation of care.

Contrary UK evidence has, however, been reported by Collins and Klein (1980), and more recently by O'Donnell and Propper (1991). Both studies used the General Household Survey data for information on self-reported morbidity ('not sick', 'acutely sick', 'chronic sick without restrictions' and 'chronic sick with restrictions') and use of health care services. Collins and Klein concentrated on primary health care use and found no consistent bias supporting the hypothesis that lower socioeconomic groups (SEGs) make lower use of services when standardised for self-reported morbidity. In fact, for two morbidity groups they found the reverse. For example, for men reporting acutely sick the utilisation rate for SEG 1 (professional class) was 40.9 per cent compared to 71.0 per cent for SEG 6 (unskilled, manual class). The remaining morbidity groups showed no class gradients.

The authors concluded that the NHS does better than its equity principle of equal access for equal need because, if anything, there is a slight pro-poor distribution. However, this conclusion is potentially misleading because utilisation, not access, has been measured.

The authors also commented on why other work found pro-rich distributions of health care. The confounding factor in these other pieces of work was the inclusion of 'not sick' people who use health care. They obviously use GP services for other purposes (e.g. health prevention and promotion) and as they constitute a large proportion of the primary care user group (39 per cent 'not sick' people used primary care services) this group can mask the effects of utilisation on other morbidity groups. Indeed, in Collins and Klein's analysis the 'not sick' group exhibited a slightly pro-rich distribution, as might be expected given that higher SEGs tend to be more highly motivated to use preventive and health promotion services.

O'Donnell and Propper extended Collins and Klein's analysis to cover all NHS services and also report a pro-poor distribution of utilisation within morbidity groups during 1985. They suggest that this distribution is consistent with (rather than better than) equal access for equal need, because supplementary data indicate that, as health status in poorer income groups is, on average, lower, so need will be greater. Yet again their measures were of utilisation rather than of access, making their conclusion, once more, potentially tentative.

Waiting for health services is another important indicator of access in the UK health care system. Equal access for equal need in this context means appropriate use of waiting times as a filter in the passage of a patient from family practitioner to hospital outpatient clinic and subsequently to inpatient admission. According to Bloom and Fendrick (1987), waiting time in the UK NHS does not appear to affect those most in need particularly unfavourably. They examined waiting times for people needing non-emergency care using Hospital Inpatient Enquiry data for England and Wales in 1984. The median wait for all inpatients was 14 weeks. Broken down by specialty, this wait varied by a factor of 7. Outpatient waiting times varied from a low of 2 weeks for internal medicine to a high of 12 weeks for neurosurgery and orthopaedic surgery. Intra-regional variations (i.e. variations within each of the 15 regions) were greater than inter-regional variations.

By examining who waits, it was found that those assigned relatively low 'medical priority' waited. Only one in four admissions had been placed on a waiting list prior to admission; the others were 'booked' admissions (i.e. dates were offered to patients 2–3 weeks prior to admission). The case mix of waiting lists consisted overwhelmingly of low-risk and low-complexity medical problems, for example, chronic diseases of tonsils and adenoids and chronic pharyngitis.

There is, however, no evidence about the social class effects, if any, of the use of waiting lists. Moreover, the criteria by which 'need' was assessed in this study were limited to medical factors.

Potter and Porter (1989) used Bloom and Fendrick's data, in combination with data from the RAND Corporation and the University of Minnesota Centre for Health Services Research, to demonstrate that mean waiting times for general practitioner care in the UK and the USA were one day and three days respectively. Outpatient waiting times were about equal, while access to specialists in the USA was, in general, greater, although those requiring urgent care in the UK received such care.

Of the recent reforms to the UK NHS (Secretaries of State, 1989a and b), the opportunity for certain general practitioners to become budget holders is of interest here because it may have a detrimental effect on waiting times for hospital appointments and admissions. It is too soon to evaluate these reforms, but speculation raises concern about the development of a two-tier waiting system (*The Guardian*, 17 April 1991). The concern is that it will be in the interest of GP budget holders to search for hospitals which give their own patients the shortest waiting times. Hospitals, anxious to attract contracts, may encourage queue jumping for these patients in preference to patients in equal or greater need whose GPs are not budget holders. If this scenario is borne out, it would clearly destroy the equity principle of equal access for equal need for non-emergency hospital care. Likewise, hospitals in the UK seem to have greater freedom to accept privately-funded patients, which also threatens the principle of equal access for equal need.

The UK NHS is also concerned with equality of geographical access. Le Grand (1982) explains that supply factors such as the distribution of medical facilities and staff are crucial access determinants.

The work of the Resource Allocation Working Party (RAWP) has been based on this concern for geographical access. The RAWP terms of reference were to secure 'a pattern of distribution [of NHS resources except GP services] responsive objectively, equitably and efficiently to relative need' (DHSS, 1976). The RAWP budgetary formula for regional health authorities (RHA) was derived from regional populations weighted to reflect the need for services (there were seven categories of service, excluding GP services) and adjustments made for cross-boundary flows. Need was measured using age, sex and standardised mortality ratios (SMRs). The policy was implemented within the constraints of zero resource growth. This meant that, as a typical RHA budget was of the order of £1 billion, a 0.1 per cent shift in resources (about £1 million) would be a significant gain to one region and a significant loss to another. Since the inception of the policy, resources have been redistributed mainly from the South of England (particularly the London regions) to the North. Table 9.4 shows the extent of redistribution of revenue that has been achieved during the ten years from 1977–78 to 1986–87. The data show that North-western and Northern regions gained the most, while North-west Thames, North-east Thames and South-east Thames lost the most as the revenue of regions with similar needs became more equal.

Important criticisms of the RAWP formula called for a review in 1985 (DHSS, 1986b), and in the NHS reforms (Secretaries of State, 1989a and b) the intention to abandon it altogether was announced, because 11 of the 14 regions are within 3 per cent of their target. Although there seems to be

Table 9.4 Distance from the target revenue expressed as a percentage of each health region's RAWP allocation in England during the financial years 1977–8 and 1988–9

Region	Distance from target, 1977–8	Distance from target, 1977–8
East Anglia	−6	−4.0
West Midlands	−6	−1.3
Trent	−10	−2.7
South-west	−5	−1.4
Yorkshire	−4	−1.4
Northern	−10	−1.6
North-west	−11	−1.4
Wessex	−6	−1.8
Mersey	−4	1.5
Oxford	7	−2.6
South-west Thames	6	1.0
South-east Thames	12	1.7
North-west Thames	14	7.3
North-east Thames	15	4.5

Source: OHE (1989).

some confusion over the replacement formula it is to be based on capitation adjusted for age and some measure of health other than SMRs (Secretaries of State, 1989a and b). The choice of this other health measure will be crucial in determining resource allocations to different districts and general practices (see Carr-Hill *et al.*, 1990).

Judgement

More recent and methodologically sophisticated evidence supports equal social class utilisation for equal need, although the measurements of morbidity and social class remain problematic. The evidence does not relate to the objective of equal social class access for equal need. The NHS's performance on equal geographical access for equal need has improved over time, although the evolution of the recent NHS reforms will determine whether this success continues.

Finland: Objective – Equality of Geographical Utilisation

The Finnish health care system is decentralised. The communes (or local authorities) are financially autonomous. However, to ensure a fair distribution of resources across such a large a country as Finland, with its marked differences in population density, income level and occupational structure, central government pays subsidies to communes according to their income (in 1982 this varied from 35 per cent to 70 per cent). This policy, part of the Primary Health Care Act 1972, seeks to promote geographical equity in provision and utilisation of health care services (Purola *et al.*, 1974). Haro's (1987) assessment of this policy is to recognise some improvement in equity in provision because the less-prosperous Northern and Eastern Central Hospital Regions received higher per-capita government subsidies to compensate for their higher than average per-capita health care expenditure.

The policy also marked the beginning of a major reallocation of resources from specialised care to primary health care. Over the period 1963–71 the annual average growth of real expenditure on specialised care was 8.5 per cent compared with 3.7 per cent on primary health care. By the period of 1978–83 this situation had more than reversed, with figures of 1.0 and 8.1 per cent, respectively (Pekkurinen *et al.*, 1987). Kalimo *et al.* (1982) support these findings and conclusions. However, Salmela (1988) is less impressed by these achievements. During the period 1973–84 the 'great differences between municipalities in the supply and use of health services decreased very slowly'. Salmela's analysis also reported inconsistencies in the resources allocated for inpatient services when controlling for age and sex. Vohlonen and Pekkurinen (1990) support Salmela, reporting the need to make uneven regional allocations of new resources to compensate for the inequity arising over the period 1973 to 1982.

Judgement

More recent analysis is less enthusiastic than older studies about attempts to promote equality of expenditure across geographical areas and between specialised and primary care, although there is agreement that some inequality has been removed.

CONCLUSIONS

In this chapter selected evidence has been presented to demonstrate the performance of various health care systems' in relation to equity criteria. Unfortunately, it has not been possible to compare different health care delivery systems directly one with another because there is no universal and absolute measure of equity in health care delivery. It is possible to derive international comparisons for equity in health care finance. However, results from the seminal work in this area are yet to be published at the time of writing. Some important findings can be inferred from the evidence produced so far on equity in finance and delivery.

Regarding the fairness with which health care systems are financed, largely publicly financed systems in developed countries, especially those predominantly tax-financed, are the most successful at meeting equity objectives. However, this does not mean that, political and public opinion willing, further improvements cannot be made. In the UK and Canada health care payments are extracted primarily on the basis of ability to pay (although a case could be made for making them still more progressive), while such progressivity is not present in US health care. Instead, we find US health care extremely inequitable, with only the highest income decile contributing a smaller proportion to health care monies than is their proportionate share of income. Dutch health care contributions are paid at a rate more reflective of proportional income distribution.

Although US society at large, and health professionals in particular, are concerned about the equity consequences of their health care system, it seems they are not prepared to pay for equity improvements by financing a change to some form of social insurance system. It has been tentatively argued that the recent growth in social-insurance-financed health care systems in LDCs is the fairest way of financing these countries' health care costs.

Coverage of health care insurance (or access to health services in the case of publicly financed systems) is not at issue in developed countries, except in the USA where the problem is significant. LDCs are also likely to face problems with insurance coverage. The US health care system clearly discriminates against ethnic minorities and the poor. Frequently they have no cover, or they remain inadequately protected, particularly against the expense of catastrophic illness. These problems seem to be growing rather than contracting in the wake of numerous financial developments and reforms, especially HMO arrangements and prospective payment systems.

Three of the four countries (Canada, the UK and Finland) selected for in-depth analysis of horizontal equity achievements have, in our judgement, been cautiously encouraging. They all have largely publicly financed systems. The Canadian equity objective of equality of utilisation for equal need has been a success. There are national data to confirm the hypothesis that financial status does not adversely affect health outcome. However, we argue that the equity objective itself is somewhat misleading; it should be equality of access for equal need that is sought. At the same time, however, we recognise the inherent difficulties of measuring access compared with the relative ease with which utilisation may be assessed.

The recent reforms of the UK NHS may threaten to undermine the concept of equality of access, but this can only be judged on the basis of evidence in the longer run. Currently, the most recent and methodologically sound evidence claims outstanding success with equality of access. However, careful scrutiny shows that the measures used are in fact, once again, measures of utilisation. Thus we feel that the claims made by both Collins and Klein and also by O'Donnell and Propper need to be re-evaluated in terms of access.

Finland, yet again, represents a cautionary tale, but agreement exists between studies that some geographical inequity has been removed over time, particularly since the introduction of the Primary Health Care Act 1972.

Other examples have been cited in this chapter of largely publicly financed systems that have not been very successful at combating horizontal inequities. This evidence goes to prove that simply having a publicly financed health care system will not guarantee equity. However, compared with the US, these equity failings, particularly in developed countries, are less severe, as basic levels of provision (e.g. emergency care and primary care) are usually available to everyone.

For the US system, some encouragement may be taken from the knowledge that geographical equity is achieved through a federally subsidised rural health care programme. On the other hand, we find that the most rapidly growing sector of the health care sector, HMOs, is clearly selective in the type of individuals enrolled (i.e. low health-risks). This does not bode well for equity in the long term let alone in the short term where, already, an estimated 15 to 17 per cent of the non-elderly population have inadequate health insurance, and some 9 per cent have none.

Of the four possible solutions that can simultaneously counter the effects of adverse selection and support caring externalities, only two (providing free health care and making health care insurance compulsory) have been tested to date. It could, perhaps, be worth experimenting with the other two solutions (experience-rated premiums with subsidies and selective community rating) in appropriate settings to see if greater equity can be achieved. For example, experience-rated premiums with subsidies could be tried in the US setting, while selective community rating could be tried in a system that favours a substantial private insurance market (e.g. the Netherlands).

The main lessons from this chapter are that, first, predominantly private health care systems appear less equitable. Secondly, predominantly publicly financed systems do better. While public finance cannot ensure equity in principle and private finance does not preclude it, in the real world it is clear that publicly financed systems are likely to do better in the pursuit of equity. This may well be in large part because the reason why many systems are public is precisely because of the importance placed on equity objectives.

PART 4
Future Challenges

CHAPTER 10

Future Considerations: Setting the Health Care Budget

INTRODUCTION

So far we have considered how best to finance health care at the level of individual actors (such as consumers and doctors) and corporate actors (such as hospitals) within the health care sector. This leaves two questions unanswered: Ideally, how should the health care budget be set? and: What should the budget actually be? Despite the difficulties involved in answering these questions, it is our contention that in future the best evidence relating to them will come from the application of economics to health care and other health-producing activities.

In an unregulated competitive health care market, it would be simple to answer the question of what the level of the health care budget should be: 'Leave it to the market.' There would never be any reason even to address the question explicitly, as the 'appropriate' level of spending would be determined by the 'invisible hand' guiding transactions between fully informed patients and doctors.

As we have seen, however, most health care markets are (justifiably) heavily regulated. In such systems, there is no automatic mechanism, like the market, to guide the system to the appropriate level of spending. The aims of this chapter are twofold: first, to demonstrate that there are techniques of economic analysis which can contribute significantly to setting the budget for health care; and, second, to show that there is no one 'correct level of spending' in this regard, despite the fact that much analysis assumes that there is.

The techniques can be used to address two of the main issues in connection with total spending on health care either as a percentage of gross domestic product (GDP) (sometimes gross national product, GNP) or per head of population. They are:

(1) What are the determinants of total health care spending?
(2) Is such spending too large or too small?

167

It is important to examine the first of these because it may be that the variables affecting the total spend are those about which little can be done directly. For instance, if GDP is *the* important determinant, little can be done by way of direct health care policy in setting the budget; governments should aim to increase GDP if they want to enhance the budget for health care. Cultural factors may also be difficult to manipulate in policy terms. Also, attempting to answer question (1) involves looking at health care spending and its determinants across countries at a very broad level, which is problematical (see below).

Question (2) is more realistic; it is basically asking 'Where do we go from here?' In answering this, it is necessary to consider the benefits (i.e. enhanced well-being) which health services contribute to the community relative to the resources spent. It may be that more should be spent on health care but only if the benefits outweigh the costs. Likewise, it may be that less should be spent, but only if there are some treatments whose costs outweigh their benefits. In the latter case, more well-being would be produced by diverting the health care resources to some other beneficial non-health-care activity.

Answering the second question involves looking not only at the size of the health care budget, but also at what we get for the resources spent. Again, some studies attempt to do this using naive and problematical international comparisons of spending on health care and its broad outputs; our views on this approach are more fully outlined below. Accepting that different countries have different starting points in terms of the size of the health care budget, there are still two techniques, currently much underused in health care policy analysis, which can take us a long way in helping to set the right level of health care budget within a country. These are economic evaluation and the analysis of the determinants of health.

WHAT ARE THE DETERMINANTS OF TOTAL HEALTH CARE SPENDING?

Apart from natural curiosity, the main reason for being interested in this question is because it is thought that an understanding of the determinants of spending might yield insights into whether and how expenditure can be controlled, particularly in those countries where spending is high (and rising fast) in relation to others.

There is enormous international variation in the size of health care expenditures per head, even when one has attempted to make the comparisons as consistent as possible and has used purchasing power parities to convert national currencies into dollars of (roughly) equal purchasing power. Table 10.1 shows the results for OECD countries.

Table 10.1   Per-capita health expenditures, 1980

Country	Exchange rates		Basis GDP PPPs		Health PPPs	
	$	Rank	$	Rank	$	Rank
USA	1087	1	1087	1	809	8
Germany	1065	2	818	4	825	7
France	1036	3	837	3	941	2 ·
Netherlands	983	4	773	5	865	3
Norway	963	5	772	6	1071	1
Denmark	879	6	667	8	665	11
Luxemburg	845	7	714	7	806	9
Canada	787	8	853	2	663	12
Belgium	747	9	596	10	675	10
Austria	718	10	603	9	828	6
Finland	677	11	559	11	853	4
Japan	569	12	537	13	832	5
UK	530	13	468	15	653	13
Ireland	480	14	510	14	509	15
Italy	479	15	541	12	636	14
Spain	334	16	376	16	405	16
Greece	175	17	211	18	289	18
Portugal	151	18	238	17	379	17
Mean	695		620		706	

Source: OECD (1987).

Perhaps the most consistent finding in this literature has been that the main determinant of the amount a country spends per head or as a share of GDP is income. It is what may be termed the 'luxury good' view of health care; luxury goods are those for which a percentage increase in income (in this case, national income) leads to a greater percentage increase in the amount of the good consumed (in this case, health care). The result that health care is a luxury good was originally found by Kleiman (1974) in an international cross-section study, but was most prominently researched by Newhouse (1975, 1977). There is a remarkable consistency between the studies which find that, of every £1 increase in GDP per head, health spending will rise by about 8 pence per head; this is a greater proportionate change for health care than for GDP. There is broad agreement that the income elasticity (percentage rise in spending divided by percentage rise in income) lies between +1.18 and +1.36. Results from the studies by Newhouse (1977), Parkin *et al.* (1987) and Culyer (1988) are displayed in Table 10.2. Only the results of Parkin *et al.* (1987) cast some doubt on the general finding, so that a 10 per cent increase in GDP can be expected on average to lead to a roughly 25 per cent increase in health care spending.

Table 10.2 Studies of the association between national income and health care spending

Author	Method	Income elasticities
Newhouse (1977)	Single-variable regression analysis of per capita GDP on per capita medical care expenditure from 13 developed countries. Expenditure measured in US dollars at annual average echange rates.	+1.35
Parkin *et al.* (1987)	As above, but from 23 countries.	+1.18
Culyer (1988)	As above, but from 20 countries.	+1.35
Parkin *et al.* (1987)	As above, but from 18 countries and using purchasing power parities, instead of exchange rates.*	+0.90
Culyer (1989)	As above, but from 20 countries and using purchasing power parities instead of exchange rates.	+1.35

* Purchasing power parities provide a measure of the command of one dollar over resources which is more consistent across countries than simple exchange rates.

Table 10.3 Expenditure in health in low-, middle- and high-income economies

Country	% of Central Government expenditure spent on health (1983)
Low-income economies	
1. Nepal	4.5
2. India	2.4
3. Sri Lanka	5.1
4. Pakistan	1.0
Middle-income economies	
5. Indonesia	2.2
6. Philippines	6.8
7. Papua New Guinea	9.3
8. Thailand	5.1
9. South Korea	1.6
10. Singapore	6.4
Industrial economies	
11. Germany, Federal Republic	18.6
12. Australia	7.1
13. Canada	6.3
14. USA	10.7

Source: Asian Development Bank *et al.* (1988), pp. 39–40.

More impressionistic evidence from Table 10.3 also supports the basic finding that the level of health spending is largely determined by national income. In this table, poorer countries tend to spend smaller proportions of government expenditure on health care: the percentage of public expenditure on health care ranges from 1 to 5.1 per cent in low-income countries, from 1.6 to 9.3 per cent in middle-income countries and from 6.3 to 18.6 per cent in high-income countries (Note 26).

The finding of an elasticity between $+1.18$ and $+1.36$ is surprising for many reasons. One is that it is counter-intuitive to be told that health care is a luxury rather than a necessity ('luxury' also having the connotation of 'indulgence'). A second is that it is rather surprising that so much of the international variation in spending per head (more than 90 per cent in Newhouse's work) is explained by income alone. It also seems to imply that to get increased proportionate resourcing for health care a country should aim to get rich. Nothing is said about the effectiveness of health care systems in improving or maintaining the health of the community. Precious little is left over to be explained by cultural factors, disease prevalence, age of population, degree of socialisation of medical care, method of paying doctors, and the other factors that are commonly offered as likely determinants (Maxwell, 1981).

Many authors claim (but mostly on non-quantitative grounds) that financing, in particular, must play some role. Thus Feldstein (1977) argued that the uncontrolled nature of hospital reimbursement by insurance companies in the USA both stimulated technical progress towards more costly provision and weakened incentives for cost control. The introduction of Medicare and Medicaid in the USA led – at least initially – to cost inflation (Davis, 1973; Feldstein, 1977; Zweifel, 1984). It has also been widely felt that, in the UK, stringent public expenditure controls have held costs down. The divergence in trends in health care costs in Canada and the USA since the completion of the introduction of compulsory public insurance in the Canadian system of health care financing around 1971 demonstrates the importance of the method of overall financing of the health system. The impact on health care spending of the introduction of compulsory public insurance in Canada is demonstrated in Figure 10.1 by comparison with spending in the USA and the UK. Contrary to this, Sweden is often cited as a high-spending but publicly financed health care system. What this illustrates is that a highly regulated system *can* choose to spend more or not. Less regulation may give less freedom to make such a choice.

How such choices are articulated from consumer to provider is difficult to characterise. In Sweden, this is done through the localised democratic system; a local community can decide to spend more on health care and raise the money through increased taxation. Such 'choices' will reflect cultural expectations. Aaron and Schwartz (1984) have argued that, to

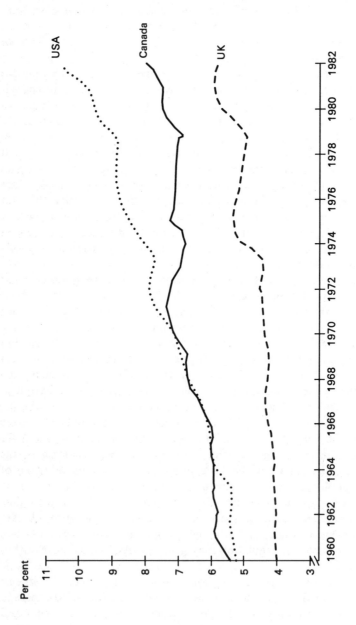

Figure 10.1 Health care expenditure as a percentage of GDP: USA, Canada and UK, 1960–82. *Source:* Culyer (1988).

some extent, Americans collectively 'choose' to spend more than Britons on certain treatments which are still beneficial to patients (e.g. coronary artery bypass grafts), while British planners and doctors 'choose' not to provide as much of other treatments whose benefits they see as not worth the costs incurred (e.g. intensive care).

It is likely that small sample sizes, inadequate data on certain variables and different definitions of variables across countries contribute to supporting the 'luxury good' view, which denies any role at all to determinants other than GDP. Parkin *et al.* (1987) point to problems of use of highly aggregated data which do not account for differing patterns across countries in terms of spending on institutional/non-institutional care or the mix of personnel. Leu (1986) tentatively concluded that the higher the public/private ratio in total funding, the higher the total spend; while the more centralised the health budgeting system, the lower the spend. This seems to be confirmed by Culyer's detailed study of Canada (Culyer, 1988) and by the work of Evans (1982, 1984 and 1987). Public finance enables the consumption of care that would not otherwise be taken up; centralisation enables the squeezing of fee schedules and tighter control on budgets. Moreover, none of the above studies of determinants of spending explicitly combines resource use (or cost) with enhanced or maintained well-being; they give no indication of the 'right' level of spending. It is necessary to know the relationship between input and outputs before an optimal budget can be set. It is this issue to which we now turn.

WHAT IS THE APPROPRIATE LEVEL OF SPENDING?

There is much controversy in deciding where societies are on an input–output curve like that in Figure 10.2. Are they at point (a) – as many doctors urge – where the pay-off to increased spending is high? Or are they at (b) – the point Enthoven (1980) has called 'flat-of-the-curve' medicine, where the pay-off to higher spending is zero? Or are they at (c) – as Illich (1976) has argued – where the pay-off is negative and health services manufacture ill-health?

Unfortunately, this evidence is hard to assess. It consists on the one hand of very broad indicators of 'input' and 'output' whose correspondence with the true inputs and – especially – the true outputs is very approximate and whose causal connection is tenuous. On the other hand, there are more precise methods which do represent a way forward in that much more investment in these activities will take countries much closer to setting an optimum health care budget. The techniques are economic evaluation and analysis of determinants of health. These methods do ask a more limited, but perhaps more relevant, question: Given our current level of spending, where do we go from here?

Future Challenges

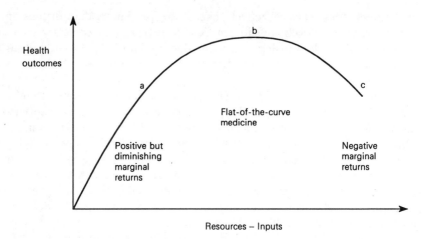

Figure 10.2 Diminishing marginal returns to health care

Where Do We Go from Here? Relating Broad Inputs to Broad Outputs

The 'broad' approach has been to examine mortality, morbidity and health care expenditure across (usually OECD) countries. An 'international comparisons industry' has become established using such data not because it tells us what we want to know but rather 'because its there'. An underlying implication of this work is that there is a 'magic number' (a percentage of GDP spent on health care) to which all societies should be moving.

From the twenty-one OECD countries for which a comparison can be made (see Table 10.4), take the position of Australia. Some countries appear to spend less than Australia and achieve better health outcomes (e.g. Denmark and Japan). However, other countries spend more, but do not necessarily do better than Australia in terms of health outcomes (e.g. the USA and France).

Can anything be inferred from these data about the allocation or misallocation of health care resources in Australia? Unfortunately not. Although the mortality data of Table 10.4 may provide crude indications of the health-related quality of life, they are not measures of the potential product of health care. Health care is productive only if it changes mortality or morbidity for the better – by reducing the rate or by preventing or slowing its rise. For instance, relating overall health care spending to specific perinatal mortality rates does not really make much sense. To examine this issue properly, spending on perinatal services should be related to perinatal mortality while one attempt to control for other factors, such as

Table 10.4   Health care expenditure per capita, male life expectancy and perinatal mortality (OECD countries)[a]

	Per capita expenditure[b] ($US)	Male life expectancy at age 40[c] (years)	Perinatal mortality rate[d]
Australia	798	33.9	1.30
Austria	684	32.5	1.20
Belgium	636	32.0	1.30
Canada	1058	34.0	1.07
Denmark	736	33.9	0.90
Finland	629	31.8	0.79
France	996	33.2	1.23
Germany	883	32.9	1.05
Greece	256	36.4	1.87
Iceland	832	36.5	0.76
Ireland	532	32.0	1.36
Italy	607	33.7	1.70
Japan	673	35.9	1.10
Luxemburg	719	31.3	1.11
Netherlands	851	34.7	1.07
New Zealand	481	33.1	1.05
Norway	822	34.7	0.96
Sweden	1239	34.9	0.77
Switzerland	990	35.1	0.91
UK	539	32.7	1.20
USA	1388	33.3	1.26

Source: OECD (1985).

[a] Portugal, Spain and Turkey are omitted here because the data for these countries are incomplete. [b] 1982 (calculated in current US dollars using purchasing power parity exchange rates). [c] 1980. [d] 1981.

cultural and social incentives to attend antenatal clinics and lifestyle factors such as nutrition. The problem of measuring the contribution of health care to health improvements is discussed in the following subsection.

High mortality may be of a sort that is immune to attack by health care or that is more effectively tackled by other means (such as public-health measures, better housing, education). There is, moreover, the ever-present problem of ensuring that the attribution of cause and effect is correct, that is, that the observable health care input is not piggy-backing on an already declining mortality rate or coinciding with service and environmental factors that are not part of health care. Approaches aimed at addressing the contribution to health or health care relative to other factors is discussed in the next-but-one subsection.

In short, the use of international comparisons is naive. Therefore, it is not surprising that, when based on such methods, a judgement of the effective impact of health care is elusive. No matter how good the data are in the future, it always will be. It is the method that is at fault, not the data. What is required is a method which tells us, within a country, what are the costs and benefits of changing the current uses of health care resources and what are the costs and benefits of expanding or contracting the health care budget.

There is some evidence, based on changes in health care expenditures and changes in life expectancy in OECD countries, that there is a qualitative link between relatively slow rates of growth in expenditures and slow rates of increase in life expectancy (Wolfe, 1986; Wolfe and Gabay, 1987) and slow rates of decline in infant mortality (Maxwell, 1981). These analyses are more sophisticated than the usual more simplistic comparisons reviewed in this subsection. Even so, adjustments for other 'contaminating' factors are at best very approximate and the relationship is by no means readily observable.

The establishment of measures of the costs and benefits of health care requires detailed evaluation of its effectiveness and efficiency (as advocated by Cochrane in 1972). The rigorous evaluation culture which he tried to promote in the UK NHS has still to take off in many countries (including the UK). This was based largely on the use of randomised controlled trials (RCTs). Techniques of economic evaluation, which are also much under-used, fit neatly with the concept of RCTs. One particular technique is outlined in the following subsection.

Where Do We Go from Here? Economic Evaluation

It is clear that progress on what to spend on health care cannot be made without more precise data on the productivity of health care interventions. This requires economic evaluation in which the costs of such interventions are related to their benefits.

In the narrowest sense, benefits can be measured in lives saved or life years saved, as in cost effectiveness analyses. In the widest sense, these benefits can be measured in monetary units, as in cost–benefit analyses. Monetary estimates of benefit can be generated through willingness-to-pay techniques. Willingness-to-pay measures are very experimental (Donaldson, 1990). However, a more limited improvement to the use of life years saved has received much attention over the last decade. This improvement involves adjusting life years for their quality, resulting in quality adjusted life years (or QALYs).

Torrance (1986) provides an excellent review of the development of QALYs. Table 10.5, which draws on a wide variety of studies done for several health care programmes, contains his estimates of marginal cost per QALY to be gained from a number of health care procedures. The interpretation one is invited to put on these data is that since a QALY obtained by, say, coronary bypass surgery costs $4200 while one from neonatal intensive care for babies with very low birthweights cost $31 800, the former programme ought to be expanded relative to (or perhaps at the expense of) the latter. In this way, with a limited health care budget, resources would be allocated to those areas where the marginal returns, in terms of health gains to the community, are greatest relative to marginal expenditure. This would ensure maximisation of the community's health given the resources available for health care.

Table 10.5 Comparative cost–utility results for selected health care procedures

	Adjusted Cost/QALY gained
	1983 $US
PKU Screening	< 0
Post-partum anti-D	< 0
Ante-partum anti-D	1220
Coronary artery bypass surgery for left main coronary artery disease	4200
Neonatal intensive care, 1000–1499-g infants	4500
T4 (thyroid) screening	6300
Treatment of severe hypertension (diastolic 105 mmHg) in males age 40	9400
Treatment of mild hypertension (diastolic 95–104 mmHG) in males age 40	19 100
Oestrogen therapy for postmenopausal systems in women without a prior hysterectomy	27 000
Neonatal intensive care, 500–999-g infants	31 800
Coronary artery bypass surgery for a single vessel disease with moderately severe angina	36 300
School tuberculin testing program	43 700
Continuous ambulatory peritoneal dialysis	47 100
Hospital haemodialysis	54 000

Source: Torrance (1986).

Note: These figures are drawn from studies that used similar but not identical methods. Generally, costs were net health care costs; however, discount rates and preference weights were not completely consistent. Differences in methods should be considered when comparing the relative cost-utility. For details, see the original sources, which are given in the source for this table.

The measures will, of course, be neither complete nor fully comparable, but they will represent the best judgement of those who are qualified to know about the expected gains (experimental judges have included panels of doctors, nurses, patients, managers and the general public). Moreover, the way in which they have been compiled is such that those who dissent from the result may with reasonable ease identify the source of the disagreement and assess the effect, if any, of making changes in the assumptions and judgements that are more to their liking. The technique can be applied to an expansion or a contraction of the budget for health care, ensuring health gains are maximised in the case of an expansion and that health losses are minimised in the case af a contraction. In any event, these measures are simply aids to judgement and not substitutes for it. As Andersen and Mooney (1990) point out, we have a duty to measure the effectiveness of health care in some form. If we do not have evidence that spending at a level of $5x$, $3x$ or $2x$ is better than one at x, is it surprising that cost cutting politicians choose x?

The potential of QALYs for use in decision making regarding the *size* of the health care sector depends on the widespread adoption of the technique in health services. If a marginal cost per QALY could be calculated for all existing and proposed health care interventions, a 'league table' of costs per QALY for all services could be constructed. Given a fixed level of funding for services, presumably a cut-off point could be established above which services are funded (at the margin) and below which they are not. Those arguing the case for increased funding would then be able to present such results to governments and say 'By not giving £Y extra funding for health services, X QALYs will be sacrificed.' Claims about 'harm to the community from a lack of funding' or the 'need for more efficiency in health services' would be more easily substantiated or dismissed. Thus, QALYs would be used to *inform* the decision about appropriate health care spending rather than to substitute for the decision making process; because health care would be competing with other public sector areas, the decision would have to be taken on the basis of a concept of welfare which embodies more than health (QALYs).

As it is, the experimental techniques used to derive QALYs are varied and of varying reliability. Like all techniques, they are again no substitute for hard thinking. They do have the great merit of exposing certain key issues and isolating those elements about which uncertainty or controversy exists. In particular, they reveal the need for making value judgements about the following:

— those aspects of 'life' or 'health' in terms of which quality is to be measured;
— the scaling of those aspects, either individually or in groups;
— the weighting of the various aspects;
— the interpersonal weights to be applied (is one QALY to be treated as of equal value to whomever it may accrue?);

- the variability of the weights (is one additional QALY worth the same to a person who currently expects none as it is to a person already expecting several?);
- the weighting of QALYs received at different times (is a QALY expected five years hence as valuable as one to be received in the next year?); and
- who should be asked to make these various value judgements.

These issues have recently been extensively discussed in the British context by Williams (1985, 1986), Donaldson *et al.* (1988) and Loomes and McKenzie (1989).

The 'solution' which QALYs potentially offer for budget setting within health care and for setting the overall health care budget lies many years ahead. Measures embodying more than just health may also have been developed by then. The literature has, however, focused attention on the nature of the factual and value judgements that reaching a conclusion requires to be made. Of necessity, their making in present circumstances will be crude. In the medium term it is clear that the burden of the literature focuses attention both on the need for more research into suitable outcome indicators and for developing systems that better direct resources towards their more highly productive uses.

Where Do We Go From Here? Other Sectors' Contributions to Health

Another point to bear in mind in endeavouring to determine where we go from here is the fact that health care is but one input into the process by which the health of the individual is improved or maintained. In Figure 10.3, it is illustrated that income, education, genetic endowment, lifestyle, work environment, work status, housing and health care all affect an individual's stock of health. This stock of health, in turn, produces healthy time for the individual. The diagram in Figure 10.3 is a basic representation of a model relating health outcome to health inputs which was first introduced by Grossman (1972) and developed by others (Muurinen, 1982; Wagstaff, 1986). However, social science disciplines and epidemiologists would also lay legitimate claims on this area of research.

Whatever the academic property rights, in the context of health care financing, the interesting question is whether an extra amount of money spent on another input would be more productive in terms of health improvements than spending that same amount on health care. It may be that arguing for more health care resources is to the detriment of health if such resources are won at the expense of those resources being put into a more health-productive input.

Inputs *Outputs*

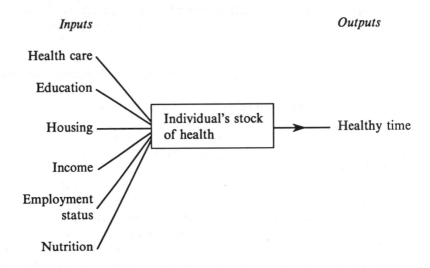

Figure 10.3 Grossman model of inputs to and outputs from health

Impressionistic evidence tells us that, if a major goal of public policy is health improvement, then developing countries would be better off implementing broader social and educational policies than in developing high-technology health care. Some detailed studies provide more such impressionistic evidence. For example, the evaluation of alternative ways of treating people post-myocardial infarction indicated that health care only affects survival if it is received very soon (within six hours) after the infarction. As many patients do not enter the health care system that rapidly, their health is no better improved by health care than by remaining at home (Hill *et al.*, 1978; Mather *et al.*, 1978).

Many studies have found positive associations between deprivation and mortality rates (Townsend *et al.*, 1988; Carstairs and Morris, 1989). In such studies, measures of 'deprivation' comprise aspects such as overcrowding in housing, employment status (particularly unemployment), social class and whether or not one has a car. Higher income and schooling was found to have a positive effect on health as well as access to health care (Grossman, 1975; Corman and Grossman, 1985). In the latter study, availability of organised family planning, abortion and neonatal intensive care were associated with lower neonatal mortality rates.

Using cross-sectional data, a US study analysed the potential changes in mortality rates which would be associated with 10 per cent increases in some variables. It can be seen from Table 10.6 that, once again, an increase in education (represented by years of schooling) has more potential for reducing mortality than does an increase in per-capita health spending (Auster *et al.*, 1972). The small impact of increased spending on health care may be characteristic of many developed nations. Cigarette consumption has the expected sign, an increase leading to greater mortality. Higher income is also associated with increased mortality, suggesting that the positive health effects of increased income may be outweighed by the negative effects.

Table 10.6   Percentage changes in age-specific mortality rates resulting from a 10 per cent increase in several variables

	10% increase in			
	Income	*Education*	*Cigarette consumption*	*Per capita health expenditure*
Percentage change in mortality	+2.0	–2.2	+1.0	–0.65

Source: Culyer (1976).

As with QALYs, the 'solution' to the health and health care budget setting problem which can be offered by more and wider analysis of determinants of health lies many years in the future. Once again, it points us in the direction of searching for better measures of health outcome as well as evidence on the effects on health of not only health care but also investment in other health-producing activities. In determining where we go from here, it will then be possible to examine whether or not the greatest health improvements for the community will result from a larger or smaller budget for health care.

CONCLUSIONS

In analysing the major determinants of health care spending, it seems that GDP is the main factor: one spends what one can afford. This should not be held to be an 'iron law'; nor does it say anything about what is the 'correct' level of spending. Many other factors play important roles, such as the centralisation of budgeting systems, and the tight control of fee schedules and hospital budgets.

Regarding the appropriate level of the health care budget, little can be offered by way of evidence from economic studies on what the 'correct' level is; largely because there is no universally correct level. In the absence of market forces, the level which is set, or reached, will, to a large extent, depend on various cultural factors.

International comparisons are naive and unhelpful. There does not seem to be any point in refining a method of comparison that does not tell us what we want to know. The real challenge is for countries to decide for themselves by use of the appropriate techniques of economic evaluation and of the analysis of the determinants of health. This will not result in a uniform level of spending across countries, but it will help to decide where increases and decreases in available resources are best targeted. If the determination of the size of the health care budget is not to be left in the hands of those providing unsubstantiated arguments in favour of either expansion or 'cuts', the future for health care budget setting must, to a certain degree, rest with the development of these techniques.

CHAPTER 11

Health Care Financing Reforms: Challenges for the 1990s

INTRODUCTION

The financing arrangements of many health care systems world wide are under reform, or at least their reform is anticipated. The key to judging such reforms is whether they make things better or worse for the population at large. Our primary objective has been to show the essential role of economics in assessing performance within this climate of change. The two powerful economic criteria against which change should be assessed are, of course, efficiency and equity; the former being concerned with the need to finance services in a way that maximises the well-being of the community and the latter with access to health services for less well-off groups in need. When examined against these criteria, the economic arguments are as strong as the social and ideological arguments in favour of extensive government intervention in health care financing.

We have seen that reforms can be directed towards various levels of health care finance: micro-level changes, such as prospective payments for hospital care, or fundamental changes, like for instance the Canadian move to social insurance funding. Whatever the details of these reforms, the crucial economic issues that are of interest are:

- the nature of the financial intermediary that stands between the consumer and the provider;
- the form of 'insurance premium' and the principles on which it is based;
- the size of out-of-pocket payments made by the consumer at the point of use;
- payment mechanisms for professional providers; and
- reimbursement arrangements for institutions.

Paying due attention to the costs, benefits and equity implications of each of these is essential if informed judgements on reforms are to be made.

THE CONTRIBUTION OF ECONOMIC THEORY

The first and second parts of this book set out the economic arguments behind the inevitability that some level of government intervention in health care financing will exist, and the sorts of forms it might take.

Indeed, extensive government intervention is difficult to avoid if maximisation of the community's health is an objective of health care. Rarely in the case of any commodity do market forces work sufficiently well to produce that highly desirable outcome, maximum satisfaction at least cost to society. However, the nature of health care is such that all the basic assumptions underlying a market approach break down. Thus, although there are differences of opinion concerning the 'correct' balance between market forces and government intervention (as is evident from the diverse array – one might even say disarray – of financial arrangements that exist in health care systems around the world), the characteristics of health care make it uniquely susceptible (and, in our view, rightly so) to significant government intervention. These characteristics (the risk and uncertainty associated with contracting illness; external effects; and asymmetrical information about health care between providers and consumers combined with problems of professional licensure), make it likely that government intervention will dominate the financing of health care. The evidence on prevalence of NHS and social-insurance-based systems (including their growth in LDCs) bears witness to this.

Usually government finance of health care takes the form of income tax, a hypothecated tax or payroll taxes. Unevaluated ways of government finance include 'voucher systems', lotteries and charitable donations.

The setting of health care objectives represents an intricate piece of juggling by policy makers to ensure that seeking too much efficiency does not counter too much equity, or vice versa. A trade-off between these two objectives is normally inevitable. This makes it important that both objectives are made explicit so that societies, or their representatives, can be well placed to judge for themselves the acceptability of trading off some amount of the ideal level of one for some greater level of the other.

Equity itself is a difficult notion to comprehend and agree upon beyond some strong, basic understanding that some 'fair' distribution is desirable. Its pursuit in practice can be hampered by conflict between different definitions of equity.

We believe that the most desirable definitions are (1) financing based on ability to pay (a progressive income-conditioned tax basis) and (2) equality of access. However, it is not possible to measure equality of access in absolute terms; rather, barriers to access need to be taken into account (e.g. geographical or time). These may capture only partially the notion of access. Even so, data on such variables may be difficult to come by and so proxy measures, particularly related to utilisation, are often used. We recognise that such proxies are unsatisfactory, but accept that in many instances they may be the best available. We have found considerable support in policy statements and pronouncements for our chosen definitions of equity objectives, although they are by no means uncontested.

In comparison with the complexities surrounding equity objectives, efficiency definitions are uncontentious. They have been described as technical efficiency and allocative efficiency. The appropriate 'rules' to measure and monitor them fall under the familiar auspices of economic evaluation: cost effectiveness analysis; cost–utility analysis; and cost–benefit analysis.

Where there may be a more contentious area is not on efficiency per se but in defining benefit. Although we have not pursued this at any length in the book, we believe that while health dominates the outputs of health care systems it does not monopolise them; there is also utility in the process of health care which, on occasions, may be more important than utility from outome.

EMPIRICAL FINDINGS — HOW HEALTH SERVICES SHOULD BE FINANCED

Throughout the third part of this book we have reported on available evidence (and often lack of it) of the performance of different financing arrangements. This has been done in as objective a way as possible. We make no pretence at having achieved comprehensiveness, as the literature is far too large for that, but feel we have reported adequately on the main published literature. Where we report crucial gaps in information (e.g. on the question of how best to pay doctors) we find it alarming that reforms can be undertaken without any prior, controlled experimentation (as in the recent UK NHS reforms).

There is no unique and unambiguous conclusion that can be summarised easily. Instead, in what follows we attempt to bring the information in the book into some perspective – inevitably with important value judgements coming into play. These are summarised by looking at:

- the role of the financial intermediary;
- financing and the supply side;
- financing and the demand side.

In doing so our aim is to address the question, 'What health care financing arrangements should and should not be in place in order to operate a fair and efficient system?'

The Financial Intermediary

First, what should be the role of the financial intermediary that stands between the consumer and the provider? Ideally, it should provide an environment for health care providers and consumers to act efficiently and equitably. In reality, any financial intermediary is susceptible to encouraging inefficient behaviour, because it breaks accountability links between those who bear the cost of health care with those who provide the benefits and those who obtain them. However, as we have seen in Chapters 6, 7 and 8, financial intermediaries can with varying degrees of success make attempts at re-establishing some accountability.

Government-based intermediaries seem best placed to offer a basis to cope with access problems of the sort created by unregulated health care insurance. By taking on the role of compulsory purchasers of health care insurance they can detach the basis for setting premium rates from experience of illness.

The most appropriate roles for the financial intermediary are to ensure comprehensive access to health care services or to insurance and to support an environment for the promotion of efficiency. Government-based intermediaries are best placed to achieve this and the 'insurance premium' should be a compulsory one, set at levels according to ability to pay.

Financing and the Supply Side

We further believe that the overall success of any reform to improve efficiency rests with the way in which the supply side of health care is financed, particularly the way in which doctors are paid. Given the characteristics of health care, it must be the case that ways of dealing with doctor-induced moral hazard and the institutions doctors work in are easily the most influential. Doctors need to be given incentives to influence the amount and type of care they supply. As they are also better informed than consumers about the technological relationship between health care and health, they are often in the position of determining health care consumption. The hospital sector is also important, because it accounts for a significant part of expenditure in any health care system. It is therefore crucial in playing an important role not only in determining the level and nature of hospital activity but also in controlling total health service costs.

There are few empirical data available concerning the effect of different methods of payment on doctors' performance, other than overconsumption when fees are used for reimbursement. It strikes us, therefore, that fees should only be part of a tightly controlled remuneration package that rewards efficient behaviour at least cost (e.g. fees targeted for preventive health goals). Salaried payments probably lead to less consumption as compared with fee income. The problem is knowing the effects of these systems across different patient groups, particularly with regard to access and outcome. It certainly appears to be the case that HMO-style care favours the selection of healthier individuals.

As there is such a lack of evidence on how best to pay doctors, we are forced to suggest that individual health care systems postulate their own judgements of how well they think reforms of doctors' remuneration will work. As medical practices tend to vary socially and culturally, it would not be surprising to learn of radically different remuneration packages improving efficient behaviour in different countries. For example, the social status and remuneration levels accorded Western doctors and Eastern European doctors are poles apart. Consequently, it is quite possible that, for example, a remuneration package in an Eastern European country would place greater importance on payment for 'good practice' and less on FFS remuneration than in a Western country – but that both would work equally effectively.

The second major element in achieving efficiency will come from financing reforms for institutions. Although costing issues are important to the financial incentives facing health care institutions, they are not of sole importance. Efficiency is about value for money. Thus the fact that the HMO-style financial and organisational arrangement has undoubtedly been shown to achieve significant cost savings is not sufficient to assure efficiency. Indeed, the evidence points quite strongly to either the selection of healthier individuals in non-randomised comparisons with FFS arrangements or the reduction in quality of care in randomised comparisons with FFS arrangements.

However, the relative efficiency of most reimbursement mechanisms has yet to be determined. Cost minimisation has, too frequently, been placed high on the political and administrative agendas without due attention being paid to effects on patient outcome. What should be of importance is the identification of cost reductions which can be achieved at little or no detrimental effect on patient outcome. Beyond politicians' having greater concern for cost control than for the health of the populations they serve, problems with health outcome measurement are largely responsible for this misguided focus on cost minimisation.

Price control of hospital budgets has been widely researched. The fact that the findings of such studies are indeterminate is striking. Competitive arrangements (e.g. HMOs or internal markets) may reduce costs, but the effects on patient outcomes are unknown. There is some HMO evidence to suggest even that patient outcomes can be worse for low-income initially sick individuals.

In the case of the US Medicare PPS system, which uses diagnostics-related groups to set prices, cost per case and cost per admission can be reduced, but compensatory increases in throughput mean total costs may actually rise. Cost shifting and patient shifting are also potential problems under such a financing system. The way forward for reimbursing institutions is, we suggest, to develop the idea behind clinical budgeting. This first means coming to terms with what is meant by 'best clinical practice' before setting reimbursement levels according to efficient modes of practice. It could be that DRGs become the price mechanism used, but they do not have to be. For example, it might be more relevant to price spare capacity at marginal cost.

Financing and the Demand Side

The final economic issue that should be considered in assessing efficient health care financing is the question of the size of out-of-pocket payments made by consumers at the point of consumption. We have deliberately left this issue to the end because we feel minimal responsibility should be placed on consumers.

Probably the most conclusive evidence on consumer moral hazard comes from the use of charges in the US private insurance market. Although charges help to reduce frivolous demand, the opportunity cost is high. Frivolous demand is not always easy to separate from necessary demand and low-income groups (particularly children) have been shown to be most disadvantaged by a corresponding reduction in the consumption of necessary care that accompanies the introduction, or raising, of charges. Furthermore, the scale of reduced consumption suggested by published findings is contingent upon doctor behaviour, because doctors' demand-inducing powers have a strong influence on consumption patterns. Because of both these factors, the relevance of charges to efficiency, over and above some nominal amount, must be highly contestable. With respect to equity, charges are almost inevitably bad.

Among those in developed countries, the US health care system is clearly the most inequitable, both in terms of gaining access to health services and in its financing arrangements. Access is mostly a problem for different social groups rather than across urban/rural areas. Not only are basic payments regressive but gross inequities have been demonstrated in financial protection against catastrophic coverage. LDCs, not surprisingly given their stringent resource supply, also have serious problems with comprehensively protecting their population from the risk of ill-health. It is likely that basic payments are regressive, although it is felt by some that greater use of private health insurance by richer groups may actually contribute to equity in finance and delivery.

Some people may believe that public financing restricts choice. We have deliberatley left out this issue because we could not find any evidence to support or refute it (however 'choice' is to be defined). It is possible that private financing allows more choice, but it is equally conceivable that, because of the nature of health care, utility is gained from a situation of restricted choice. Consumers prefer to pass on decisions to their doctors.

DETERMINING THE SIZE OF THE BUDGET

Any health care financing system will, to a large extent be culture-specific. However, within systems, debates will still go on about what the size of the health care budget should be. No such debates will be adequately resolved without more data on patient outcomes and well-being. Such data would facilitate not only comparisons between types of health care with each other but also comparisons of levels of health care spending with those of other sectors of the economy. Economic evaluation could then be used to make within-system comparisons, while analyses of determinants of health could be used to compare different sectors' contributions to health. Production of outcome data, plus development of these techniques, represent the most 'profitable' way forward for informed debate on health care spending. Decision making would then not be left totally in the hands of those providing unsubstantiated arguments for health care expansion or 'cuts'.

CONCLUSIONS

Our overall, if rather depressing, conclusion must be that much more evidence is required on the effects of different ways of financing health care. So far, however, it is clear that 'solutions' based on simple (even simplistic) neoclassical models which assume the existence of well-informed consumers uninfluenced by providers are very naive. Neither charges nor competitive reforms go well with health care. Where competition involves public bodies acting on behalf of consumers, the situation may be improved; but this type of competition remains unevaluated. The key to the health care market lies on the supply side, and financing reforms should be concentrated there. Such future reforms, however, can be properly informed only by adequate evaluation, which in turn depends primarily on the future development of outcome measures, measures of access and incentive structures.

Notes

1. Social insurance means insurance operated by a government or government-approved agency, but not a private insurance company.
2. See Chapter 3 for an explanation of why 'free marketeers' accept that many public-health interventions should be provided (or regulated by) governments.
3. Smith, despite having been a professor of moral philosophy, is generally regarded as one of the first economists. He, and some contemporaries, tend to be labelled 'classical' economists. More recently, economists subscribing to the school of thought which promotes the use of market mechanisms in the allocation of many goods, including health care, have become known as 'neoclassical' economists. Neoclassical economists developed and updated many of the ideas of the classical economists, but would still subscribe to many of Smith's basic insights. For a short and non-technical discussion of the development of economic thought see Whynes (1988), Chapters 3 and 4.
4. Even Smith (1776) recognised the disadvantages of collusion:

   'People of the same trade seldom meet together even for merriment or diversion but the conversation ends in a conspiracy against the public, or some contrivance to raise prices.'

   Many neoclassical economists tend not to heed the possibilities of such behaviour when espousing the virtues of 'free' markets.
5. Only consumers themselves truly know how much anxiety, pain and suffering an illness has caused and, consequently, they may have an incentive to overstate their case when making a claim. Thus, an insurance company would never offer payment as recompense for experiencing such effects.
6. For a more precise definition of 'opportunity cost', see the section on 'efficiency' in Chapter 5.
7. Between the demise of the first Australian public insurance scheme in 1976 and the introduction of the second in 1984 there was a government-subsidised private insurance scheme. See Palmer and Short (1989) for a more detailed description.
8. Continuing the Mercedes Benz analogy, there may be an externality effect in the case of access to transport in general, though not to Mercedes Benz cars in particular. This is demonstrated to some extent by the degree of subsidisation of public transport systems in many countries. Thus, in terms of problems of access (or, in health care, adverse selection) and externalities, it could be argued that transport and health care are, more or less, similar. The main difference between transport and health care seems to be that, in many countries, the provision of a two-tiered service ('Mercedes Benz' versus 'public transport') in transport is more acceptable to the population than is a two-tiered service in health care.
9. Some public health interventions are good examples of what economists call 'public goods'. The market fails in the context of public goods because of the free rider problem. People disguise what they are willing to pay for a service

that must be provided to everybody in a particular population or not be provided at all. These 'free riders' want to consume the service but let others pay for it. Given the incentive for everyone to behave in such a manner, some worthwhile public health interventions might never be funded. Examples of such interventions are clean air, clean water, water fluoridation and health-promotion campaigns in the media. Thus, there is a clear role for government intervention which is accepted by proponents of markets for health care (Logan *et al.*, 1989). This role, however, is much narrower than that which the externalities argument seeks to justify.

10. Smith's earlier work, *The Theory of Moral Sentiments*, was in the field of social philosophy rather than economics. However, he saw the contents of this work and the later *Wealth of Nations* as part of a greater whole which he intended to bring together in a third (and never completed) work on the principles of law and government.

11. There is also the debate about whether such notions can be incorporated into the externalities argument above.

12. Navarro (1989), however, would dispute this point on the basis of evidence from surveys of the US population.

13. Strictly, adverse selection is a phenomenon of private health insurance. Private health insurance did not exist to a great extent in the UK before 1944. However, in the quotations from the National Health Service policy document, there is obviously a concern about exclusion from care of certain 'needy' groups as a result of market forces and only partial coverage by the UK government, which amounts to the same thing.

14. Much of the finance in these two countries actually comes from direct taxation.

15. The UK government proposal was that major acute hospitals (i.e. those with over 250 beds) currently within the NHS be allowed to opt out of health authority board control to become independent hospital trusts. Such a hospital would no longer be under the jurisdiction of its district health authority, but would be seeking to attract funds from that authority. The first wave of 57 such trusts including some ambulance and community services, came into existence on 1 April 1991.

16. In practice, however, informational asymmetries may remain.

17. Note that the provision of opportunity is a supply-side phenomenon rather than relying on the demand-side (via the burden placed on the consumer) to achieve the equity objective.

18. Note that this does not mean that inequalities cannot be reduced. This still requires a definition of 'health inequalities' and, furthermore, clarification of the scale of reduction in inequalities to be pursued.

19. In fact, although registration of doctors in these countries actually commenced in the mid-nineteenth century, it was not until the early twentieth century that unqualified practitioners, or 'quacks', were effectively prevented from practising by law (Peterson, 1978; Allen, 1982).

20. Perfect agency would require doctors to weight equally the patient's benefit and the hospital's financial interests. As Evans (1984) has pointed out, this would also require the doctor to be a 'perfect schizophrenic'!

21. The point about supplier-induced demand and the theory of Ellis and McGuire (1986) demonstrate that, partly contrary to our earlier assertions, some theories about the response of individual actors (in this case, doctors) to reimbursement mechanisms can also be brought to bear when predicting how institutions (like hospitals) might respond to different mechanisms.

22. Of course, the incorrect classification may have been the earlier code. Either way, it is difficult to justify reimbursing hospitals for 'upcoding'.

23. A hospital's market area comprised zip code areas (ZCAs) contributing to at least three per cent of a hospital's total discharges. A hospital was considered to have a competitor if a second hospital drew at least 3 per cent of a ZCA's total discharges from at least one of the ZCAs of the first hospital. Degree of competitiveness was measured by a Hirschman–Herfindahl index, for which an area with a single monopoly supplier would receive a score of 1 and an area with several competitors, each with equal shares, would receive a score close to 0. The degree of competition faced by a hospital was defined as the weighted average of indices in the ZCAs in its market area, with the proportion of patients from each ZCA used as the weight. For more details, see Melnick and Zwanziger (1988).

24. The marginal cost, in this context, would be the cost of admitting one more patient. With spare capacity, staffing and other costs are unlikely to be affected by the admission of one more patient. However, average cost data would include these staffing and other costs. Therefore, the marginal cost is likely to be less than the average. The most competitive price for hospital care is one which reflects marginal cost.

25. Negative KI values represent regressivity, and positive values progressivity. The details can be found in Wagstaff *et al.* (1989).

26. The proportion of government expenditure on health care is displayed in Table 10.3 because LDCs have difficulty in keeping track of expenditures in the private sector.

References

Aaron HA and Schwartz WB (1984). *The Painful Prescription*. Brookings Institute, Washington, DC.

Abel-Smith B (1986). Funding health for all — is insurance the answer? *World Health Forum*, 7: 3–11.

Abel-Smith B and Dua A (1988). Community-financing in developing countries: the potential for the health sector. *Health Policy and Planning*, 3: 2; 95–108.

Akin JS (1988). Health insurance in developing countries: experience and prospects. In *Health Care Financing: Regional Seminar in Health Care Financing, 27 July–3rd August, 1987, Manila, Philippines*. Asian Development Bank, Manila; Economic Development Institute of the World Bank, Washington; East-West Center, Honolulu.

Allen J (1982). Octavius Beale reconsidered: infanticide, babyfarming and abortion in NSW in the 1930s. In Sydney Labour History Groups (Eds). *What Rough Beast? The State and Social Order in Australian History*. Sydney, George Allen and Unwin.

Andersen TF and Mooney GH (1990). *The Challenges of Medical Practice Variations*. Basingstoke, Macmillan Press.

Andersen TF, Madsen M and Loft A (1987). Regionale variatione i anvendelsen af hysterektomi. *Ugeskrift for Lager*, 36: 2415–2419.

Angelus T (1990). Personal communication.

Archibald GC and Donaldson DJ (1976). Paternalism and prices. In Allingham M and Burnstein ML (Eds), *Resource Allocation and Economic Policy*. London, Macmillan.

Arrow KJ (1963). Uncertainty and the Welfare Economics of Medical Care. *American Economic Review*, LIII, 5: 941–967.

Ashton T (1991). Personal Communication.

Asian Development Bank (1988). *Health Care Financing: Regional Seminar in Health Care Financing, 27 July–3 August, 1987, Manila, Philippines*. Asian Development Bank, Manila; Economic Development Institute of the World Bank, Washington, East-West Center, Honolulu.

Asvall JE (1990). Foreword. *Social Science and Medicine*, 31: 3; 223.

Auster R *et al*. (1972). The production of health: an exploratory study. In Fuchs VR (Ed), *Essays in the Economics of Health and Medical Care*. New York, National Bureau of Economics Research, Columbia University Press.

Australia, Budget Statements (1989). *Budget Statements 1988–89*. Budget Paper No. 1. Canberra, Australian Goverment Publishing Service.

Baillit H, Newhouse J, Brook R, Duan N, Goldberg G, Hanley J, Kamberg C, Spolsky V, Black A and Lohr K (1985). Does more generous dental insurance coverage improve oral health? *Journal of the American Dental Association*, 110: 701–707.

Barer M, Evans R and Labelle R (1988). Fee controls as cost control: evidence from the frozen North. *Milbank Quarterly*, 66: 1–64.

Barer ML, Evans RG and Stoddart GL (1979). *Controlling Health Care Costs by Direct Charges to Patients: Snare or Delusion?* Ontario Economic Council Occasional Paper No. 10. Toronto, Ontario Economics Council.

Bays CW (1977). Case-mix differences between non-profit and for-profit hospitals. *Economic Inquiry*, 26: 21–36.

Beck RG (1974). The effects of co-payment on the poor. *Journal of Human Resources*, 9: 129–142.

Becker ER and Sloan FA (1985). Hospital ownership and performance. *Economic Inquiry*, 23: 21–36.

Berki SE and Ashcraft MLF (1980). HMO enrollment: who gains what and why? A review of the literature. *Milbank Memorial Fund Quarterly*, 58: 588–632.

Berki SE, Ashcraft MLF, Penchansky R *et al.* (1977). Enrolment choice in a multi-HMO setting: the roles of health risk, financial vulnerability and access to care. *Medical Care*, 15: 95–114.

Birch S (1986). Increasing patient charges in the National Health Service: a method of privatising primary health care. *Journal of Social Policy*, 15: 163–184.

Birch S (1989). Hypothesis: charges to patients impair the quality of dental care to elderly people. *Age and Ageing*, 18: 136–140.

Black Report (1980). *Inequalities in Health: Report of a Research Working Group.* London, Department of Health and Social Security.

Blaxter M (1984). Equity and consultation rates in General Practice. *British Medical Journal*, 288: 1963–1967.

Blewett N (1988). Opening address to the Public Health Association of Australia and New Zealand Conference, Sydney, August 1987. *Community Health Studies*, 12: 106–111.

Bloom BS and Fendrick AM (1987). Waiting for care: queuing and resource allocation. *Medical Care*, 25: 131–139.

Blumberg MS (1980). Health status and health care by type of private health coverage. *Milbank Memorial Fund Quarterly*, 58: 633–655.

Borgenhammer E (1987). Equity in health care; Experiences from Sweden. *International Journal of Health Planning and Management*, 2: 159–173.

Bowden D (1987). *Resource Management and Budgeting for Clinicians.* Paper presented to joint meeting of the Health Economics Study Group and the Institute of Health Services Management. University of York, 7th–9th July, 1987.

Brook RH, Ware JE, Rogers WH, Keeler FB, Davies AR *et al.* (1983). Does free care improve adults' health? Results from a randomized controlled trial. *New England Journal of Medicine*, 309: 1426–1434.

Broyles AW, Manga P, Shillington *et al.* (1983). The use of physician services under a national health insurance scheme. *Medical Care*, 21: 1037–1054.

Buchanan JL and Cretin S (1986). Risk selection of families electing HMO membership, *Medical Care*, 24: 39–50.

Butler JRG (1984). On the relative efficiency of public and private enterprises: some evidence from hospitals. In Tatchell PB (Ed), Economics and Health 1983: *Proceedings of the Fifth Australian Conference of Health Economics.* Canberra, Australian National University.

Carr-Hill RA, Maynard AK and Slack R (1990). Morbidity variation and RAWP. *Journal of Epidemiology and Community Health*, 44: 271–273.

Carrin G and Vereecke M (1992). *Strategies for Health Care Finance in Developing Countries with a Focus on Community Financing in Sub-Saharan Africa.* Basingstoke, Macmillan Press.

Carroll NV and Erwin WF (1987). Patient shifting as a response to Medicare prospective payment. *Medical Care*, 25: 1161–1167.

Carstairs V and Morris R (1989). Deprivation: explaining differences in mortality between Scotland and England and Wales. *British Medical Journal*, 299: 886–889.

Chazou Y (1988). *Restructuring affects the whole health service.* Moscow, Novosti Press Agency Publishing House.

Chassin MR, Kosecoff J, Winslow CM, Kalm KL, Merrick NJ *et al.* (1987). Does inappropriate use explain geographic variations in the use of health services? *Journal of the American Medical Association*, 258: 2533–2537.

Clarkson KW (1972). Some implications of property rights in hospital management. *Journal of Law and Economics*, 15: 363–384.

Cochrane AL (1972). *Effectiveness and Efficiency: Random Reflections in Health Services*. London, Nuffield Provincial Hospital Trust.

Collins E and Klein R (1980). Equity and the NHS: self-reported morbidity, access and primary care. *British Medical Journal*, 281: 1111–1115.

Commonwealth Department of Health (1986). *Health Maintenance Organisations: A Development Program under Medicare*. Canberra, Australian Government Publishing Service.

Constitucao da Republica Portuguesa (1982). Lisbon, Rei dos Livros.

Cooper MH and Culyer AJ (1971). An economic survey of the nature and intent of the British NHS. *Social Science and Medicine*, 5: 1–13.

Corman H and Grossman M (1985). Determinants of neonatal morbidity rates in the USA: a reduced form model. *Journal of Health Economics*, 4: 213–236.

Council on Ethical and Judicial Affairs (1990). Black–White disparities in health care. *Journal of the American Medical Association*, 263: 17; 2344–2346.

Creese AL (1990). *User Charges for health care: a review of recent experience*. Geneva, SHS Paper No.1, World Health Organization.

Cromwell J and Mitchell JB (1986). Physician-induced demand for surgery. *Journal of Health Economics*, 5: 293–313.

Cullis JG and Jones PR (1985). National health service waiting lists: a discussion of computing explanations and a policy proposal. *Journal of Health Economics*, 4: 119–135.

Cullis JG and West P (1979). *The Economics of Health*. Oxford, Martin Robertson.

Culyer AJ (1971). The nature of the commodity health care and its efficient allocation. *Oxford Economic Papers*, 23: 189–211.

Culyer AJ (1976). *Need and the National Health Service: Economic and Social Choice*. London, Martin Robertson.

Culyer AJ (1985). *Economics*. Basil Blackwell, Oxford.

Culyer AJ (1986). *The Withering of the Welfare State and Whither the Welfare State?* 1985 Woodward Lectures in Economics, University of British Columbia, Vancouver.

Culyer AJ (1988). *Health Expenditure in Canada*. Toronto, Canadian Tax Foundation.

Culyer AJ (1989). Cost containment in Europe. *Health Care Financing Review*, 1989 (Annual Supplement), 21–32.

Culyer AJ (1991). The normative economics of health care finance and provision. In McGuire A, Fenn P and Mayhew K (Eds) *Providing Health Care: the Economics of Alternative Systems of Finance and Delivery*. Oxford University Press, Oxford.

Culyer AJ and Cullis JG (1976). Some economics of hospital waiting lists. *Journal of Social Policy*, 5: 239–264.

Culyer AJ, Maynard A and Williams A (1981). Alternative systems of health care provision: an essay on motes and beams. In Olsen M (ed), *A New Approach to the Economics of Health Care*. Washington DC, American Enterprise Institute.

Culyer AJ and Simpson H (1980). Externalities, models and health: a look back over the last twenty years. *Economic Record*, 56:222–230.

Dahlgren G and Diderichen F (1986). Strategies for equity in health and health services in Sweden – some experiences and suggestions. Leeds, Paper presented for the WHO Meeting on Social Justice and Health, July.

Daniels N (1981). Health care needs and distributive justice. *Philosophy and Public Affairs*, 10, 2: 34–58.

Danskernes Sundhand (1985). *Det dankse sundhadsvaesen. En status med perspectiver frem mod ar 2000*. Indenrigsministeriet og Sundhedsstyrelsen.

Davey Smith G, Bartley M and Blane D (1990). The Black Report on socioeconomic inequalities in health 10 years on. *British Medical Journal*, 310: 373–377.

Davis K (1973). Hospital costs and the Medicare Program. *U.S. Social Security Bulletin*, 38: 8.

Davis K (1989). National health insurance: A proposal. *American Economic Review*, 79: 4; 349–352.

Davis K and Russell LB (1972). The substitution of hospital outpatient care for inpatient care. *Review of Economics and Statistics*, 54: 109–120.

Dearden B (1991). First welfare state at the end of the road. *Health Service Journal*, 8 August: 15.

de Ferranti D (1985). Paying for health services in developing countries: a call for realism. *World Health Forum*, 6: 99–105.

Deeble JS (1982). Unscrambling the omelet: public and private health care financing in Australia. In McLachlan G and Maynard A (Eds) *The Public/Private Mix for Health: the Relevance and Effects of Change*, London. Nuffield Provincial Hospitals Trust.

Department of Health and Social Security (1976). *Sharing resources for health in England*. Report of the Resource Allocation Working Party. London, HMSO.

Department of Health and Social Security (1986a). *Resource management (management budgeting) in Health Authorities*. Health Notice, NH (86) 34, November 1986, London, HMSO.

Department of Health and Social Security (1986b). *Review of the Resource Allocation Working Party Formula*. Report by the NHS Management Board. London, HMSO.

Diehr P, Martin DP, Liebely R, Krueger L, Silberg N and Barchets (1987). Use of ambulatory health care services in a preferred provider organisation. *Medical Care*, 25: 1033–1043.

Directorate General for Research and Documentation (1988). The Health Systems of European Community Countries. Environment, Public Health and Consumer Protection Services Series No. 12. Luxemburg.

Donaldson C (1990). Willingness to pay for publicly provided goods: a possible measure of benefit? *Journal of Health Economics*, 9: 103–118.

Donaldson C and Gerard K (1989a). Paying general practitioners: shedding light on the review of health services. *Journal of the Royal College of General Practitioners*, 39: 114–117.

Donaldson C and Gerard K (1989b). Countering moral hazard in public and private health care systems: a review of recent evidence. *Journal of Social Policy*, 18, 2: 235–251.

Donaldson C and Gerard K (1991). Minding our Ps and Qs? Financial incentives for efficient hospital behaviour. *Health Policy*, 17: 51–76.

Donaldson C, Atkinson A, Bond J and Wright K (1988). Should QALYs be programme-specific. *Journal of Health Economics*, 7: 239–257.

Donaldson C, Lloyd P and Lupton D (1991). Primary health care consumerism amongst elderly Australians. *Age and Ageing*, 20: 280–286.

Dowd BE, Johnson AN and Madson RA (1986). Inpatient length of stay in the Twin Cities health plans. *Medical Care*, 24: 694–710.

Dranove D (1988). Pricing by non-profit institutions: the case of hospital cost shifting. *Journal of Health Economics*, 7: 47–57.

Draper D, Kahn KL, Reimisch EJ, Sherwood MJ, Carrey MF *et al.* (1990). Studying the effects of the DRG-based prospective payment system on quality of care. *Journal of the American Medical Association*, 264: 1956–1961.

Dukes MJG and Lunde I (1981). The regulatory control of non-steroidal anti-inflammatory agents. *European Journal of Clinical Pharmacology*, 19: 3–10.

Eggers PW (1980). Risk differential behaviour between Medicare beneficiaries enrolled and not enrolled in an HMO. *Health Care Financing Review*, 1: 3; 91–99.

Ellis RP and McGuire TG (1986). Provider behaviour under prospective reimbursement: cost sharing and supply. *Journal of Health Economics*, 5: 129–251.

Enthoven AC (1980). *Health plan: the Only Practical Solution to the Soaring Cost of Medical Care*. Reading, Massachussetts, Addison-Wesley.

Enthoven A and Kronick R (1989a). Consumer choice health plan for the 1990s. Universal health insurance in a system designed to promote quality and economy. (First of two parts), *New England Journal of Medicine*, 320: 29–37.

Enthoven A and Kronick R (1989b). Consumer choice health plan for the 1990s. Universal health insurance in a system designed to promote quality and economy. (Second of two parts), *New England Journal of Medicine*, 320: 94–101.

Epstein AM, Stern RS and Weissman JS (1990). Do the poor cost more? A multihospital study of patients' socioeconomic status and use of hospital resources. *New England Journal of Medicine*, 322: 16; 122–128.

Evans RG (1974). Supplier-induced demand: empirical evidence and implications. In Perlman M (Ed), *The Economics of Health and Medical Care*. New York, John Wiley and Sons.

Evans RG (1982). Health care in Canada: patterns of funding and regulation. In McLachlan G and Maynard A (Eds) *The Public/Private Mix for Health: The Relevance and Effects of Change*. London, Nuffield Provincial Hospitals Trust.

Evans RG (1984). *Strained Mercy: the Economics of Canadian Medical Care*. Toronto, Butterworths.

Evans RG (1987). Public health insurance: the collective purchase of individual care. *Health Policy*, 7: 115–134.

Evans RG (1990). The dog in the night-time: Medical practice variations and health policy. In Anderson TF and Mooney GH (Eds), *The Challenge of Medical Practice Variations*. London, Macmillan.

Evans RG (1990). Tension, compression and shear: directions, stresses and outcomes of health care cost control. *Journal of Health Politics, Policy and Law*, 15: 101–128.

Evans RG, Lomas J, Barer ML, Labelle R, Fooks C *et al.* (1989). Controlling health expenditures – the Canadian reality. *New England Journal of Medicine*, 320: 571–577.

Fallon M (1988). The doctors in excess. *The Guardian*, 17 February 1988.

Farley JP (1985). Who are the underinsured? *Milbank Memorial Fund Quarterly*, 63: 476–503.

Feldstein MS (1977). The high cost of hospitals – what to do about it. *Public Interest*, 48: 40.

Fisher CR (1987). Impact of the prospective payment system on physician charges under Medicare. *Health Care Financing Review*, 8: 101–102.

Fitzgerald JF, Fagan LF, Tierney WM and Dittus RS (1987). Changing patterns of hip fracture care before and after implementation of the prospective payment system. *Journal of the American Medical Association*, 258: 218–221.

Foot M (1973). *Aneurin Bevan: a Biography, 1945–1960, Volume II*. Davis-Poynter, London.

Fox J (1989). *Health Inequalities in European Countries*. Aldershot, Gower.

Foxman B, Valder RB, Lohr KL, Goldberg GA, Newhouse JP and Brook RH (1987). The effect of cost sharing on the use of antibiotics in ambulatory care: results from a population-based randomised controlled trial. *Journal of Chronic Diseases*, 40: 429–437.

Frank RG, Salkever DS and Mullen F (1990). Hospital ownership and the care of uninsured and Medicaid patients: findings from the National Hospital Discharge Survey 1979–1984. *Health Policy*, 14: 1–11.

Friedman E (1991). The uninsured: from dilemma to crisis. *Journal of the American Medical Association*, 265: 2491–2495.

Fuchs V (1978). The supply of surgeons and the demand for operations. *Journal of Human Resources*, 13 (suppl.): 35–56.

Fuchs VR and Hahn JS (1990). How does Canada do it? A comparison of expenditures for physicians' services in the United States and Canada. *New England Journal of Medicine*, 323: 884–890.

Garnick DW, Luft MS, Gardner LB, Morrison EM, Barrett H, O'Neill A and Harvey B (1990). Services and charges by PPO physicians for PPO and indemnity patients: an episode of care analysis. *Medical Care*, 128: 894–906.

Gaumer G (1986). Medicare patient outcomes and hospital organisational mission. In Institute of Medicine, *For-profit Enterprise In Health Care*. Washington DC, National Academy Press.

Gibbens FJ, Sen I, Vaz FS and Bose S (1988). Clinical budgeting and drug management on long–stay geriatric wards. *Age and Ageing*, 17: 328–332.

Ginsburg PB (1988). Public insurance programs: Medicare and Medicaid. In HR Frech III (Ed) *Health Care in America: the Political Economy of Hospitals and Health Insurance*. Pacific Research Institute for Public Policy, San Francisco.

Ginsburg PB and Carter GM (1986). Medicare case-mix index increase. *Health Care Financing Review*, 7: 51–65.

Giraldes dRM (1990). The equity and efficiency principle in the financing system of the NHS in Portugal. *Health Policy*, 14: 13–38.

Goldsmith M (1988). Do vouchers hold the key to the funding dilemma? *The Health Service Journal*, 21 January p78.

Gottschalk P, Wolfe B and Haveman R (1989). Health care financing in the USA, UK and Netherlands: distributional consequences. In *Changes in Revenue Structures*. Proceedings of the 42nd Congress of the International Institute of Public Finance, Athens, 351–373.

Goyert GL, Bottoms SF, Treadwell MC and Nehra PC (1989). The physician factor in caesarean birth rates. *New England Journal of Medicine*, 320,11: 706–709.

Grant C and Lapsley H (1989). *The Australian Health Care System, 1988*. Australian Studies in Health Service Administration, No. 64, University of New South Wales.

Gray A (1991). A mixed economy of health care: Britain's health service sector in the inter-war period. In McGuire A, Fenn P and Mayhew K (Eds) *Providing Health Care: the Economics of Alternative Systems of Finance and Delivery*. Oxford, Oxford University Press.

Green D (1986). *Which Doctor?* London, Institute of Economic Affairs.

Greenspan AM, Kay HR, Berger BC, Greenberg RM, Greenspan AJ and Gaughan MJS (1988). Incidence of unwarranted implantation of permanent cardiac pacemakers in a large medical population. *New England Journal of Medicine*, 318: 158–163.

Griffin CC (1988). User charges for health care in principle and practice. In *Health Care Financing, Regional Seminar in Health Care Financing*, 27 July–3 August. 1987, Manila, Philippines. Asian Development Bank, Manila; Economics Development Institute of the World Bank, Washington; East–West Center, Honolulu.

Grivell AR, Forgie MJ, Fraser CG and Berry MN (1981). Effect of feedback to clinical staff of information on clinical biochemistry requesting patterns. *Clinical Chemistry*, 27: 1717–1720.

Grol R, Mokkink H and Shelleris P (1988). The effects of peer review in general practice. *Journal of the Royal College of General Practitioners*, 28: 10–13.

Grossman M (1972). *The Demand for Health: a Theoretical and Empirical Investigation*. National Bureau of Economic Research Occasional Paper No. 119. New York, Columbia University Press.

Grossman M (1975). The correlation between health and schooling. In Terleck NE (Ed) *Household Production and Consumption*. National Bureau of Economic Research, New York.

Guterman S and Dobson A (1986). Impact of the Medicare prospective payment system for hospitals. *Health Care Financing Review*, 7: 97–114.

Hall J (1991). *Equity, Access and Health*. Sydney, Department of Public Health, University of Sydney, PhD. Thesis.

Hankansson S, Majnoni d'Intignano B, Roberts J and Zollner H (1988). *The Leningrad Experiment in Health Care Management 1988*. Report of a visit to the USSR. Copenhagen, World Health Organization Report SSR/MPN 501.

Haro AS (1987). Health expenditure by area in Finland – an indicator of equity. *Health Policy*, 7: 299–315.

Harris BL, Stergachis A and Reid DL (1990). The effect of drug copayments on utilisation and cost of pharmaceuticals in a Health Maintenance Organisation. *Medical Care*, 28: 908–917.

Hayward RA et al. (1988). Inequities in health services among insured Americans. *New England Journal of Medicine*, 318: 1507–1512.

Haywood RA, Shapiro MF, Freeman HE and Corey CR (1988). Inequities in health services among insured Americans. *New England Journal of Medicine*, 318: 1507–1512.

Health Care Financing Administration (1989). *Health Care Financing Review. International comparison of health care financing and delivery: data and perspectives*. Annual Supplement. Washington, DC.

Health Targets and Inequalities (Health for All) Committee (1988). *Health for All Australians*. Canberra, Australian Government Publishing Service.

Heller PS (1982). A model of the demand for medical and health services in peninsular Malaysia. *Social Science and Medicine*, 16: 267–284.

Hellinger FJ (1987). Selection bias in health maintenance organisations: Analysis of recent events. *Health Care Financing Review*, 9: 2; 55–63.

Helms LJ, Newhouse JP and Phelps CE (1978). Co-payments and the demand for medical care: the California Medicare experience. *Bell Journal of Economics*, 9: 192–208.

Hemenway D, Killen A, Cashman SB, Parks CL and Bicknell WH (1990). Physicians' responses to financial incentives: evidence from a for profit ambulatory care centre. *New England Journal of Medicine*, 322: 1059–1063.

Henke K-D (1989). Response to Jonsson. *Health Care Financing Review, Annual Supplement*, 93–6.

Herzlinger RE and Krasker WS (1987). Who profits from non-profits. *Harvard Business Review*, 93–106.

Hickson EB, Altemeier WA and Perrin JM (1987). Physician reimbursement by salary or fee-for-service: effect on physician practice behaviour in a randomised prospective study. *Paediatrics*, 80: 344–350.

Hill JD, Hampton JR and Mitchell JPA (1978). A randomised trial of home versus hospital management for patients with suspected myocardial infarction. *Lancet*, 1: 837–841.

Hillman AL, Pauly MV and Kerstein JJ (1989). How do financial incentives affect physicians' clinical decisions and the financial performances of health maintenance organisation? *New England Journal of Medicine,* 321: 86–92.

Himmelstein DU and Woolhandler S (1986). Cost without benefit: administrative waste in U.S. health care. *New England Journal of Medicine,* 314: 441–445.

Himmelstein DU, Woolhandler S and the Writing Committee of the Working Group on Program Design (1989). A national health program for the United States. *New England Journal of Medicine,* 320: 102–105.

Hoyer G (1985). Transinnleggesber og trangsretensjon i psykiatriske institusjoner - en sammentignrng av regelverk og praksis i de skemdincenyke land. *Nordisk Psykrorisk Trdsskritt,* 29: 147–157.

Hurst J (1985). *Financing health care in the USA, Canada and Britain.* London, Kings Fund Institute.

Illich I (1976). *Limits to Medicine. Medical Nemesis: The Expropriation of Health.* London, Marian Boyers.

Indulski JA, Smolen MM and Wlodarczyz C (1989). Some economic aspects of the Polish NHS reform project. Paper presented to the *First European Conference on Health Economics,* Barcelona, Sept. 1989.

Institute of Medicine (1986). *For-profit Enterprise in Health Care.* Washington DC, National Academy Press.

Irwin WG, Mills KA and Steele K (1986). Effect on prescribing of the limited cost in a computerised group practice. *British Medical Journal,* 293: 857–859.

Italian Ministry of Justice (1978). *Legge 838: Institutizione del Sernzio Sanitario.* Supplement to Tazzotta Ufficcale, 28 December 1978, Rome.

Jonsson B (1989). What Americans can learn from Europeans. *Health Care Financing Review, Annual Supplement,* 79–83.

Jørgensen K and Kristiansen AL (1991). *Brugerbetaling I Sundhedsvaesement.* Copenhagen, AKF.

Juba D, Lave JR and Shaddy J (1980). An analysis of the choice of health benefit plans. *Inquiry,* 17: 62.

Kahn KL, Keeler EB, Sherwood MJ, Rogers WH, Draper D *et al.* (1990b). Comparing outcomes of care before and after implementation of the DRG-based prospective payment system. *Journal of the American Medical Association,* 264: 1984–1988.

Kahn KL, Rogers WH, Rubenstein LV, Sherwood MJ, Reinisch EJ *et al.* (1990a). Measuring quality of care with explicit process criteria before and after implementation of the DRG-based prospective pricing system. *Journal of the American Medical Association,* 264: 1969–1973.

Kalimo E, Nyman K, Klaukka T, Tuomikoski H and Savolainen E (1982). *Need, use and expenses of health services in Finland 1964–1976.* (In Finnish, with an English summary.) Helsinki, Research Institute for Social Security, Finland, A: 18.

Keeler EB and Rolph JE (1988). The demand for episodes of treatment in the health insurance experiment. *Journal of Health Economics,* 7: 337–367.

Keeler EB, Brook RH, Goldberg GA *et al.* (1985). How free care reduced hypertension of participants in the Rand Health Insurance Experiment. *Journal of the American Medical Association,* 154: 1926–1931.

Kirkmann-Liff BL (1990). Physician payment and cost containment strategies in West Germany: suggestions for medicare reform. *Journal of Health Politics, Policy and Law,* 15: 69–99.

Kleiman E (1974). The determinants of national outlay on health. In Perlman M (Ed) *The Economics of Medical Care.* New York, Macmillan.

Kosecoff J, Kahn KL, Rogers WH, Reinisch EJ, Sherwood MJ *et al.* (1990). Prospective payment system and impairment at discharge. The 'quicker-and-sicker' story revisited. *Journal of the American Medical Association*, 264: 1980–1983.

Krasnik A, Groenewegen P, Pedersen PA, Scholter P, Mooney G *et al.* (1990). Changing remuneration systems: effects on activity in general practice. *British Medical Journal*, 300: 1698–1701.

Kristiansen IS (1989). Personal communication.

Langwell KL and Hadley PJ (1989). Evaluation of the Medicare competition demonstrations. *Health Care Financing*, 11: 2; 65–80.

Le Grand J (1978). The distribution of public expenditure: the case of health care. *Economica*, 45: 125–142.

Le Grand J (1982). *The Strategy of Equality*. London, George Allen and Unwin.

Leavy R, Wilkin D and Metcalfe DHH (1989). Consumerism and general practice. *British Medical Journal*, 298: 737–739.

Leeder SR (1987). Looking forward to better health. *Medical Journal of Australia*, 146: 340–341.

Leenen H (1984). Equality and inequality in health care. *Nederlands Tijdschrift voor Gezondheidsrect*, 53–67.

Lees DS (1962). The logic of the British National Health Service. *Journal of Law and Economics*, 5; 111–118.

Leu RE (1986). The public/private mix and institutional health care costs. In Culyer AJ and Jonsson B (Eds), *Public and private health services: complementaries and conflicts*. Oxford, Basil Blackwell.

Lewin LS, Derzov RA and Margulies R (1978). Investor-owned and non-profits differ in economic performance. *Hospitals: Journals of the American Hospital Association*, 55: 52–58.

Lewin LS, Eckels TJ and Miller LB (1988). Setting the record straight: The provision of uncompensated care by not-for-profit hospitals. *New England Journal of Medicine*, 318: 18.

Lindsay CM (1980). *National Health Issues: The British Experience*. Welwyn, Roche Laboratories.

Lindsay CM and Feigenbaum B (1984). Rationing by waiting lists. *American Economic Review*, 74: 404–417.

Loft A and Mooney G (1989). Trying to judge what is best medical practice. *International Journal of Health Planning and Management*, 4: 159–166.

Logan J, Green D and Woodfield A (1989). *Healthy Competition*, Centre for Independent Studies, Sydney.

Logan R *et al.* (1972). *Dynamics of Medical Care*, Memoir No. 14, London School of Hygiene and Tropical Medicine, London.

Lohr KN, Brook RH, Kamberg CJ, Goldberg GA, Leibowitz A *et al.* (1986). Use of medical care in the Rand Health Insurance Experiment: diagnosis and service-specific analyses in a randomised controlled trial. *Medical Care*, 24 (supplement).

Longman New Universal Dictionary (1982). Harlow, Longmans.

Loomes G and McKenzie L (1989). The use of QALYs in health care decision making. *Social Science and Medicine*, 28: 299–308.

Lowry MF (1987). Variations between paediatricians in the treatment of childhood asthma. *Paediatric Reviews and Communications*, 1: 55–65.

Luft HS (1978). How do HMOs achieve their 'savings'? *New England Journal of Medicine*, 298, 24: 1336–1343.

Lupton D, Donaldson C and Lloyd P (1991). Caveat emptor or blissful ignorance? Patients and the consumerist ethos. *Social Science and Medicine*, 33: 559–568.

Macintyre S (1989). The role of health services in relation to inequalities in health in Europe. In Fox J (ed) *Health Inequalities in European Countries*. Aldershot, Gower.

Manga P, Broyles RW and Douglas AE (1987). The determinants of hospital utilisation under a universal public insurance program in Canada. *Medical Care*, 25: 658–670.

Manning WG, Leibowitz A, Goldberg GA, Rogers WH and Newhouse JP (1984). A controlled trial of the effect of a prepaid group practice on use of services. *New England Journal of Medicine*, 310: 1505–1510.

Manning WG, Newhouse JP, Guan N, Keeler EB, Leibowitz A and Marguis MS (1987). Health insurance and the demand for medical care: evidence from a randomised experiment. *American Economic Review*, 77: 251–277.

Margolis H (1982). *Selfishness, Altruism and Rationality*. Cambridge, Cambridge University Press.

Mather HG, Morgan DC, Pearson NG, Read RLQ, Shaw DB, Steed GR, Thorne MG, Lawrence CJ and Riley IS (1978). Myocardial infarction: a comparison of home and hospital care of patients. *British Medical Journal*, 1: 925–929.

Maxwell R (1981). *Health and Wealth*, Lexington, Massachusetts, Lexington Books.

Maynard A, Marinker M and Gray DP (1986). The doctor, the patient and their contract III. Alternative contracts: are they viable? *British Medical Journal*, 242: 1438–1440.

Maynard AK and Tingle R (1975). The objectives and performance of the mental health services in England and Wales in the 1960s. *Journal of Social Policy*, 4: 151–168.

McClelland A (1991). *In Fair Health? Equity and the Health System*. Canberra, National Health Strategy Unit, Background Paper No. 3.

McGuire A, Henderson T and Mooney G (1988). *The Economics of Health Care: An Introductory Text*. London, Routledge and Kegan Paul.

McLachlan G and Maynard A (1982). The public/private mix in health care: The emerging lessons. In McLachlan G and Maynard A (Eds), *The Public/Private Mix in Health Care: The Relevance and Effects of Change*. London, Nuffield Provincial Hospitals Trust.

McLaughlin C (1988). The effect of HMOs on overall hospital expenses: is anything left after correcting for simultaneity and selectivity? *Health Services Research*, 23: 421–441.

McPherson K, Strong PM, Epstein A and Jones L (1981). Regional variations in the use of common surgical procedures: within and between England and Wales, Canada and the United States of America. *Social Science and Medicine*, 15A: 273–288.

McPherson K, Wennberg JE, Horind OB and Clifford P (1982). Small–area variations in the use of common surgical procedures: an international comparison of New England, England and Norway. *New England Journal of Medicine*, 207, 21: 1310–1314.

Melnick GA and Zwanziger J (1988). Hospital behavior under competition and cost containment policies: the California experience, 1980 to 1985. *Journal of the American Medical Association*, 260: 2669–2675.

Merrick NJ, Brook RH, Fink A and Solomon DH (1986). Use of carotid endarterectomy in five California veterans administration medical centers. *Journal of the American Medical Association*, 256: 2531–2535.

Minev D, Bogdana D and Miliva N (1990). The Bulgarian country profile: The dynamics of some inequalities in health. *Social Science and Medicine*, 31: 8; 837–846.

Ministerio de Sanidad y Consumo (1989). *The Spanish Health Care System: Highlights*. Madrid.

Ministry of Health, Ethiopia (1984). Financial planning for health care development in Ethiopia. *World Health Statistics Quarterly*, 37: 421–427.

Mooney GH (1987a). What does equity in health mean? *World Health Statistics Quarterly*, 40: 296–303.

Mooney GH (1987b). *Equity and efficiency: an inevitable or unethical conflict?* Sydney, Paper presented to the First Conference of the Public Health Association of Australia and New Zealand, August 24–27.

Moore GT (1991). Let's provide primary health care to all uninsured Americans – now! *Journal of the American Medical Association*, 265: 2108–2109.

Morgan M *et al.* (1987). Can hospital use be a measure of need for medical care? *Journal of Epidemiology and Community Health*, 41: 269–274.

Morris AL, Roos LL, Brazauskas R and Bedard D (1990). Managing scarce resources: A waiting list approach to cardiac catheterization. *Medical Care*, 28: 9; 784–792.

Morrisey MA, Sloan FA and Valvona J (1988). Medicare prospective payment and post hospital transfers to subacute care. *Medical Care*, 26: 685–698.

Moser WL (1987). The evolution of health care delivery in American industry. *Geneva Papers on Risk and Insurance*, 12, 45: 297–307.

Musgrave RA (1959). *The Theory of Public Finance – A Study in Public Economy.* New York, McGraw-Hill.

Musgrove P (1986). Measurement of equity in health. *World Health Statistics Quarterly*, 39: 325–335.

Mushlin AI, Panzer RJ, Black ER, Greeland P and Regenstreif DI (1988). Quality of care during a community-wide experiment in prospective payment to hospitals. *Medical Care*, 26: 1081–1091.

Muurinen JM (1982). The demand for health: a generalised Grossman model. *Journal of Health Economics*, 1: 5–28.

Mwabu GM and Mwangi WM (1986). Health care financing in Kenya: a simulation of welfare effects of user fees. *Social Science and Medicine*, 22: 7; 763–767.

Myers CN (1988). Thailand's community finance experiments: experience and prospects. In *Health Care Financing: Regional Seminar in Health Care Financing, 27 July–3 August, 1987, Manila, Philippines.* Asian Development Bank, Manila: Economic Development Institute of the World Bank, Washington; East-West Center, Honolulu.

Myers LP and Schroeder SA (1981). Physician use of services for the hospitalised patient: a review with implications for cost containment. *Milbank Quarterly*, 59: 481–507.

A National Health Service (1944). Cmnd 6502. London, HMSO.

Navarro V (1989). Why some countries have national health insurance, others have national health services and the USA has neither. *Social Science and Medicine*, 28, 9: 887–898.

Needham A, Brown M and Freeborn S (1988). Introduction and audit of a general practice formulary. *Journal of the Royal College of General Practioners*, 38: 166–167.

New South Wales Department of Health (1990). *A resource allocation formula for the New South Wales Health System.* Sydney, State Health Publication, No. SDB1 90–36.

Newacheck PW (1988). Access to ambulatory care for poor persons. *Health Services Research*, 23: 401–419.Newhouse JP (1974). A design for a health insurance experiment. *Inquiry*, 16: 5–27.

Newhouse JP (1975). Development and allocation of medical care resources: Medico-economics approach. In *Development and allocation of resources – Proceedings of 29th World Medical Assembly*, Tokyo, Japan Medical Association.

Newhouse JP (1977). Medical-care expenditure: a cross-national survey. *Journal of Human Resources*, 12: 115–125.

Newhouse JP and Bryne DJ (1988). Did Medicare's prospective payments system cause length of stay to fall? *Journal of Health Economics*, 7: 413–416.

Newhouse JP and Phelps C (1974). *On having your cake and eating it too: econometric problems in estimating the demand for health services*. R.–1149–NC. Santa Monica, California, Rand Corporation.

Newhouse JP, Manning WG, Morris C, Orr L, Duan N *et al.* (1981). Some interim results from a controlled trial of cost sharing in health insurance. *New England Journal of Medicine*, 305: 1501–1507.

North of England Study of Standards and Performance in General Practice (1990). *Final Report: Volume III – the Effects of Setting and Implementing Clinical Standards*. Report No. 40. Health Care Research Unit, University of Newcastle upon Tyne.

Nozick R (1974). *Anarchy, State and Utopia*. New York, Basic Books.

O'Donnell O and Propper C (1991). Equity and the distribution of National Health Service resources. *Journal of Health Economics*, 10: 1–10.

Office of Health Economics (OHE) (1989). *Compendium of Health Statistics for 1987*. London, Whitehall, Edition 7.

Organization for Economic Cooperation and Development (1985). *Measuring Health Care, 1960–1983, Expenditure, Costs and Performance*. Paris, OECD.

Organization for Economic Cooperation and Development (1987). *Financing and Delivering Health Care: a Comparative Analysis of OECD Countries*. Paris, Social Policy Studies No. 4.

Orosz E (1990). The Hungarian country profile: Inequalities in health care in Hungary. *Social Science and Medicine*, 31: 8; 847–857.

Palmer G and Short SD (1989). *Health Care and Public Policy: an Australian Analysis*. Melbourne, Macmillan.

Parkin D, McGuire A and Yule B (1987). Aggregate health care expenditures and national income: is health care a luxury good? *Journal of Health Economics*, 6: 109–127.

Patrick DL, Stein J, Porta M, Porter CQ and Ricketts TC (1988). Poverty, health services and health status in rural America. *Milbank Quarterly*, 66: 1; 105–136.

Pattison PV and Katz HM (1983). Investor-owned hospitals and health care costs. *New England Journal of Medicine*, 309: 370–372.

Pauly MV (1968). The economics of moral hazard. *American Economic Review*, 58: 531–557.

Pauly MV (1968). Taxation, health insurance and market failure in the medical economy. *Journal of Economic Literature*, 24: 629–675.

Pauly MV (1983). More on moral hazard. *Journal of Health Economics*, 2: 81–85.

Pearson RJC, Smedby B, Bertenstam R, Logan RF, Burgess AM and Peterson OL (1968). Hospital caseloads in Liverpool, New England and Uppsala. An international comparison. *The Lancet*, September 7: 559–566.

Pekkurinen M, Vohlonen I and Hakkinen U (1987). Reallocation of resources in favour of primary care: the case of Finland. *World Health Statistics Quarterly*, 40: 313–325.

Pereira J (1989). *What Does Equity in Health Mean?* York, Centre for Health Economics, Discussion Paper 61.

Pereira J (1990). Equity objectives in Portuguese health policy. *Social Science and Medicine*, 31: 1; 91–94.

Petchey R (1987). Health maintenance organisations: just what the doctor ordered? *Journal of Social Policy*, 16: 489–507.

Peterson MJ (1978). *The Medical Profession in Mid-Victorian England.* California, University of California Press, Berkeley.

Phelps C (1986). Induced demand – can we ever know its extent? *Journal of Health Economics,* 5: 355–365.

Phelps C and Newhouse JP (1974). *Coinsurance and the demand for medical services.* R-964-1 OEO/WC. Rand Corporation, Santa Monica, California.

Porell FW and Turner WM (1990). Biased selection under an experimental enrollment and marketing Medicare HMO broker. *Medical Care,* 28: 7; 604–615.

Potter C and Porter J (1989). American perceptions of the British National Health Service: five myths. *Journal of Health Politics, Policy and Law,* 14: 341–365.

Prescott N and Jamison DT (1984). Health sector finance in China. *World Health Statistics Quarterly,* 37: 387–402.

Prescott N and Jamison DT (1985). The distribution and impact of health resource availability in China. *International Journal of Health Planning and Management,* 1: 45–56.

Purola T, Kalimo E and Nyman K (1974). *Health Services Use and Health Status Under National Sickness Insurance. An Evaluative Resurvey of Finland.* Helsinki, Social Insurance Institution, Research Institution for Social Security, A: 11.

Quam L (1989). Post-war American health care: The many costs of market failure. *Oxford Review of Economic Policy,* 5: 1; 113–123.

Rawls J (1971). *A Theory of Justice.* Cambridge, Massachusetts, Harvard University Press.

Reinhardt U (1978). Parkinson's law and the demand for physicians' services (comments on Sloan F and Feldman R, 'Competition among physicians'). In Greenberg W (Ed), *Competition in the Health Care Sector: Past, Present and Future.* Germanstown, Maryland, Aspen Systems.

Relman AS (1983a). Is cost sharing dangerous to your health? *New England Journal of Medicine,* 309: 1453.

Relman AS (1983b). Investor-owned hospitals and health care costs. *New England Journal of Medicine,* 309: 370–372.

Rice TH (1983). The impact of changing Medicare reimbursement rates on physician-induced demand. *Medical Care,* 21: 803–815.

Rice TH and Labelle RJ (1989). Do physicians induce demand for medical services? *Journal of Health Politics, Policy and Law,* 14: 587–600.

Richardson J (1987). Ownership and regulation in the health care sector. In Abelson P (Ed), *Privatisation: An Australian Perspective.* Sydney, Australian Professional Publications.

Robinson JC and Luft HS (1988). Competition, regulation and hospital costs, 1982 to 1986. *Journal of the American Medical Association,* 260: 2676–2681.

Rodriguez M, Calonge S and Rene J (1990). *An Analysis of Equity in the Financing and Delivery of Health Care in Spain.* Discussion paper presented to the Bellagio Conference, Bellagio, 12–16 November.

Roemer MI (1987). Health system financing by social security. *International Journal of Health Planning and Management,* 2: 109–124.

Roos NO, Roos LL and Henteleff PD (1977). Elective surgical rates – do high rates mean lower standards? *New England Journal of Medicine,* 297: 360–365.

Rosko MD and Broyles RW (1987). Short–term responses of hospitals to the DRG prospective pricing mechanism in New Jersey. *Medical Care,* 25: 88–99.

Rubenstein LV, Kahn KL, Reinisch EJ, Sherwood MS, Rogers WH *et al.* (1990). Changes in quality of care for five diseases measured by implicit review, 1981 to 1986. *Journal of the American Medical Association,* 264: 1976–1979.

Rushing W (1974). Differences in profit and non-profit organisations: a study of effectiveness and efficiency in general short-stay hospitals. *Administration Services Journal*, 19: 474–484.

Russell I, Donaldson C, Foy CJW *et al.* (1986). Performance review in British primary medical care: an epidemological and economic evaluation. In Bergenhoff P, Helmann D and P Novak (Eds), *Primary Health Care: Public Involvement, Family Medicine and Health Economics*. Berlin, Springer-Verlag.

Russell LB and Manning CL (1989). The effect of prospective payments on medical expenditures. *New England Journal of Medicine*, 310: 439–444.

Sagar MA, Easterling DV, Kindig DA and Anderson OW (1989). Changes in the location of death after passage of Medicare's prospective payment system: a national study. *New England Journal of Medicine*, 320: 433–439.

Salisbury C (1989). How do people choose their doctor? *British Medical Journal*, 299: 608–610.

Salmela R (1988). *Political-administrative guidance and its effectiveness in decreasing the regional differences in the supply and use of health services in the 1970s and 1980s in Finland (in Finnish)*. Social Science Original Reports 1/1988. Kuopio, University of Kuopio.

Schwartz WB and Aaron HA (1984). Rationing hospital care: lessons from Britain. *New England Journal of Medicine*, 310: 52–56.

Secretaries of State for Health, Scotland, Wales and N. Ireland (1989a). *Working for Patients*. London, HMSO.

Secretaries of State (1989b). *Funding Contracts for Health Services*. London, HMSO, Working paper 2.

Sen A (1977). Rational fools: a critique of the behavioural foundations of economic theory. *Philosophy and Public Affairs*, 6; 317–344.

Skinner A (1986). Introduction. In Smith A, *An Inquiry into the Nature and Causes of the Wealth of Nations* (1986 edition). Hardmondsworth, Penguin.

Sloan FA and Vraciu RA (1983). Investor-owned and not-for-profit hospitals: addressing some issues. *Health Affairs*, 2: 25–37.

Sloan FA, Morrisey MA and Valvona J (1988). Medicare prospective payment and the use of medical technologies in hospitals. *Medical Care*, 26: 837–853.

Sloan FA, Valvona J and Mullner R (1986). A statistical profile. In Sloan FA, Blumstein JF and Perrin JM (Eds), *Uncompensated Hospital Care: Rights and Responsibilities*. Baltimore, Johns Hopkins University Press.

Smith A (1759). *The Theory of Moral Sentiments*. London, Strachan and Cadell.

Smith A (1776). *An Inquiry into the Nature and Causes of the Wealth of Nations*. London, Strachan & Cadell. 1986, Harmondsworth, Penguin Classics.

Smith T (1985). Limited lists of drugs: lessons from abroad. *British Medical Journal*, 290: 532–534.

Stanton B and Clemens J (1989). User fees for health care in developing countries: a case study of Bangladesh. *Social Science and Medicine*, 29: 10; 1199–1205.

Stoddart GL and Labelle RJ (1985). *Privatisation in the Canadian Health Care System*. Prepared for the Minister of National Health and Welfare, Minister of Supply and Services, Canada.

Sui AL, Sonnenberg FA, Manning WG *et al.* (1986). Inappropriate use of hospitals in a randomised trial of health insurance plans. *New England Journal of Medicine*, 315, 20: 1259–1266.

ten Have H (1988). Ethics and economics in health care: a medical philosopher's view. In G Mooney and A McGuire (Eds) *Medical Ethics and Economics in Health Care*. Oxford, Oxford Medical Publications.

The Guardian (1991). Questions of health. April 17, p.18.

Thorpe KE, Siegel JE and Dailey T (1989). Including the poor: The fiscal impacts of Medicaid expansion. *Journal of the American Medical Association*, 261: 7; 1003–1007.

Titmuss RM (1970). *The Gift Relationship*. London, George Allen and Unwin.

Torrance GW (1986). Measurement of health state utilities for economic appraisal. *Journal of Health Economics*, 5: 1–30.

Townsend P, Phillimore P and Beattie A (1988). *Health and Deprivation: Inequalities and the North*. London, Croom Helm.

Trevino FM, Moyer EM, Valdez RB and Stroup–Benham CA (1991). Health insurance coverage and utilisation of health services by Mexican Americans, Mainland Puerto Ricans and Cuban Americans. *Journal of the American Medical Association*, 265: 2; 233–237.

Tussing D and Wojtowycz M (1986). Physician induced demand by Irish GPs. *Social Science and Medicine*, 23: 851–860.

Tymowska K (1987). Health service financing in Poland. *International Journal of Health Planning and Management*, 2: 147–157.

University of Minnesota Center for Health Services Research (1987). *Comparison of Utilisation Rates and Satisfaction with Services According to Type of Coverage*. University of Minnesota, Minneapolis.

Valdez RB (1986). *The effects of cost sharing on the health of children*. 2–3270–HHS. Santa Monica, California, RAND Corporation.

van de Ven WMM (1989). *A Future for Competitive Health Care in the Netherlands*. NHS White Paper Series, Occasional Paper No. 9, Centre for Health Economics, University of York.

Vayda E (1973). A comparison of surgical rates in Canada and in England and Wales. *New England Journal of Medicine*, 289: 1224–1229.

Vayda E, Barnsley JM, Mindell WR and Cardillo B (1984). Five–year study of surgical rates in Ontario's counties. *Canadian Medical Association Journal*, 131: 111–115.

Vayda E, Mindell WR and Rutkow IM (1982). A decade of surgery in Canada, England and Wales, and the United States. *Archives of Surgery*, 117: 846–853.

Vohlonen I and Pekkurinen M (eds) (1990). *Variation in Hospital Productivity: Effects of Planning, Administration and Monitoring* (in Finnish, with an English summary). Helsinki, The National Board of Health, Health Services Research, No 57.

Wagner EH and Bledsoe T (1990). The Rand Health Insurance Experiment and HMOs. *Medical Care*, 28: 191–200.

Wagstaff A (1986). The demand for health: theory and applications. *Journal of Epidemiology and Community Health*, 40: 1–11.

Wagstaff A, van Doorsler E and Paci P (1989). Equity in the finance and delivery of health care: some tentative cross-country comparisons. *Oxford Review of Economic Policy*, 5,1: 89–112.

Walden DC, Wilensky GR and Kasper JA (1985). *Persons with Changing Insurance Status in 1977: NHCES data preview 21*. Rockville, National Center for Health Services Research.

Waller D, Agass M, Mant D, Coulter A, Fuller A and Jones L (1990). Health checks in general practice: another example of inverse care? *British Medical Journal*, 300: 1115–1118.

Ware JE, Brook RH, Rogers WH, Keeler EB, Davies AR *et al.* (1986). Comparison of health outcomes at a health maintenance organisation with those for fee-for-service care. *Lancet*, i: 1017–1022.

Watt JM, Derzon RA, Renn SC, Schromm CJ, Hahn JS and Pollan GD (1986). The comparative economic performance of investor-owned chain and not-for-profit hospitals. *New England Journal of Medicine*, 314: 89–96.

Weinberger M, Autl KA and Vinicor F (1988). Prospective reimbursement and diabetes mellitus: impact upon glycemic control and utilisation of health services. *Medical Care*, 26: 77–83.

Weisbrod BA (1978). Comment on MV Pauly. In Greenberg W (Ed) *Competition in the health care sector. Proceedings of a Conference Sponsored by Bureau of Economics, Federal Trade Commission*, Germanstown, Maryland, Aspen Systems.

West P (1981). Theoretical and practical equity in the National Health Service in England. *Social Science and Medicine*, 15c, 117–122.

Whitehead M (1988). *The Health Divide*. London, Penguin.

Whynes D (1988). *Invitation to Economics*. Oxford, Basil Blackwell.

Wickings, I, Childs T, Coles J and Wheatcroft C (1985). *Experiments using PACTs in Southend and Oldham HAs. A Final Report to the DHSS of the PACTs Projects at Southend HA and Oldham HA, 1979–1985*. CASPE Research, King Edward's Hospital Fund, London.

Wilensky GR (1988). Filling the gaps in health insurance. *Health Affairs*, 7: 133–149.

Wilensky GR and Rossiter L (1983). The relative importance of physician-induced demand in the demand for medical care. *Milbank Memorial Fund Quarterly*, 61: 252–257.

Williams A (1985). Economics of coronary artery bypass grafting. *British Medical Journal*, 291: 326–329.

Williams A (1986). The cost-benefit approach to the evaluation of intensive care units. In Reis Miranda D and Langrehr D (Eds) *The ICU – A Cost–Benefit Study*. Amsterdam, Elsevier.

Williams A (1988). Health economics: the end of clinical freedom? *British Medical Journal*, 297: 1183–1186.

Winslow CM, Kosecoff JB, Chassin M, Kanouse DE and Brook RH (1988a). The appropriateness of performing coronary artery bypass surgery. *Journal of the American Medical Association*, 260: 505–509.

Winslow CM, Solom DH, Chassin MR, Kosecoff JB *et al.* (1988b). The appropriateness of carotid endarterectomy, *New England Journal of Medicine*, 318, 12: 721–727.

Wolfe B (1986). Health status and medical expenditures: is there a link? *Social Science and Medicine*, 22: 943–999.

Wolfe B and Gabay M (1987). Health status and medical expenditures: more evidence of a link, *Social Science and Medicine*, 25: 888.

Wolfe B and Gottschalk P (1987). The distribution of health care financing in the overall population among the elderly. *Social Justice Research*, 1: 3; 315–328.

Woolhandler S and Himmelstein DU (1991). The deteriorating administrative efficiency of the USA health care system. *New England Journal of Medicine*, 324: 1253–1258.

World Health Organization (WHO) (1982). *Plan of Action Implementing the Global Strategy for Health for All*. Geneva, World Health Organization.

World Health Organization (1985). *Targets for all: targets in support of the European regional strategy for health for all*. Copenhagen, WHO Regional Office for Europe.

Wouters AV (1990). The cost of acute outpatient primary care in a preferred provider organisation. *Medical Care*, 28: 573–585.

Wouters AV and Hester J (1988). Patient choice of providers in a PPO. *Medical Care*, 26, 3: 240–255.

Wyszewianski L (1986). Families with catastrophic health care expenditures. *Health Services Research*, 21: 5; 615–634.

Yelin EH, Shearn MA and Epstein WV (1986). Health outcomes for a chronic disease in prepaid group practice and fee for service settings: the case of rheumatoid arthritis. *Medical Care*, 24: 236–247.

Yoder RA (1989). Are people willing and able to pay for health services? *Social Science and Medicine*, 29: 35–42.

Yule BF, Fordyce ID, Bond CM and Taylor RJ (1988). *The 'Limited List' in General Practice: Implications for the Costs and Effectiveness of Prescribing*. Discussion Paper No. 01/88, Health Economics Research Unit, University of Aberdeen.

Zwanziger J and Auerbach RR (1991). Evaluating PPO performance using prior expenditure data. *Medical Care*, 29: 142–151.

Zwanziger J and Melnick GA (1988). The effects of hospital competition and the Medicare PPS program on hospital cost behaviour in California. *Journal of Health Economics*, 7: 310–320.

Zweifel P (1984). *Kosten-versicherungsspirale im gesundheitswesen*. Zurich, University of Zurich, mimeograph.

Subject Index

211

Author Index